MILDRED MOSCOSO

strengthening women's voices

Building Women Communicators for Environmental Conservation

amic

Nanyang
Technological University

EASTERN UNIVERSITIES PRESS
by Marshall Cavendish

Published 2003 by Eastern Universities Press
An imprint of Marshall Cavendish International
(Singapore) Private Limited
A member of Times Publishing Limited

Times Centre, 1 New Industrial Road,
Singapore 536196
Tel:(65) 6213 9288
Fax: (65) 6284 9772
E-mail: tap@tpl.com.sg
Online Book Store:
http://www.timesacademic.com

Printed by Vine Graphic Pte Ltd, Singapore
on non-acidic paper

National Library Board (Singapore)
Cataloguing in Publication Data
Strengthening Women's Voices: Building Women
Communicators for Environmental Conservation /
Mildred Moscoso. – Singapore:
Eastern Universities Press,- 2003.

p. cm.
ISBN: 981-210-236-1

1. Women in conservation of natural resources – Asia,
   Southeastern.
2. Communication in conservation of natural
   resources- – Asia, Southeastern.
3. Environmental education – Asia, Southeastern.
4. Environmental protection- – Asia, Southeastern.
I. Title.

GE90
363.70071059 — dc21
SLS2003033749

London • New York • Beijing • Shanghai
• Bangkok • Kuala Lumpur • Singapore

Contents

Introduction   vii

Instructions for the Facilitator   ix

Acknowledgement   xi

Chapter 1   1
The ASEAN Environmental Scenario

Chapter 2   23
Environmental Communication

Chapter 3   32
Women and the Environment

Chapter 4   76
Communication Planning

Chapter 5   113
Preparation and Production of Media
Resources: Print Media

Chapter 6   167
Preparation and Production of Media
Resources: Community Radio Broadcasts

Chapter 7   202
Preparation and Production of Media
Resources: Small Format Video and Cable TV Production

Chapter 8   **249**
Preparation and Production of Media
Resources: Community Theatre

Final Word to the Facilitator   **287**

Production Team   **290**

Index   **294**

Asian Media Information and Communication Centre

The Asian Media Information and Communication Centre was established as a non-profit NGO in 1971 with the support of the Government of Singapore and the Friedrich-Ebert Stiftung of the Federal Republic of Germany.

The Centre is now housed in the School of Communication and Information of Nanyang Technological University, Singapore. It has a close working partnership with the School, collaborating in media training, research, conferences and publications.

AMIC functions as a resource centre to gather and disseminate knowledge about communication and its effects in Asia. By addressing the subject both on a practical level through training programmes and professional consultations, as well as on a theoretical level through research and seminars, it ensures the relevance and applicability of its activities. Research studies analyse the processes of communication and change, while training programmes contribute to an improvement of standards and effectiveness.

Part of AMIC's role is the promotion of an awareness of the nature, structure and roles of media in society, to encourage ethical and social responsibility of the media, to support democratic access and participation in media development and production, and to provide opportunities for empowerment of disadvantaged sectors in the communication/media environment.

As a catalyst for effective mass communications, AMIC cooperates with governments and national bodies as well as working in close association with international organizations such as the World Bank, UNESCO and The Commonwealth Secretariat.

Asian Media Information and Communication Centre

Jurong Point PO Box 360
Singapore 916412
Tel: (65) 67927570
Fax: (65) 67927129
email: enquiries@amic.org.sg

School of Communication and Information
Nanyang Technological University

The School of Communication and Information at NTU is Singapore's premier media education and research institution. It was established in 1992 to meet the increasing demand for well-trained personnel in the media industry and information services in Singapore and the region.

The School offers a four-year programme leading to a Bachelor's degree (with Honours) in Communication Studies, as well as postgraduate programmes by coursework or research leading to Master's and Doctoral degrees.

The School is committed to excellence in education. This commitment starts with an innovative curriculum designed to provide the best possible combination of theory and practical training. Faculty are recruited internationally from academe and industry. State-of-the-art laboratory facilities for print, multimedia, advertising and promotions, audio/radio and video/television productions are housed in the S$22.6 million SCI Building.

The School aims to be a centre of excellence in research. To develop research that analyses communication topics and policy issues important to Singapore and the region, the School has established and continues to maintain an international network of communication scholars and professionals through collaborative projects, conferences and other exchanges. Affiliation and collaboration with world-class institutions, leadership in providing a forum for communication scholarship in the region and ongoing programmes of research all contribute to this goal.

School of Communication and Information
Nanyang Technological University
31 Nanyang Link
Singapore 637718
Tel: (65) 67904578
Fax: (65) 67913082
email: wwwscs@ntu.edu.sg
http://www.ntu.edu.sg/sci/

Introduction

Strengthening Women's Voices was born as a result of the Asian Media Information and Communication Centre (AMIC) Workshop on Capacity Building of Women Communicators to Promote Environmental Awareness and Conservation, sponsored by the Swedish International Development Agency (Sida), and held in Bangkok, Thailand from November 5 to 9 2001.

The workshop brought together media practitioners, representatives from grassroots women's organisations and researchers from seven Asian countries: Cambodia, Lao PDR (hereafter referred to as Laos), Indonesia, Malaysia, Philippines, Thailand and Vietnam. I was blessed to be one of the participants in the workshop. For me, it was an eye opener as it showed how interconnected we were in the ASEAN region, and indeed in the whole world, in terms of environment; and how we can help each other in alleviating the ills that have beset it. Through country reports we were shown the status of women in the ASEAN region and how they can be advocates for the environment despite the limitations certain cultures have set upon them.

Most of the training time was spent on teaching skills on the production of communication materials such as brochures, posters, video and street theater presentations in order to promote environmental awareness and conservation at the community level. The community and community media were emphasised because it is in the communities where environmental problems are felt more keenly and where affirmative action to help solve these problems should begin.

The lessons and insights from the workshop were put to good use in the production of this AMIC-sponsored training manual. And I feel doubly blessed for being part of the production team who put this manual together.

This training manual is a guide for you, trainers and facilitators, in conducting training that focuses on strengthening ASEAN women's capabilities as communicators for the environment, as well as the conceptual principles behind it.

Though we believe this manual can be followed as it is, we rely on your wisdom as trainers and facilitators to choose which of these topics are needed by your participants. You are in the best position to know which contents of the manual will be most useful to your audience. Thus, you may follow the manual as it is or choose the specific topics you feel are most urgently needed and start from there.

Although this manual is far from comprehensive and has been produced with ASEAN women communicators in mind, we believe the lessons inside will be useful for both men and women everywhere who take their role as advocates and stewards of the environment seriously.

However, *Strengthening Women's Voices* is just what the title says. It is our meagre contribution to promoting environmental awareness and conservation by strengthening the capabilities of women communicators as advocates for the environment whose voices must be heard. After all, by virtue of being women, they have unwittingly earned the role of nurturers of nature. So if their voices have not been heard before or come in whispers, this manual tries to strengthen their voices as effective advocates for the environment.

As for the women who are already advocates of the environment, we are hoping that this attempt to help strengthen their capabilities will result in the recognition of their role in environmental awareness and conservation.

Thus, let us empower women to take their place among their men in the fight against environmental degradation. The time has come when men need not do it alone and women need not hide their strength and ability nor silence their voices. All our efforts are needed in the global attempt to save our environment.

This is our humble contribution and we dedicate it to the women of the ASEAN Region. *Let your voices be heard!*

MILDRED O. MOSCOSO
Project Coordinator

Instructions for the Facilitator

Before you begin using the manual, here is information you will find useful.

WHAT THE TRAINING MANUAL IS ABOUT

What you have in your hands is a manual to guide you in conducting an 11-day training session entitled, "Capacity Building of Women Communicators to Promote Environmental Awareness and Conservation". This training session was adapted from a five-day workshop with the same title held from November 5 to 9 2001 in Bangkok, Thailand. This training was organised by the Asian Media Information and Communication Centre (AMIC) with support from the Swedish International Development Cooperation Agency (SIDA) for women representatives from the ASEAN region.

AMIC commissioned the College of Development Communication (CDC), University of the Philippines Los Baños (UPLB) through the University of the Philippines Development Foundation, Inc. (UPLBFI) to develop this training manual for women communicators so that they may be able to conduct and facilitate a training course for community women on environmental awareness and conservation.

Whom this Manual is for

This manual is for the trainers and/or facilitators who will conduct the training. They should have at least a basic knowledge of communication, communication theories and communication planning.
It would also be most helpful if they have a deep understanding of the environmental issues in their communities or areas.

The training participants, on the other hand, are community women who will be involved in environmental communication efforts in their own areas. The only requirement they should fulfill is that they have a desire to help in promoting environmental awareness and conservation in their own communities.

What are the Objectives of the Manual

The manual aims to:
1. present an overview of the ASEAN environmental scenario;

2. provide concepts about environmental communication;
3. discuss women and their relationship with the environment and what they can do to conserve the environment and how;
4. teach the different steps of communication planning;
5. train women communicators to prepare and produce media resources, namely: low-cost print materials; community radio broadcasts; small-format video programmes and community theater.

How the Manual is Organised

The manual is divided into eight chapters for your easy reference. The first three chapters provide the foundation for empowering women to be advocates for the environment. The next five chapters focus on specific communication skills that they would need in order to communicate effectively for environmental conservation and preservation, with emphasis on using these skills at the community level.

Each chapter contains lessons, discussions and activities appropriate for each major topic. Some chapters have case studies and appendices which you will find useful in your discussion of the topic.

A **facilitator's guide** is found at the end of each chapter which tells the facilitator at a glance how the lessons can be taught and the activities managed effectively. In other words, the facilitator's guide serves as your navigation instrument throughout the chapter.

How Long the Training Should be

This training manual was designed for an 11-day training course. The whole training schedule is found in the Guide for the Whole Training Course found at the end of this manual. However, you may opt to deviate from the original design.

Each chapter has a specific number of days and hours for its session. The facilitator's guide at the end of every chapter gives the specific time duration for each topic. Thus, if you feel that your participants are already knowledgeable about a certain topic or if you sense that some information is more urgently needed than the others, then you can opt to shorten the training session by focusing only on the topics with the information your participants need. These chapters have been designed in such a way that they may be conducted by themselves or as part of the whole training course. This is a decision you make as the trainer/facilitator based on the needs of the participants and also on the capability of the sponsoring organisation or agency.

Acknowledgement

This book was made possible by funding from the Swedish International Development Cooperation Agency (Sida).

CHAPTER 1

The ASEAN Environmental Scenario

DINAH PURA T. DEPOSITARIO
MIDRED O. MOSCOSO

OBJECTIVES

By the end of this chapter, the participants should be able to:

1. Identify key environmental issues in the ASEAN member countries; and
2. Identify specific environmental issues in their communities.

INTRODUCTION

When five Southeast Asian countries joined together in 1967 to form the Association of Southeast Asian Nations (ASEAN), their stated purpose was to promote economic development and regional cooperation among the original member nations – Indonesia, Malaysia, Philippines, Singapore, and Thailand. The founders reasoned that by banding together, their economic clout would be greater than if they acted alone in a competitive way (Jafaar, 1999). Since then, ASEAN has expanded to include other neighbouring countries, namely: Brunei Darussalam, Cambodia, Laos, Myanmar, and Vietnam. These ASEAN Member Countries (AMCs) have consistently maintained and fostered close collaboration among themselves in addressing not just economic issues but also other vital concerns. One of the most pressing of these concerns is the environment.

Southeast Asia has one of the richest and most varied natural environments in the world. The use of natural resources plays a big part in the well-being of its nations and the 500 million people who depend on these resources for both consumption and production. Along with the rich and varied resource mix comes the challenge of caring for and nurturing the environment (ASEAN, 2001). This challenge comes at a significant time when most AMCs are in the throes of recovering from the Asian economic crisis that has beset the region while at the same time, facing many environmental problems.

The leaders of ASEAN view the protection of the environment and the sustainable use and management of natural resources as essential to the long-term economic growth of their countries and the region (ASEAN, 2001). Indeed, these countries, albeit different in many respects, share a "common aspiration for continued socio-economic progress while maintaining balanced development based on the principle of environmentally sound sustainable development" (ASEAN, 2000).

However, this is not an easy goal to achieve. Present environmental problems besetting the region are becoming more pervasive and more complex. Thus, with regards to helping solve these problems and promoting the sustainable use and management of the nations' natural resources, action should not only come from associations such as ASEAN and the leaders of AMCs' but from everyone.

This manual, *Strengthening Women's Voices: Training Manual for Capacity Building of Women Communicators for Environmental*

Awareness and Conservation, is a modest attempt to contribute to this movement to involve **everyone** – men and women – in helping save the environment.

This first chapter of the manual looks at some highlights of the different environmental concerns of the ASEAN region. These have been grouped and divided into three parts: water and aquatic ecosystems, terrestrial ecosystems and the atmosphere. Information for this chapter largely relies on the Second ASEAN State of the Environment Report 2000.

LESSON 1. WATER AND AQUATIC ECOSYSTEMS

Compared to most regions of the world, ASEAN has adequate renewable water resources but seasonal and other pressures are increasing. The region is a major global producer and exporter of fish products, but the resources on which they depend – clean water, mangrove forests and coral reefs – are deteriorating. ASEAN has established over 90 marine and coastal Protected Areas covering nearly 100,000 sq km to protect these resources.

Let us now look at the status of some of these water and marine resources in the region.

1. Quality of Freshwater Bodies

Degradation of water quality from water pollution has been a ubiquitous environmental problem in the ASEAN region for some decades now, especially in the urban areas. Water pollution is caused mainly by the discharge of untreated or inadequately treated wastewater from domestic, industrial and agricultural pollutant sources, as well as surface runoff from other indirect sources. The extent and severity of water pollution problems in AMCs vary widely depending on the pollution loads and the capacity of the water to assimilate waste. In general, rivers and coastal waters near large cities (such as Metro Manila, Bangkok, and Jakarta) is severely polluted by domestic and industrial wastewater. In rural areas, water pollution is normally caused by agricultural and localised industrial waste discharge.

2. Coastal and Marine Resources

A coastal zone is defined as a land within 60 km inland of the sea. The marine environment consists of coastal waters – and coastal ecosystems including estuaries, mangroves, coral reefs and sea grasses – and high seas. The coastal zone and marine environment are closely linked, both ecologically and economically.

Though coastal and marine ecosystems are very fragile, they are being subjected to serious threats from human activities including waste discharged from coastal populations, industries, and agriculture; shipping and accidental oil spills; and siltation due to soil erosion in the hinterlands. Coastal resources in the ASEAN region are declining rapidly due to over-fishing, destructive fishing methods such as dynamite and cyanide fishing, and the destruction of mangrove forests for aquaculture.

A. Mangroves

Mangroves include trees, shrubs, palms or ground ferns growing in intertidal zones. Mangroves play an important role in coastal zone ecology by supporting marine species that use the mangrove environment during all or part of their life cycles. Mangroves exist in all AMCs except Laos. In 1997, their global extent was approximately 18 million ha, about 35% of which was in Southeast Asia.

The following section discusses the status of mangrove forests in selected AMCs.

Cambodia. The main threats to Cambodia's mangrove forests are intensive shrimp farming and charcoal production in Koh Kong province, fuelwood extraction, and conversion to salt farming in the Kampot province. Although the conversion of mangrove shrimp farms is fairly recent, it already affects coastal people and coastal biodiversity adversely. Approximately 840 ha of 16,000 ha of the Koh Kong's mangrove forest was used for intensive shrimp farming in early 1994, with 105 entrepreneurs taking part. By the end of the year, 1,240 ha had been converted. Moreover, there is large-scale cutting of mangrove trees for charcoal. During the 1980s, this was limited to local use and was in effect sustainable. However, by 1992, 300 kilns were producing 24,000 tonnes of charcoal, mostly for illegal export.

Indonesia. In terms of total coverage, Indonesia's mangrove forest is believed to be the largest in the world. Mangroves are found on almost all islands although tree size and extent vary. However, growing populations demand more land to produce food, build settlements, and create employment, thereby stimulating the conversion of mangroves to

4

coastal aquaculture, rice paddy fields and settlements. Cutting of mangroves for firewood is also common in many coastal areas. Moreover, aside from a general lack of awareness of the important functions of the mangrove ecosystem, there is widespread perception of the mangrove belt as exploitable public property.

Malaysia. In Malaysia, mangrove forests are mainly found along sheltered coastlines protected from strong waves, mainly in the states of Kedah, Perak, Selangor, and Johor in Peninsular Malaysia and Sabah and Sarawak in East Malaysia. As elsewhere, mangroves are being converted to other land uses such as agriculture and shrimp farming. The forests have decreased about 47% in area, from approximately 505,300 ha in 1980 to 269,000 ha in 1990.

Philippines. Mangrove loss in the Philippines has been high, declining from 450,000 ha in 1920 to 120,500 ha in 1994, due to overexploitation by coastal dwellers and land conversions to either settlements or agriculture, salt beds, and industry. However, aquaculture remains the major cause – around half of the 279,000 ha lost from 1951 to 1998 were converted to culture ponds. Ninety-five percent (95%) of the Philippines' brackish water were ponds from 1952-1987, and were derived from mangroves. Some 300 m of shoreline at the mouth of Naisud River, have reportedly been eroded in the past decade because the loss of mangrove and beach vegetation has exposed the area to strong wave action especially during typhoons (which average 20 per year) and the northeast monsoon winds.

Thailand. As a result of changes in land use accompanying rapid economic development, Thailand has lost 54% of its original mangrove cover from 1961 to 1996. Major causes have been conversion to aquaculture ponds; clear felling for timber, charcoal, and wood chip production; and conversion for agriculture and industrial, and urban development. Much of the loss of mangroves was for short-term economic gain involving unregulated and illegal activities that also destroyed endangered species.

Vietnam. During the last war, a large area of mangroves - 104,123 ha of mangroves - was destroyed by herbicides. After reunification in 1975, many localities replanted forests. However, most mangroves, both natural and the replanted forests, have been destroyed due to extensive shrimp farming. From 1991 to 1994, areas southwest of Ca Mau Cape were invaded by illegal migrants who built thousands of shrimp ponds, resulting in the death of mangrove forests. In 1995, the government banned shrimp ponds in the area; since then, full recovery of more than 30,000 ha of denuded mangroves was achieved within the four years since the ban (Hong, 1999). In Vietnam, mangrove trees have recently been planted to protect sea dykes from erosion. An action plan for mangrove reforestation is also being developed to achieve rapid rehabilitation of ecosystems in some coastal zones, with the help of local communities.

B. Coral Reefs

Coral reefs are the marine equivalent of tropical forests and among the most productive and diverse of natural ecosystems. They provide a wide variety of habitats for a huge number of species. Their abundant biological diversity includes not only corals and commercially important species associated with the reef, but also an immense number of other plant and animal types. Of the approximate 600,000 sq km of coral reefs worldwide, about 10% have already been degraded beyond recovery while another 30% are likely to decline significantly within the next 20 years. Coral reef ecosystems in more remote areas are probably in better condition. If this trend is not reversed, it is estimated that most reefs will be severely depleted within the next 40 years.

The following section describes the conditions of coral reefs in selected AMCs:

Indonesia. Reef conditions in Indonesia vary from place to place. Off the Java and Sumatra coasts, reefs are damaged from overexploitation, sedimentation, and organic pollution. To the far east and northeast, reef ecosystems tend to be in excellent shape – particularly those which are relatively inaccessible to coastal dwellers. In Central Indonesia, reefs are degraded from blast fishing, cyanide fishing, and overfishing/collection. On the other hand, in Eastern Indonesia, population pressures are lower on the coral reefs and if destructive fishing is controlled here, many damaged reefs in this area may recover. Forest clearing and sedimentation, both associated with human population growth, are expected to severely affect reef health in Western Indonesia. Coral reef ecosystems of Palau Seribu, which provide both fishery resources as well as tourist opportunities for Jakarta are being severely damaged by mainland pollution and overfishing.

Malaysia. The coral reefs of Malaysia suffer from organic and sediment pollution as well as overexploitation although not as extensive as some other AMCs. However, construction-related sedimentation has badly affected reefs in the Palau Redang marine reserve. Moreover, all reefs in Peninsular Malaysia are expected to decline significantly over the next 20 years as a result of sedimentation and water pollution. The reefs of Sabah are also experiencing overexploitation.

Philippines. Coral reefs are in decline throughout the Philippine archipelago due to sedimentation, port construction, entrophication, blast fishing, cyanide fishing, and muro-ami fishing which involves the use of weights on ropes to smash corals and drive fish into awaiting nets. Coral cover is rapidly declining and fish populations are now low due to overfishing. The loss of 80% of the mangrove area and over half of the total forest area since 1920 has stressed reefs with sedimentation and has caused fish populations to decline. Large areas of Scarborough reef off Luzon and other large, offshore reefs have also been denuded of fish and corals from blast-fishing, and muro-ami fishing within the last two years. Between 1966 and 1986, the productivity of coral reefs in the Philippines dropped by one third as the national population doubled.

Singapore. The coral reefs of Singapore are valuable ecotourism destinations. However, they are being severely degraded by the construction of ports, oil processing facilities and other forms of coastal development. Though coral cover is reduced (less than 50%) on near-shore reefs, coral cover is still relatively high on the outer reefs. Threats to the reefs include sediment loads which limit coral distribution to depths of less than 10 m as well as fish and coral collection for the aquarium trade.

Thailand. Thailand's near-shore reefs are suffering from coastal development while offshore reefs have relatively high coral cover. Domestic and industrial pollution from Bangkok and Pattaya have almost totally destroyed the reefs in the northern Gulf of Thailand. Reefs off the western coast of the Gulf are in much better shape with coral cover often exceeding 50%. However, recent reports show that coral cover is declining by 20% annually due to tourist -related coastal clearing and sewage pollution. Healthy reefs with over 75% coral cover can be found in the Andaman Sea just off Similan and Surin Islands. However, in Phuket, reefs are being stressed by overfishing, tourist activities, and the release of sewage and sediment into shallow Phangnga Bay. Moreover, in the Gulf of Thailand, the fishery industry is in near collapse.

3. Fishery Resources

Asia dominates global aquaculture output, particularly China, which produced 27,072 thousand tons in 1998 with a value of US $25.5 billion. Four AMCs were among the top nine producers in the world together producing 2.88 million tons valued at nearly US $ 6 billion. Similarly, three AMCs were in the top 12 list of countries for world marine and inland fish capture in 1998, all together accounting for 8.4 million tons of fish, about 14% of the global total.

Pressure on marine fishery resources in AMCs has continued, rising in line with high domestic and export demand. The main concern is overfishing, which has resulted in a decline in the productivity of a large number of species. A number of small local pelagic fish are also nearing full exploitation. These include the mackerel and round scad in the Straits of Malacca and the Gulf of Thailand, the round scad in the Philippines, and the sardines in the Straits of Bali. Meanwhile, the larger coastal pelagic fish have only been moderately exploited in recent years. Cephalopods (e.g., squids and cuttlefish) are perhaps the only major marine resource in some Indonesian and Vietnam waters, with potential for further development. Cephalopods capture has increased from 165,000 tons in 1984 to 270,000 tons in 1994, 43% of which was contributed by Thailand.

There are other environmental problems affecting fishery resources and these include deteriorating marine water quality, degradation of coastal areas caused by inadequate waste management, and ineffective management of coastal zones. In addition, some AMCs have substantial difficulties with illegal and destructive fishing methods using cyanides or explosives to catch fish from reefs.

To summarise, the issues and concerns about water and aquatic ecosystems include the following:

*   ***Quality of Freshwater Bodies***
    In general, rivers and coastal waters near large cities in the region are severely polluted by domestic and industrial waste water. On the other hand, in rural areas, water pollution is normally caused by agricultural and localised industrial waste discharge.
*   ***Coastal and Marine Resources***
    The fragile coastal and marine ecosystems in the ASEAN region are under serious threat from destructive human activities such

as indiscriminate waste disposal from coastal populations, industries and agriculture; over fishing and destructive fishing methods like dynamite and cyanide fishing; conversion of mangrove forests to agriculture, aquaculture and industrial uses; and degradation of coral reefs due to over-exploitation, over-fishing, destructive fishing methods, sedimentation, pollution, and too many tourist activities.

- *Fishery Resources*

Four AMCs were among the top nine producers of global aquaculture output, together producing 2.88 million tons valued at nearly US$6billion.

However, over-fishing has caused a decline in the productivity of a large number of fish species in the ASEAN region. A number of small local pelagic fish are also nearing full exploitation. Other problems affecting fishery resources of AMCs include: deteriorating marine water quality, inadequate waste management in coastal areas, ineffective management of coastal zones and difficulties with illegal and destructive fishing methods.

LESSON 2. TERRESTRIAL ECOSYSTEMS

Lesson 2 of this chapter discusses land/soil resources and terrestrial ecosystems in AMCs, as well as deforestation, threatened biodiversity, and waste management.

The following portion discusses the various concerns of land/soil resources and terrestrial ecosystems and the status of the AMCs in relation to these concerns:

1. Land Degradation

Land degradation is a significant environmental problem taking place in almost all AMCs. It occurs in various ways such as nutrient depletion, structural decline and compaction, biological decline, chemical deterioration (through increased levels of alkalinity and salinity, for example), and soil erosion. Land degradation is caused by several factors including deforestation, excessive application of farm chemicals, inadequate management of soil quality, and improper irrigation. These problems are closely linked to forest management and agricultural development.

Soil erosion by water is the most pervasive form of land degradation found in ASEAN affecting nearly 14% of all its land. This varied widely among the countries, from 3.1% (Myanmar) to 39% (Philippines). About 75% of the soil erosion was due to topsoil loss, 21% to terrain deformation, and 4% to off-site effects. Sizeable areas in Malaysia (12.9 million ha), Indonesia (12.1 million ha), and the Philippines (11.4 million ha) were affected by topsoil loss. In both Malaysia and the Philippines, topsoil loss affected as much as 39% of the total land area. The percentage was also significant in Vietnam (22%) and Thailand (15%). However, the impact on soil productivity was only moderate for all AMCs except for the Philippines where about 5.6 million ha suffered strong to extreme land productivity impacts. Terrain deformation by water erosion affected only Indonesia (10.5 million ha) and Myanmar (6 million ha). Finally, off-site effects were notable only for the Philippines (2.7 million ha).

Decline in soil fertility was the major chemical deterioration in ASEAN, affecting 56 million ha of land. Nearly 26 million ha in Thailand (about 50% of land area), experienced this problem with a moderate impact on productivity. On the other hand, only 0.4 million ha of land in Vietnam were strongly affected. Fertility decline was insignificant in Indonesia and in the Philippines. About 2 million ha of land in Thailand suffered from increased soil salinity, a growing problem in the northeast and southern regions particularly along the coast. In the northeast, the cause is irrigation which uses high-salinity water. In the south, salinisation has been caused by the expansion of brackish aquaculture. This problem is increasingly common in the agricultural areas of the coastal zones in most AMCs. Soil acidification has moderately affected 0.9 million ha of land in Vietnam and about 1.6 million ha in Thailand.

2. Soil Contamination

Excessive use of agricultural chemicals can contaminate soil and agricultural produce. It does this by leaving chemical residues through the uptake of chemicals by the produce soil salinisation and soil acidification. Pollutants in contaminated soil can find their way into groundwater aquifers, surface water, and the ecosystems through food chains. These chemical residues on agricultural produce can be harmful to human health. These problems are becoming more common in ASEAN. Pesticides used in Vietnam, Cambodia, and Lao PDR are reported to exceed the safety levels recommended by the Food and Agriculture Organisation (FAO).

3. Forest Cover and Deforestation

Forest cover and deforestation vary widely among AMCs. From 1970s to 1990, ASEAN lost 31.4 million ha of forest, at a rate of about 15,700 sq km per year. During this 20-year period, Indonesia, Thailand, Myanmar, and Vietnam accounted for 86% of the total decrease in forest cover and deforestation, while Brunei Darussalam and Malaysia increased their net forest cover.

There was an increase in deforestation within AMCs between 1990 to 2000; the average annual loss grew by 23,260 sq km per year. Indonesia, Myanmar, Malaysia, and Thailand accounted for well over 90% of the total loss. Vietnam, on the other hand was the only country with a net gain in forested area.

Nevertheless, ASEAN remains among the most heavily forested regions of the world, coming a close second to South America. However, during the past decade, the annual rate of deforestation within ASEAN exceeded 1%. With the world deforestration rate at 0.23% per year and the overall deforestration rate of Asia less than 0.1% annually, the deforestration rate of ASEAN is still considerably higher than other regions of the world.

4. Biological Diversity

The UN Convention defines biodiversity as "*the variability among living organisms from all sources, including terrestrial, marine and other aquatic ecosystems and the ecological complexes of which they are part, and this includes diversity within species, between species and between ecosystems*". In the world, nations which are also called mega-diversity countries, collectively contain over two-thirds of the Earth's biological resources. In terms of plant and animal species at risk, these countries may account fully for 80% of the planet's most endangered biodiversity and are therefore known as "hotspots" or

11

biologically rich areas under greatest threat of destruction. Seven of the world's 25 recognised biodiversity hotspots are in Asia and three are in ASEAN: Indonesia, Malaysia and the Philippines. The rain forests in the Philippines have the highest levels of endemism in Indo-Malaya, although the country also has the highest percentage (4%) of threatened plant species.

Biodiversity is under tremendous threat in the ASEAN region with a variety of inevitable underlying causes. Unlike economic losses, which can usually be reversed or reduced with appropriate policies and actions, loss of biological diversity is essentially irreversible.

Moreover, it is not known how many species of plants have already become extinct in the ASEAN region.

In recognition of this grave threat to biodiversity, AMCs have established over 1,000 terrestrial "protected areas" covering 18,000 sq km, or nearly 10% of the total land area of AMCs.

5. Solid Waste Management

In the cities of ASEAN, solid waste generation is substantial. Poorly controlled disposal can lead to public health hazards, soil pollution, and water pollution. Municipal Solid Waste (MSW) consists mostly of decomposable organic materials, inert matter, and sometimes smaller amounts of hazardous materials from hospitals and elsewhere. Proper management of MSWs renders them harmless to humankind if removed and transported to a location where treatment and/or final disposal can eliminate potential hazards. Methods of disposal vary, and is dictated by land availability, environmental performance required at the disposal site, and affordability.

Management of MSWs in most ASEAN cities faces common issues and problems. Collection and disposal have long been treated as part of social services rather than public utilities with charges kept low relative to true cost. For example, households in Bangkok are charged 40 Baht (about US$0.95) or less per month for MSW service. Therefore, MSW operations must be subsidised from other sources of revenue. The capacity of most local governments in MSW management requires strengthening. In Bangkok, collection efficiency is only 1.3 tons/day/worker compared to 3.2 tons/day/worker in Kuala Lumpur and 8.5 tons/day/worker in Singapore. Low productivity of collection in Bangkok is due mainly to traffic congestion and the time spent by workers in sorting out saleable materials from collected wastes (BMA, 2000).

6. Hazardous Wastes

Management of Toxic and Hazardous Wastes (THW) has generally been regarded as a significant problem primarily in those AMCs with a large and relatively broad-based industrial sector. These countries are Indonesia, Malaysia, the Philippines, Singapore, and Thailand. In the remaining five countries (Brunei Darussalam, Cambodia, Laos, Myanmar, and Vietnam), THW has been regarded as less serious, the main concern being to prevent illegal exports of THW from other countries into AMCs.

In 1999, industries in Singapore reportedly generated about 118,000 tons of toxic industrial wastes. Of this, 70% was recovered or reclaimed for reuse and the remaining 30% was treated for disposal by landfill. In addition, about 9,000 tons of infectious wastes from hospitals and clinics were collected and treated. On the other hand, in Malaysia, nearly 399,000 tons of THW were collected in 1998. Of this, 53% went to recovery facilities, 14% was centrally treated, 6% was treated on-site, and 2% was exported for special treatment. The remaining 25% was uncollected and probably stored on-site.

Another THW issue is the proper containment or destruction of large volumes of toxic chemicals used during wars between 1960s-70s and/or have been stored for long periods since then.

THW management in AMCs is at a relatively early stage with Indonesia, Malaysia, Singapore, Thailand, and the Philippines spearheading the establishment of legal and institutional frameworks to help set up THW management facilities and procedures. With the exception of the Philippines, all four have granted concessions to the private sector to construct central THW processing facilities.

In summary, here are the issues and concerns about terrestial ecosystems:

- *Land Degradation*
  Land degradation is a major environmental problem in almost all AMCs and soil erosion by water is the most pervasive form of

soil degradation in the region. On the other hand, decline in soil fertility was the major form of chemical deterioration of land in ASEAN.

- *Soil Contamination*

  Among AMCs, soil contamination through excessive use of agricultural chemicals is becoming common. Pollutants in the contaminated soil, subsequently find their way into groundwater aquifers, surface waters and the ecosystems, thereby causing more contamination.

- *Forest Cover and Deforestation*

  ASEAN remains among the most heavily forested regions of the world and yet its deforestation rate per year is still considerably higher than other regions. Deforestation among AMCs is largely caused by excessive clearance and forest fires so the land can be used for agriculture, industry, mining activities and others.

- *Biodiversity Diversity*

  Biodiversity is under grave threat in the region. Seven of the world's 25 recognised biodiversity "hotspots" or biologically rice areas under greatest threat of destruction, are found in Asia. Three of these are in the ASEAN region: Indonesia, Malaysia and Philippines. Many plants and animal species from these countries are at risk of extinction. Furthermore, biodiversity loss is essentially irreversible.

- *Solid Waste Management*

  The cities of ASEAN generate substantial solid waste. Poor management and disposal of these wastes can lead to public health hazards, soil pollution, and water pollution. However, solid waste management in most ASEAN cities faces problems, one of which is that the capacity of most local government in solid waste management needs to be strengthened.

- *Management of Toxic and Hazardous Wastes*

  Management of Toxic and Hazardous Wastes (THW) has been considered a major problem in AMCs with a large industrial sector. These countries are Indonesia, Malaysia, Philippines, Singapore and Thailand. THW management in AMCs is currently at an early stage. Nevertheless, the mentioned countries are spearheading the establishment of legal and institutional frameworks to help set up THW management facilities and procedures.

LESSON 3. ATMOSPHERE

Lesson 3 of this chapter reviews air quality in ASEAN. In the larger cities, total suspended particulates, which can cause respiratory illnesses, are sometimes more than double the World Health Organization (WHO) guidelines. However, nitrogen and sulphur dioxides are well within the guidelines, and dramatic progress has been made in reducing lead concentrations in ambient air, most notably in Malaysia, Singapore, and Thailand. Transboundary haze from land and forest fires was a serious problem, particularly in 1997-1998, over much of Southeast Asia. An estimated 70 million people were affected, and 9 million ha of land and forests in Indonesia were damaged, with a cost estimated at US$9 billion. ASEAN has taken the lead role in addressing this problem through a substantive regional programme of monitoring, prevention, and mitigation.

Below are some environmental concerns of the region about the atmosphere:

1. Air Pollution

With increasing industrialisation and urbanisation in ASEAN member countries, air pollution has become a more serious problem. A major source of air pollution in AMCs is the combustion of fossil fuels, especially from motor vehicles and thermal electric power stations.

In terms of urban air quality, the combustion of fossil fuels and biomass by transportation industries, agriculture, and households releases huge volumes of pollutants. For most ASEAN cities, the rapid growth in transportation has caused the release of various gases and particulate matter into the atmosphere with severe impact on people's health.

Air quality in most urban centres in ASEAN is improving but remains unsatisfactory. Urban air pollution is significant in major cities such as Bangkok, Jakarta, Manila, Hanoi, Ho Chi Minh City, and Kuala Lumpur; as well as in some secondary cities such as Surabaya and Bandung in Indonesia; Cebu and Davao in the Philippines; and Chiang Mai and Hatyai in Thailand. Urban areas with high usage of three-wheel vehicles and motorcycles tend to have relatively higher air pollution as these vehicles generally use inefficient 2-stroke engines which can release 10 times the emission of automobile engines.

As for rural air quality, it should be noted that indoor air pollution in some rural (and even in urban) areas of ASEAN may be a worse health hazard than outdoor pollution for those who depend on wood, charcoal, and other biomass fuels. When burned using inefficient stoves with poor ventilation, particulate concentrations may exceed WHO guidelines by 10 times or more (ADB & ESCAP, 2000). Over time, there is a high risk of emphysema, other lung problems, and serious eye irritations mainly affecting women. Moreover, this is compounded by numerous factories in the region with poorly controlled emissions.

2. Transboundary Haze Pollution

Recurrent episodes of transboundary haze pollution arising from land and forest fires have been, and still are, one of the most pressing environmental problems facing ASEAN today. Over the past two decades, the recurring climatological disturbance known as El Niño Southern Oscillation (ENSO) has repeatedly set the stage for large-scale wildfires and the associated transboundary smoke haze in the region. There have been several large-scale fire-and-haze episodes since the early 1980s, particularly during the dry seasons of 1983, 1987, 1991, 1994, and 1997-1998. These episodes have inflicted massive damage by destroying forestland and its ecology, as well as endangering human health and economic well-being in the most affected AMCs, particularly in Brunei Darussalam, Indonesia, Malaysia, and Singapore. The land and forest fires in 1997-1998 were particularly severe, with the United Nations Environment Program (UNEP) labelling the blaze as among the most damaging in recorded history.

The impact of these catastrophic fires on the environmental, economic and social dimensions of the region were profound. The total economic loss in terms of agriculture production, destruction of forest lands, health, transportation, tourism, and other economic endeavours has been estimated at US$9.3 billion (ASEAN & ADB, 2001). About 20 million people in Indonesia suffered from respiratory problems during the worst episodes. The haze incidents seriously affected tourism and impeded other economic activities in the affected regions. Airports in the eight affected provinces closed on 313 occasions, seriously disrupting air traffic.

Below is a summary of the issues and concerns about the atmosphere:

- *Air Pollution*

  Air pollution is a major problem in the region because of increasing industrialisation and urbanisation in most ASEAN member countries. Urban air pollution is significant in major cities and in some secondary cities in ASEAN due to combustion of fossil fuelds and biomass from transportation industries, agriculture and households. Indoor air pollution in some rural (and even in urban) areas in the region, not only exists, but may even pose as a worse health hazard than outdoor pollution.

- *Transboundary Haze Pollution*

  Transboundary haze pollution from land and forest fires has been one of the most serious problems in the region in recent years. The recurring climatological disturbance known as the El Niño Phenomenon has repeatedly set the stage for large-scale wildfires and the associated transboundary smoke haze in the region. These large-scale fire-and-haze episodes have inflicted massive damage. The total economic loss in terms of agriculture production, destruction of forest lands, health, transportation, tourism and other economic endeavours has been estimated at US$9.3 billion (ASEAN and ADB, 2001).

TABLE 1.1 KEY ENVIRONMENTAL ISSUES AND CAUSES IN ASEAN MEMBER COUNTRIES

Country	Shared Issue	Key Cause
Brunei Darussalam	Seasonal smoke and haze; solid wastes	Transboundary pollution from land and forest fires
Cambodia	Soil erosion; sedimentation; water pollution; deforestation; loss of biodiversity; threats to natural fisheries	Unmanaged waste and effluent discharge into Tonle Sap lake; destruction of mangrove wetlands through extensive industrial and aquaculture development
Indonesia	Deforestation; loss of biodiversity; water pollution; air pollution in urban areas; national and transboundary seasonal smoke and haze; land degradation; pollution of Malacca Straits	Deficiencies in urban infrastructure—unmanaged industrial and municipal effluents and waste; vehicular congestion and emissions; extensive land clearance and forest fires for pulp wood and oil palm production; extensive and unmanaged mining activities; national and transboundary industrial pollution; tourist developments in coastal regions beyond carrying capacity
Laos	Deforestation; loss of biodiversity; soil erosion; limited access to potable water; water-borne diseases	Land clearance; shifting cultivation; inadequate water supply and sanitation infrastructure
Malaysia	Urban air pollution; water pollution; deforestation; loss of biodiversity; loss of mangrove habitats; national and transboundary smoke and haze	Vehicular congestion and emissions; deficiencies in urban infrastructure—industrial and municipal effluents; extensive land clearance and forest fires for pulp wood and oil palm production; unmanaged coastal developments; tourist developments in coastal regions beyond existing carrying capacity
Myanmar	Deforestation; loss of biodiversity; urban air pollution; soil erosion; water contamination and water-borne diseases	Land clearance; excessive mineral extraction; vehicular congestion and emissions; deficiencies in urban infrastructure-unmanaged industrial and municipal effluents

TABLE 1.1 (con't)

Country	Shared Issue	Key Cause
Philippines	Deforestation in watershed areas; loss of biodiversity; soil erosion; air and water pollution in Manila leading to water-borne diseases; pollution of coastal mangrove habitats; natural disasters (earthquakes, floods)	Illegal forest cutting; land clearance; rapid urbanisation and deficiencies in urban infrastructure-unmanaged industrial and municipal effluents, inadequate water supply and sanitation; tourist developments in coastal regions beyond existing carrying capacity
Singapore	Industrial pollution; limited natural fresh water resources; waste disposal problems	Seasonal smoke and haze; limited land available for waste disposal
Thailand	Deforestation; loss of biodiversity; land degradation and soil erosion; shortage of water resources during dry season and flooding during rainy season; conflict among water users; coastal degradation and loss of mangrove habitat; urban air pollution; pollution from solid waste; hazardous materials & wastes	Sporadic development and destruction of watersheds; unmanaged aquaculture; tourist growth exceeding carrying capacity; deficiencies in urban and rural infrastructure; freshwater resources polluted by domestic/industrial wastes and sewage runoff
Vietnam	Deforestation and soil degradation; loss of biodiversity; loss of mangrove habitat; water pollution and threats to marine life; groundwater contamination; limited potable water supply; natural disasters (floods)	Land clearance for industry; extensive aquaculture and overfishing; growing urbanisation and infrastructure deficiencies; inadequate water supply and sanitation particularly in Hanoi and Ho Chi Minh City

Source: Adapted from ESCAP & ADB, 2000 as cited in the 2nd ASEAN State of the Environment Report 2000.

It is obvious that the general environmental problems in the ASEAN region are interconnected and do not occur in a vacuum. What happens in one part of a community affects the country which in turn affects the rest of the region, and the rest of the world. The reverse is also true in that what happens in the rest of the world subsequently affects the region.

Try the activity below to see the concrete relationship between the environmental concerns we have in our communities and the major problems mentioned in the chapter.

Environmental degradation is indeed a big problem being faced not just by the ASEAN region but by the rest of the world. The nations collectively feel the effect of this problem, but it is the individuals, specially the poor and marginalised, who directly feel the brunt of its effects.

It is clear that the environment has a profound effect upon everyone. However, it is the women and children, the poor women and children in particular, who suffer the worst consequences of environmental degradation.

Chapter 3 will explain why women are most affected by environmental degradation and how they can be the most effective advocates for the environment. The succeeding chapters will help strengthen women's communication skills in helping create environmental awareness and conservation. But first, Chapter 2 will look at the value of communication in making people aware about the environment and getting them to help in its conservation.

ACTIVITY 1.1 PROBLEM TREE ANALYSIS OF KEY ENVIRONMENTAL ISSUES OF COMMUNITIES

Procedure
1. Divide the participants into groups.
2. Ask each group to identify a particular environmental issue in their community. Each group should have their own issue. No two issues should be identical.
3. After the issue has been identified, the group should identify what other problems are caused by the particular issue. These will serve as the "branches" of the problem tree.
4. After an exhaustive discussion on the "fruits" of the problem tree, ask the group to identify what causes the identified problems. These causes then become the roots of the problem tree.

5. Ask the participants to draw a tree to represent the problem, its "branches" and "root causes".
6. Ask the participants to present their group's output at the plenary. Open the floor for discussion, questions, and clarifications. Facilitate the discussion.
7. You will most probably be able to see common "root causes" of problems and even their "branches". Point this out to the group to show how environmental issues are actually interrelated.
8. A simple problem tree is shown in the next page. This serves as an example.

FIGURE 1.1 SAMPLE PROBLEM TREE DIAGRAM

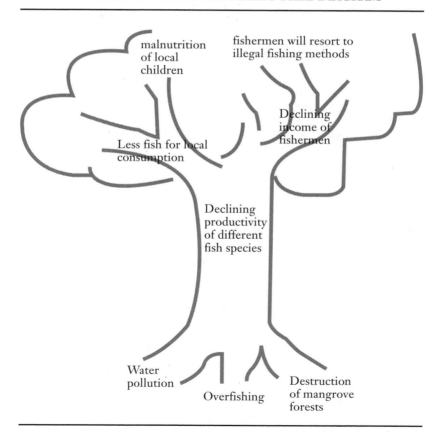

malnutrition of local children

fishermen will resort to illegal fishing methods

Declining income of fishermen

Less fish for local consumption

Declining productivity of different fish species

Water pollution

Overfishing

Destruction of mangrove forests

FACILITATOR'S GUIDE

TOPIC	OBJECTIVE	TEXT	ACTIVITY	DURATION
ASEAN	Explain why ASEAN was formed	Introduction	Discussion	15 minutes
Water and Aquatic Resources	Identify key environmental issues, particularly on water and aquatic resources, in the ASEAN member countries.	Lesson 1. Water and Aquatic Resources	Discussion	1 hour
Terrestrial Resources	Identify key environmental issues, particularly on terrestrial resources, in the ASEAN member countries.	Lesson 2. Terrestrial Resources	Discussion	1 hour
The Atmosphere	Identify key environmental issues, particularly on the atmosphere, in the ASEAN member countries.	Lesson 3. The Atmosphere	Discussion	30 minutes
Overview of ASEAN Environmental Scenario	Identify key environmental issues in the ASEAN member countries.	Summary	Discussion	30 minutes
	Identify specific environmental issues in the participants' communities	Summary	Discussion Activity1: Problem Tree Analysis	45 minutes

REFERENCES

A Bakar Binin Jafaar. 1999. **Smoke Signals in Southeast Asia**. Forum for Applied Research and Public Policy, v14 i4 pp.62.

http://www.Asiamedia.ucla.edu/Deadline(?)/ environmental%20Issues%20 in % 20Asia/Articles/Jaata.html.

The Second ASEAN State of the Environment Report 2000.

ASEAN Environment Overview 2001.

CHAPTER 2

Environmental Communication

ALEXANDER G. FLOR

OBJECTIVES
After studying this chapter, the participant should be able to:

1. Define environmental communication;
2. Enumerate the four core messages of environmental communication;
3. Name the essentials of environmental communication; and
4. Describe the importance of communication in environmental protection.

This chapter is a condensed version of combined selected chapters from the book *Environmental Communication: Principles, Strategies and Approaches of Communication Applied to Environmental Management* by A.G. Flor, written under the Textbook Writing Grants Programme of the University of the Philippines System.

INTRODUCTION

Environmentalism as we know it today began with environmental communication. The environmental movement was ignited by a spark from a writer's pen, or more specifically and accurately, Rachel Carson's typewriter. The publication of Carson's *Silent Spring* in 1962 marked the beginning of the environmental crusade that has been and is still being carried out by two generations of baby boomers and post-baby boomers. Indeed, Carson was a biologist. But, she was, as *Time* magazine put it, first and foremost, a writer.

LESSON 1. DEFINITION/ NATURE

Environmental communication is the application of communication approaches, principles, strategies and techniques to environmental management and protection. Simply put, it is the deliberate exchange of environmental information, knowledge, and even wisdom.

Environmental communication is inspired by general systems theory or GST. Among other things, GST submits that a living system has to perform three critical functions. These functions are:

- the exchange of materials with its environment and with other living systems;
- the exchange of energy with its environment and other living systems; and
- the exchange of information with its environment and other living systems.

All living systems, from the simplest to the most complex, are supposed to be equipped to perform these critical functions. They are called "critical" because they are necessary for the survival of the living system.

Communication is nothing more than the exchange of information. Hence, in its broadest sense, environmental communication is necessary for the survival of every living system, be it an organism, an ecosystem, or a social system.

Environmental communication likewise adheres to the principle that the goal of human communication is mutual understanding.

This belief is the very foundation of the Convergence Model of Communication, which was based on GST and formulated by D. Lawrence Kincaid in the 1970s.

Applied to the environmental agenda, communication should not be regarded merely as supportive to environmental management but as an integral part of it. Without this critical component, the entire environmental undertaking is jeopardised. Furthermore, environmental communication should not be source-oriented or media-centric. It should allow for greater participation of the receiver. In fact, it should enable and empower the audience not to remain passive receivers but to become active sources of information as well.

LESSON 2. CORE MESSAGES

In the past decade, there has been a general agreement among environmental communication practitioners that our core messages correspond to the four "informal" laws of ecology enumerated by the noted American biologist, Barry Commoner, in his book *The Closing Circle*. These four laws are as follows:

"Everything is connected to everything else".
This law pertains to the systems theory concept of interconnectedness. Everything within an ecosystem is interrelated and interconnected like a giant web. Extending this to the entire ecosphere, we have the Web of Life. Harming one part of this web brings consequences to the other parts.

"Everything must go somewhere".
Commoner's second law pertains to waste and its management. Waste becomes part of our environment. It cannot be discarded in the strictest sense of the word. Although it may not end up in your own backyard, it will always end up somewhere.

"Nature knows best".
Technology cannot solve all the problems of society. In fact, it may be the cause of some of these problems. Nature has its own way of compensating for inequities, keeping the equilibrium, and solving problems.

"There is no such thing as a free lunch".
Every gain has its costs. Exploiting our natural resources comes with a
price. At times, that price is higher than the benefit we get.

LESSON 3. ESSENTIALS

Based on the experiences of many, the following traits are necessary in
the practice of environmental communication:

Knowledge of Ecological Laws

The environmental communication practitioner should be familiar with
the four laws of ecology as enumerated by Barry Commoner. These so-
called informal laws were presented by Commoner in a non-technical
manner and would be easily understood by the layman. Furthermore,
most if not all of the messages in environmental communication would
fall under any of these laws.

Sensitivity to the Cultural Dimension

Although some people believe that nature and culture are two
irreconcilable dichotomies, many environmentalists consider nature
and culture as a continuum. Nature and culture actually co-evolve.
One of the best strategies of environmental communication is to
tap indigenous or popular media. Hence, the environmental
communication practitioner should be sensitive to the cultural dimension,
not merely the technical aspect, of environmental management
and protection.

Ability to Network Effectively

Environmental communication occasionally takes on an advocacy role.
Networking is essential in advocacy.

Efficiency in Using Media for Social Agenda-setting

Media sets social agendas. An environmental communication practitioner
should not only be aware of this, he should be adept at setting the
environmental agenda by using the media.

Appreciation and Practice of Environmental Ethics

The complexity and involvement which characterise environmental communication make it imperative for us to practice what we preach. Who would believe us if we do not "walk the talk"? Walking the talk comes naturally once environmental ethics are internalised. A comprehensive guide to environmental ethics may be found in Cecille-Guidote Alvarez's *Ten Commandments of Earthsaving*:

1. Thou shall plant more trees and stop illegal logging and burning of forests.
2. Thou shall protect endangered species, our indigenous heritage and biocultural diversity.
3. Thou shall not resort to destructive methods of fishing and shall rehabilitate damaged coral reefs.
4. Thou shall stop polluting the soil and waterways with garbage and toxic waste, instead recycle and compost.
5. Thou shall not resort to burning to dispose of garbage, especially plastic, to avert climate change.
6. Thou shall stop using CFCs and other ozone-depleting chemicals.
7. Thou shall stop emissions that cause mental retardation and diseases, especially of children, by keeping vehicles and factories in good running condition.
8. Thou shall not smoke.
9. Thou shall conserve water and energy.
10. Thou shall condemn war and nuclear weapons (Alvarez, 1993).

Conflict resolution, mediation, and arbitration

Environmental conflict is a common phenomenon in developing as well as developed societies, wherever and whenever projects that may impact on the environment are implemented. In many cases, such conflict is caused by the lack of information from the project proponent to affected entities, i.e., stakeholders. The environmental communication practitioner often finds herself in a role as a mediator or arbitrator, and thus, she should have conflict resolution skills.

LESSON 4. FORMS

Communication Campaigns

Environmental communication can be planned, designed and implemented as communication campaigns with specific audiences, messages, media, strategies and timetables. This is treated extensively in other parts of the manual.

Cultural Interventions

Cultural intervention as a form of environmental communication is indeed feasible. The intervention itself may not be as complicated or as grand as one would imagine. It only involves tapping and nurturing existing or spontaneously occurring cultural phenomena. It entails riding on the process of enculturation and making purposive introductions or injections into it. It cannot be done otherwise.

Indigenous Communication

Indigenous communication, in devcom parlance, is today's equivalent of folk media. In the 1960s and 1970s, development programmes particularly those associated with population, experimented with the use of folk media to promote family planning methods among the rural poor. Among the media employed were traditional forms such as puppet shows, shadow plays *(wayang kulit)*, rural theater, *balagtasan* and *balitaw*. These were the trailblazing efforts in exploring the cultural dimensions of communication campaigns. Eventually, however, the term folk media was found to be inappropriate because it was oriented towards one element in the communication process – the channel. Indigenous communication, on the other hand, was more suitable since it pays equal emphasis to other elements such as the audience and the message.

The scope of indigenous communication also went beyond the presentations mentioned above to include folklore: legends and myths. The inclusion of folklore was of course very significant particularly for purposes of environmental consciousness. Folklore is one of the most important means of enculturation. Furthermore, through its symbolisms and other literary devices, it makes abstract concepts more understandable and crude objects more significant. In traditional societies, it has instilled

28

environmental values (i.e., respect for every living creature) to succeeding generations. Myths serve life-sustaining purposes (Campbell, 1987). However inconsistent they may be to science, perhaps we are better off believing in them.

Popular Culture

There is a need to learn from the past and to revive enculturation that sustains and nurtures the environment. However, this cannot be limited to traditional vehicles only. There are also contemporary vehicles or popular media that cannot be ignored. It is true that much of contemporary popular media content is seldom socially beneficial or positive. Yet it determines to a large extent how people – particularly youth – act, speak and behave. Indeed popular media such as recordings, music videos, television and films are very powerful. They should be tapped for environmental communication purposes.

Equally important is the revival and promotional aspect of myths through the use of mass media. The synergy of folk media and mass media, particularly through radio drama, comics, audiotapes and music videos, should be fully exploited.

A long-running radio drama series on myths and legends with environmental themes supplemented by adventure-type comics laden with similar messages would provide a greater, longer-lasting impact than the one-shot radio jingles and agency propaganda comics commonly employed for environmental communication. Radio drama and adventure comics could take the place of traditional storytelling, one of the most effective means of enculturating the young. Audiotapes and videos can also be effectively tapped because these could easily be copied and multiplied. Music videos may be shown in village video halls in the countryside.

Summary

Environmentalism began with environmental communication.

Environmental communication is the application of communication approaches, principles, strategies and techniques to environmental management and protection. Simply put, it is the deliberate exchange of environmental information, knowledge, and even wisdom. It is inspired by general systems theory and adheres to the principle that the goal of human communication is mutual understanding.

Environmental communication has four major messages or themes inspired by Barry Commoner's Four Laws of Ecology:

- Everything is connected to everything else.
- Everything must go somewhere.
- Nature knows best.
- There is no such thing as a free lunch.

It has five essential traits:
- Knowledge of ecological laws.
- Sensitivity to the cultural dimension.
- Ability to network effectively.
- Efficiency in using media for social agenda setting.
- Conflict resolution, mediation, and arbitration

Environmental communication may take the form of communication campaigns. It may tap indigenous or popular media.

FACILITATOR'S GUIDE

OBJECTIVE	TEXT	ACTIVITY	DURATION
Define environmental communication	Introduction Definition/ Nature	Lecture Discussion	20 minutes
Enumerate the four core messages of environmental communication	Core Messages	Lecture Discussion *Poster Making:* Based on any of the four laws, each participant should conceptualise and draw a poster using crayons.	30 minutes
Name the essentials of environmental communication	Essentials of Environmental Communication	Lecture Discussion	10 minutes

FACILITATOR'S GUIDE (con't)

OBJECTIVE	TEXT	ACTIVITY	DURATION
Describe the forms environmental communication	Forms	Lecture Discussion Each participant shall contribute to the discussion by naming examples of environmental communication as the forms are described.	30 minutes

REFERENCES

Guidote-Alvarez, Cecille. "Environmental Communication and Culture". In Flor, Alexander G. and Ely D. Gomez (Editors) 1993. Environmental Communication: Considerations in *Curriculum and Delivery Systems Development. USAID-NRMP and UPLB-IDC, Los Baños.*

Campbell, Joseph. 1987. **The Masks of Gods**. Bantam Books (New York).

Commoner, Barry. 1971. **The Closing Circle. Nature, Man and Technology**. Bantam Books (New York).

Flor, Alexander G. and Ely D. Gomez (Editors). 1993. **Environmental Communication: Considerations in Curriculum and Delivery Systems Development**. USAID-NRMP and UPLB-IDC, Los Baños.

CHAPTER 3

Women and the Environment

DINAH PURA T. DEPOSITARIO

OBJECTIVES
At the end of this chapter, the
participants are expected to:

1. Explain the role of women in
    environmental protection; and
2. Gain insights from examples and
    cases of women and organisations
    involved in environmental
    protection.

INTRODUCTION

At first glance, it may seem that "women" and "environment" are two very unrelated terms. However, according to Davidson (1993), "it is difficult to define quite where 'environment' begins and ends for women in developing countries."

In low-income countries throughout the world, poor women interact with their environment on a daily basis. In many countries, women are responsible for childcare and a range of household duties that can be combined with childcare responsibilities. Many of these activities, such as collecting water and fuelwood, growing food, and managing the home gardens have a direct impact on the environment (Women's Empowerment, Population and Environment Factsheet, 2001).

Furthermore, in many rural families, women are in fact heads of household, as well as the main farmer. This is true particularly where men migrate to the urban areas or go abroad to look for work. This is also true in situations of armed conflict or strife where men go off to fight and leave the women behind. This is a reality in the case of widows, and/or women with ill or disabled spouses or in marriages where the men do not like to work and depend on their wife and children to carry out the farming duties as well as the household chores (Martinez, 2000).

ASEAN women, like Lao women, have always had a central role in agriculture and are involved in all stages of agricultural production, but within distinct gender-based divisions. Women have been chiefly responsible for maintaining house gardens, raising livestock, and generating income through the manufacture and sale of handicrafts and non-wood products. Moreover, women are responsible for all household duties as they are the primary child carers, attend to health needs, collect water and fuel, and manage the food of the household (Dethrasavong, 2001).

There are however contradictions in society's expectations of the role of women. Cambodian women are expected "not to travel far" but, at the same time, must work somehow to provide for their family. Khmer women, on the other hand, are naturally present in all social strata, but remain excluded from politics. Thus, their role as decisionmaker is confined to the small political sphere of the family and to issues brought about by day-to-day routines. Furthermore, in terms of power relations, a woman's status in society will generally be determined by the status of her husband (Nary and Thanak, 2001; Rasmey and Sundarinet, 2001).

Just as women interact with their environment, the environment in turn has a profound effect on the women's workload, health, and the health of their families. Each ASEAN member country (AMC) has specific environmental concerns brought about by its individual socio-economic and geographical conditions. However, some concerns are common among most AMCs and often, other issues are cross-border in nature as they are shared due to proximity.

The destruction of the ecosystems by logging, aquaculture, and industries has reserved its most burdensome consequences for women. For example, in some areas, environmental degradation has caused water sources to dry up or to be polluted by industrial waste. As a result, women and girls have to walk longer distances to get potable drinking water. Likewise, the destruction of marine habitats and fishing grounds has threatened the livelihood of households that do not gain much from industries or aquaculture to begin with, thereby increasing the women's already heavy workloads.

Finally, diseases brought about by polluted air and water raise the demand for women's care. Environmental policies and programs are mostly gender-blind and make women's contributions and culpability vastly invisible. This is particularly true in the case of environmentally stressful modes of production, such as unsustainable upland farming practices (Illo, 1997).

As the primary caretakers of family well-being, women should be especially concerned that our living environment is sustainably managed and preserved for the continued existence of our future generations (Women in Action, 1991a). Fortunately, at the worldwide level, there is a growing awareness of the need to make women contribute to the identification of environmental problems as well as in the planning of activities geared at the sustainable development of their communities. The Platform for Action, adopted by the Fourth World Conference on Women in Beijing in 1995, identified the need to involve women more actively in environmental decisionmaking at all levels as well as to incorporate the gender perspective in all strategies leading to sustainable development (Chelala, 2001). The following lessons will explain the relationship between women and the environment, the role of women in environmental protection, and how women can be involved in efforts to achieve a sustainable environment.

GUIDE TO DISCUSSION 1

Objective	Discussion Question
• Acquire an overview of the relationship between women and the environment	Ask the participants to read the Introduction. Key Question: In what instances do women interact with their environment on a daily basis? Suggested answers: • Collect water and fuelwood • Grow food and manage home gardens
• Know the status of women in developing countries	Key Question: What are the commonalities in the status of ASEAN women? Suggested answers: • Women are heads of household and the main farmers • Women are responsible for all household duties as they are the primary child carers • Woman's status in the society will generally be determined by the status of her husband; attends to family's health needs • Women's contribution to their households' livelihood is largely undervalued
• Identify the environmental issues common to ASEAN countries	Key Question: What are the environmental issues common to ASEAN countries? Suggested answers: • Deforestation • Soil erosion • Water pollution • Natural disasters (e.g., floods) • Seasonal smoke and haze
• Explain the impact of environmental degradation on women	Key Question: What is the impact of environmental degradation on women? Suggested answers are: • Women's already heavy workloads are increased (e.g., walking longer distances to get drinking water) • Diseases brought about by air and water pollution will require that women take care of themselves and their families

35

WOMEN AND THE ENVIRONMENT

A. What is Ecofeminism?

Nature – the source of Earth's life support systems, has traditionally been given a feminine gender due to its life-giving and nurturing gifts. We often encounter the term "Mother Nature" and "Mother Earth" in our readings and daily interactions.

Language largely perpetuates the symbolic connections between women and the environment. Nature is often described in female and sexual terms: nature is raped, mastered, conquered, controlled, mined. "Virgin timber" is felled and cut down while "fertile soil" is tilled and land that lies "fallow" is barren or useless (Warren, undated as cited in Zimmerman, et al., 1993).

This belief gave rise to the concept of *ecofeminism*. According to Warren (undated), as cited in Zimmerman, et al. (1993), "…'ecological feminism' or ecofeminism refers to the name of a variety of positions that make visible different sorts of woman-nature connections…".

Ecofeminism recognises the caring, nurturing, and sustaining nature of women and adapts this to ecology. In more practical terms, the concept can be viewed as the "application of feminist perspectives to problems of ecology, bringing a 'political understanding' of women's situation such as unequal rights to land, access to loans or even (say) in planning their own development" (NCRFW, 1995).

A Women in Action (1991b) article defines ecofeminism as follows:

> Ecofeminism is a term used by some to describe the diverse range of women's efforts to save the earth and the recent development of feminism resulting from the new view of women and nature…
> It recognizes the value of the feminine principle that is caring, nurturing, and sustaining, and brings this to ecology, while feminism has brought a political understanding to ecology in describing patriarchy's domination of the earth.

The term was first used in 1974 by French writer Francoise d'Eaubonne to describe women's potential to effect environmental change and spans a broad range of women's concerns focusing on activism and demonstration. The underlying awareness linking the many diverse strands of activity is a growing sense of interrelatedness – that is, a healthy life is dependent upon a healthy environment, that humans exist in a symbiotic relationship with the earth, and that to disregard this is destructive to us and the planet (Women in Action, 1991b).

Thus, the concept of ecofeminism emphasises the "interconnection of the environment and women and the creation of the perfect environmental sustainable order" (Puente, undated). Women are basically the ones who deal with nature and who create waste as well. Ecofeminism therefore implies that women should assume a more aggressive role in protecting the environment.

GUIDE TO DISCUSSION 2

Objectives	Discussion Questions
• Explain why nature has been traditionally given a feminine gender	Ask the participants to read the lesson entitled "What is Ecofeminism?". Key Question: Why has nature traditionally been given a feminine gender? Suggested answer: ▪ Nature has life-giving and nurturing gifts which are traditionally feminine traits.
• Discuss the concept of ecofeminism	Key Question: What is ecofeminism? Suggested answers: ▪ Ecofeminism is a term used to describe the "diverse range of women's efforts to save the earth and the recent development of feminism resulting from the new view of women and nature". ▪ Ecofeminism is also the "the application of feminist perspectives to problems of ecology, bringing a 'political understanding' of women's situation such as unequal rights to land, access to loans or even in planning their own development."
• Discuss the implication of ecofeminism on the nature of women's role in environmental protection	Key Question: What is the implication of the concept of feminism on the role of women in the protection of the environment? Suggested answers: ▪ Ecofeminism is a term used to describe the "diverse range of women's efforts to save the earth and the recent development of feminism resulting from the new view of women and nature." This view implies that women and nature have a symbiotic relationship – that a healthy life is dependent upon a healthy environment ▪ The concept of ecofeminism suggests that women have to play an active role in the protection of the environment.

B. Why Should Women be Concerned with the Protection of the Environment?

According to the State of World Population 2001 (2001), the direct and critical relationship between women and natural resources draws its strength not from biology – that is, not because women are born female – but from gender and the socially-created roles and responsibilities that continue to fall on women in households, communities, and ecosystems throughout the world.

The different reasons why women should be involved in the protection of the environment are:

1. **Women are users and necessarily, nurturers, of natural resources. They depend on natural resources for work, their homes, and their communities. By virtue of being women, they live in much greater harmony with nature** (Van den Hombergh, 1993, as cited in NCRFW, 1995).

- Women are primarily responsible for rearing children, and for ensuring resources are sufficient to meet children's needs for nutrition, health care, and schooling. In the rural areas of developing countries, they are the main managers of essential household resources like clean water, fuel for cooking or heating, and fodder for domestic animals. Women grow vegetables, fruits and grains for home consumption and also for sale, even producing most of the staple crops (State of World Population 2001).

- Although both genders are equally dependent on the capacities of ecosystems, their relationship with the ecosystems are often different. Throughout history, women have operated as integrators, connectors, convertors, and managers of natural, and often limited, resources. They link children and the elderly, homes and markets, are involved in the production and use of domestic resources, and often convert raw materials to usable products. They are practitioners, major users, consumers, and experts in myriad ways that in the aggregate, determine many ecological capacities and qualities (Martin-Brown, 1993).

- Women comprise more than half (51%) of the world's agricultural workforce. In Southeast Asia, women provide 90% of the labour in rice cultivation. As economic opportunities open up, women in

38

developing countries are growing, processing, and marketing non-food products made from natural resources for consumption at home and increasingly, for overseas (State of World Population 2001).

2. **Given the variety of women's daily interactions with the environment, they are the most affected by its degradation** (State of World Population 2001).

According to Dizon-Anonuevo and Jimenez-Tan (1994), as cited by Moscoso (2001), women are dependent on nature for the performance of their basic functions and any crisis in the environment affects them more than anybody else within the community.

Women are often most sensitive to changes in the environment because they are in closest contact with the home and the land; in other words, they are the first line of defense (WEDO, 1999).

Degraded environments mean that women must spend more time and effort to find fuel or produce food, but their other responsibilities, such as meeting household needs and ensuring family health do not diminish (State of World Population 2001, 2001).

The following examples illustrate the impact of environmental degradation on the daily and livelihood activities of women:

- Deforestation or contamination increases the time women must spend seeking fuelwood or safe, clean water, and increase women's risk of water-born disease. In the state of Gujurat, India, women now spend four or five hours a day collecting fuelwood, when previously they would have done so once every four to five days (State of World Population 2001).
- Soil erosion, water shortages, and crop failures reduce harvest yields; soil exhausted from over-use likewise reduces the productivity of household gardens (State of World Population 2001).
- Women play a significant role in the fishing industry, with 40% engaged in activities related to fish production – cleaning nets, vending fish, etc. Environmental degradation results in the depletion of fishery resources, giving women the additional burden of financially supporting their family. Oftentimes, the men leave the coastal village to look for work in the cities, leaving women as heads of households. In the Philippines, the collapse of major fishing grounds is uprooting 38,000 fishers each year (*Newsweek*, 1994, as cited in NCRFW, 1995).

3. **As childbearers and primary caretakers of health, women are affected by adverse health impacts of environmental degradation and pollution** (State of World Population 2001).
According to Chelala (2001), a survey on public attitudes on the environment sponsored by the United Nations Environment Program (UNEP) showed that women, as compared to men, are more likely to choose a lower standard of living with fewer health risks rather than a higher standard of living with more health risks (Chelala, 2001). This is therefore one factor which makes women assume the role of protectors of the environment.

The following elaborations on health problems among women and children resulting from environmental degradation and pollution stress the need for women to be more concerned about the environment:

- Women are more affected than men by environmental issues like polluted air and water, pesticides, waste dumping, irradiated food products, population, and development. They are the primary caretakers of the vast majority of the children who lose schooldays due to asthma. They also have elevated levels of breast cancer. Likewise, their reproductive systems are altered by pesticides, nuclear waste, and water degradation (Hopey, 2000).
- Toxic chemicals and pesticides in the air, water, and earth are responsible for a variety of women's health risks. These enter body tissues and breast milk, which are then passed on to infants. In a village in China's Gansu province, discharges from a state-run fertiliser factory have been linked to a high number of stillbirths and miscarriages. Water pollution in three Russian rivers is a factor in the doubling of bladder and kidney disorders in pregnant women. Moreover, in Sudan, a link has been established between exposure to pesticides and prenatal mortality – with the risk higher among women farmers (State of World Population 2001).
- Almost all plantations in Malaysia employ women to do the tasks around the estate, including the spraying of pesticides. Often these women have either lived in these estates all their lives or are married into families that work on estates. Their job options are therefore limited and working in the estate plantations or factories become their only means of survival.
  In oil and cocoa plantations, it is the women who go on foot and

manually spray the pesticides. The pesticides produce noxius fumes when sprayed and are poisonous if consumed.

The majority of the women also suffer from impaired eyesight, miscarriages, and vomiting. One woman even reported losing most of her fingernails (Asian and Pacific Women's Resource and Action Series: Environment, 1992).

4. **Women are the biggest stakeholders of the natural resource base and are most knowledgeable of its problems and needs, that solutions cannot be arrived at without them** (NCRFW, 1995). Women have a traditional and contemporary knowledge of the natural world around them (World Bank, 1991 as cited by Joekes, 1994). The following elaboration emphasises women's natural knowledge that can be tapped for environmental protection.

They understand more clearly the connection between economics and the environment. They know because the soil, water, and vegetation which they need for their basic livelihood – necessitates specific care and good management (NCRFW, 1995). Martinez (2000) supported this view when she said that rural women engaged in farming activities are knowledgeable about what the problems are and often have their own insights and ideas of how to solve these problems.

• Women farmers tend to use and perfect traditional cropping methods developed over time to protect precious natural resources. Women employ methods such as fallowing (leaving fields uncultivated for at least a season), crop rotation (successively planting a field with different crops), intercropping (planting several different crops in a field at one time), mulching (spreading organic material on the soil around plants to avoid water evaporation) and a variety of techniques that promote soil conservation, fertility, and enrichment. Women are thus key players in the conservation of soil fertility. Planners are now recognising the value of learning from women's local knowledge to protect and sustain the environment (FAO, undated).

• Women and women's groups are at the forefront of experiments in sustainable agriculture such as introducing more flexible cropping patterns, widening species diversity, recycling organic nutrients, and using other techniques for long-term resource conservation. Traditional methods of interplanting and crop

41

rotation are blended with new styles of agroforestry to provide an alternative approach which combines environmental improvements with direct development gains for women (Davidson, 1990).

- Women's participation is increasingly seen as crucial to the success of water supply and sanitation activities. Key decisions in which women can be included are: the siting of water facilities; choice of technology; the selection of pump caretakers, water committee members and other personnel; and the choice and management of the financing system (Baden, 1993).

Furthermore, according to Chelala (2001), women have better access to local environmental issues and know better how to approach them than men. Women have often had a leadership role in reducing unnecessary use of resources, promoting environmental ethics, and recycling resources to minimise waste.

At the same time, as cited by Davidson (1993), almost all development activities in some way affect women's surroundings – especially in rural areas. Changes in agriculture, forestry, water, and waste management all have local environmental implications which affect women. Women are also directly affected by "environmental" activities – those designed to rehabilitate degraded areas, reduce pollution, or conserve genetic variety. Thus, they must be consulted on the potential, perceived negative consequences of any environmental protection project. This would be a key factor in the successful design and implementation of any project.

5. Women's involvement in natural resource management projects is needed for the sustainability of environmental protection efforts.

It is not enough that natural resource management projects have been designed and implemented. More importantly, they have to be sustained. The following stress the important role of sustainability in environmental protection efforts.

- Women play an important role in shaping societal values and attitudes of the young towards the environment. Their perspective is therefore crucial to effective environmental management

42

programs which can help improve the quality of life in the 21st century (Antrobus and Bizot, Development Alternatives for Women in a New Era- DAWN, 1993, as cited in NCRFW, 1995).

- Gender-sensitive planning in training and technology development would not only improve production today, but would also ensure the protection of the environment for tomorrow. Women need to be informed about alternative methods of cooking, farming, heating, and waste disposal (FAO, undated).

- The U.S. Agency for International Development (USAID) has focused on integrating gender concerns into its natural resource management projects in Africa. The agency has learned, over the past 10 years, that project planners who understand women's relationship to the environment have taken the first step towards finding solutions that will result in more sustainable use of resources. USAID also found that project planners and managers who consider the constraints that women face and who find ways to reduce them, have greater success at engaging the entire community in using natural resources sustainably.

GUIDE TO DISCUSSION 3

Objectives	Discussion Questions
• Explain why women should be involved in the protection of the environment.	Ask the participants to read the lesson entitled "Why Should Women be Concerned with the Protection of the Environment?" Key Question: Why should women be concerned with the protection of the environment? Suggested answers: • Women are users and necessarily, nurturers of natural resources. • Women's performance of daily as well as livelihood activities are affected by environmental degradation. • Women are affected by adverse health impacts of environmental degradation and pollution. • Women have the biggest stake in the natural resource base and have the best knowledge of its problems and needs, that solutions cannot be arrived at without them. • Women's involvement in natural resource management projects is needed for the sustainability of environmental protection.

GUIDE TO DISCUSSION 3 (con't)

Objectives	Discussion Questions
• Discuss why any crisis in the environment necessarily affects women more than anybody else within the community.	Key Question: Elaborate on why any crisis in the environment necessarily affects women more than anybody else within the community. Suggested answer: ▪ Women are dependent on nature in their performance of their basic functions. Degraded environments mean that women must spend more time and effort in performing these basic functions such as finding fuel or producing resources.

• Identify the potential health problems among women and children that can be caused by environmental degradation and pollution	Key Question: What are the potential health problems among women and children that can be caused by environmental degradation and pollution?
	Suggested answers:
	  ▪ Asthma
	  ▪ Breast cancer
	  ▪ Stillbirths and miscarriages
	  ▪ Bladder and kidney disorders
	  ▪ Drinking water coming from rivers heavily polluted by DDT and other pesticides
	  ▪ Impaired eyesight from exposure to noxious fumes while spraying pesticides such as paraquat

• Identify women's natural knowledge that can be tapped for environmental protection.	Key Question: Identify some of women's natural knowledge that can be tapped for environmental protection.
	Suggested answers:
	  ▪ Connection between economics and the environment – that the soil, water and vegetation, which they need for their basic livelihood, necessitates specific care and good management
	  ▪ Traditional cropping methods developed over time to protect precious natural resources (i.e., fallowing, crop rotation, intercroppping, mulching, etc.)
	  ▪ Their knowledge of local plants can play an important role in protecting species and preserving biodiversity

44

GUIDE TO DISCUSSION 3 (con't)

Objectives	Discussion Questions
• Appreciate why solutions to environmental problems cannot be arrived at without the involvement of women	Key Question: Why is it that solutions to environmental problems cannot be arrived at without the involvement of women? Suggested answers: ▪ Women have a traditional and contemporary knowledge of the natural world around them. Because of this, rural women are knowledgeable about what the problems are and have their own insights and ideas of how to solve the problems. ▪ Women also have better access to local environmental issues and how to approach them than men. At the same time, changes in agriculture, forestry, and water and waste management all have local environmental implications which affect women. ▪ Women are directly affected by "environmental" activities – those designed to rehabilitate degraded areas, reduce pollution, or conserve genetic variety. Thus they should be consulted on potential, perceived negative consequences of any environmental protection project.
• Explain why women's involvement in natural resource management projects is needed for the sustainability of environmental protection efforts.	Key Question: Why is women's involvement in natural resource management projects needed for the sustainability of environmental protection efforts? Suggested answers: ▪ Women play an important role in shaping societal values and attitudes towards the environment among the young. ▪ Gender-sensitive planning in training and technology development (i.e, alternative methods of cooking, farming, heating, waste disposal etc.) would not only improve production today, but would also ensure the protection of the environment tomorrow.

C. What are the Constraints on Women's Sustainable Use of Natural Resources?

In reality, women have the responsibility for managing household resources, but they typically do not have managerial control. Decision makers often overlook this reality, even though women's use and management of local environmental resources is fundamental to household and community well-being.

Some of the specific constraints to women's sustainable use of natural resources which have implications on their current and potential effectiveness as participants in environmental protection activities are:

*   National law or local customs often effectively deny women the right to secure title or inherit land, which means they have no collateral on which to raise credit (State of World Population 2001, 2001).

    According to UN statistics, women own no more than 1% of the world's land, and even where they have access to it for farming, their tenure is often costly and uncertain. Without ownership of land or secure access to it, women are denied access to credit, training, and other production support, and preventing them to engage in the long-term conservation practices they have traditionally used (Davidson, 1990).

    Furthermore, as women rarely own land they cultivate there is little incentive for them to make environmentally sound decisions. In addition, their lack of access to credit hampers them from buying technologies and inputs that would be less damaging to natural resources. These negative factors set up a cycle of declining productivity, increasing environmental degradation, and food insecurity in the future (FAO, undated).

*   Agricultural extension services are heavily biased towards men. Education and outreach efforts in support of sustainable farming and land management methods often pass them by (State of World Population 2001, 2001).

    On the other hand, due to lack of access to information, women are constrained further from effectively using natural resources because they have fewer opportunities to learn about new seeds, safer methods of pest control, efficient irrigation techniques, or crops with higher nutritional value. Such information is offered only to landowners or to male heads of households. Thus, female farmers are less productive and are more likely to use natural resources in ways that are damaging over the long term (USAID, 1998).

To cite, in Laos, when women were questioned as to whether they knew why the government tries to stop the slash and burn cultivation and tries to move highland farmers down from the mountain, almost all of them admitted to not fully understanding the reasoning, and that it was simply a government policy (Dethrasavong, 2001).

- Poverty, precarious land tenure, and lack of expert support discourage women from investing in newer technologies or long-term strategies such as crop rotation, fallow periods, sustainable levels of cultivation or reforestation. On the contrary, these factors encourage fast-growing cash crops such as cotton, which quickly exhausts the land, and woodland clearance for short-term income (State of World Population 2001).

- Such pressures on limited land resources deplete nutrients and degrade soil. Land degradation reduces yields, leading to more intensive use, further degradation, and still lower yields. Farmers may seek new land, but often find it only in frontier or marginal areas, especially if they are women and cannot close a sale or negotiate a loan (State of World Population 2001).

- Women have also suffered from well-meaning but inappropriate development activities. Some social forestry schemes, for example, with their emphasis on eucalyptus and commercially valuable species, have ignored women's interests, not only by excluding them from the benefits, but in other ways, such as diverting scarce resources, like water, to be used as inputs to the schemes (Davidson, 1990).

- In many societies, women's ideas are not valued and their initiatives do not carry as much weight as those of men. This becomes an issue when communities are given responsibility to decide how local resources will be managed. If women cannot participate in decision making about how forests, rivers, or communal lands are to be used, they may not engage in executing plans that will have a positive, long-term benefit to preserving natural resources (USAID, 1998). To cite, in many areas, women are "invisible" water managers, responsible for supplying the water needs of the family, domestic animals, and sometimes agriculture. A number of studies have

47

shown how their role in searching for potable supplies and carrying water over long distances is important for the health, economy, and social development of local communities. Yet women are frequently excluded from the planning, implementation, and maintenance of water supplies. At the same time, they suffer the consequences of intensive, irrigated agriculture and elsewhere, of polluting industries (Davidson, 1990).

The State of the World Population 2001 hit it right on target when it emphasised that sustainable development through environmental protection "demands recognition and value for the multitude of ways in which women's lives intertwine with environmental realities." Furthermore, the report added that "Women's right to own and inherit land should be enforced; individual and communal security of land tenure should be guaranteed; women should have access to credit, and to agricultural extension and resource management services, and they should be included in decisions about the services' organization and content."

GUIDE TO DISCUSSION 4

Objectives	Discussion Questions
Discuss the constraints to women's sustainable use of natural resources	Key Question: What are the constraints to women's sustainable use of natural resources? Suggested answers: • National law or local customs often effectively deny women the right to secure title or inherit land, which deny them access to other resources such as credit. • Agricultural extension services are heavily biased towards men. • Poverty, precarious land tenure, and lack of expert support discourage women from investing in newer technologies or long-term strategies. • Pressures on limited land resources deplete nutrients and degrade soils. • Women have suffered from well-meaning but inappropriate development activities. • In many societies, women's ideas are not valued and their initiatives do not carry as much weight as those of men.

THE ROLE OF WOMEN IN ENVIRONMENTAL PROTECTION

Women could be potential partners in environmental protection. However, because women in many ASEAN societies are constrained in terms of sustainable use of natural resources, their involvement in environmental protection activities could be impeded. Fortunately, development planners can design projects that can counteract the barriers to their participation. This, according to USAID (1998), might mean developing projects that are solely for women, or it could mean mainstreaming gender within a project by giving equal opportunity for participation of both women and men. Another option would be to require the development of a hybrid project that has a "women only" component within a larger project or a separate budgeting and reporting of objectives by gender within a mainstream project.

The following are examples of different types of environmental protection projects having different project designs which have involved women in Thailand, Philippines, Cambodia, and Malaysia. These projects were facilitated by different institutions (i.e, government agency, international agency, and non-government organisations), were implemented in different ecosystems (i.e., lowland and upland), and elicited various forms of environmental protection participation from women as well as men.

1. Government Agricultural Department Project Prioritising Environmental Awareness Among Homes – Thailand

As described in the Asian and Pacific Women's Resource and Action Series: Environment (1992), an environmental awareness project was carried out in rural Thailand by the Farm Women Extension Programme of the Thai Department of Agricultural Extension (DOAE), entitled "Environmental Awareness Starts at Home". The project involved selecting two pilot villages in each of the 73 provinces in Thailand. The working task force in each pilot village planned action based on the concept of people participation, self-help, and self-reliance. At least 30 farm families in each village were expected to take part in the farmhouse model project for environment improvement.

This project aimed to increase awareness of household environmental problems as well as the various types of appropriate technology that might provide solutions to them through model households that were ecologically sustainable. Conservation of resources was also part of the awareness program.

2. Soil Conservation Project Led by an International Agency – Philippines

As documented in a USAID newsletter (1998), a participatory approach to environmental project planning requires project designers to pay attention to women's needs and interests, within a mainstream project. USAID learned this in its Sustainable Agriculture and Natural Resource Management Collaborative Research Support Program (SANREM/ CRSP) in Mindanao, Philippines. The project, located in a watershed area, aimed to reduce the amount of silt running into a lake used to generate electricity. The silt build-up in the lake, due to logging activities (a male-dominated activity) and increased farming (a female-dominated activity), was interfering with the generation of electricity.

Soil conservation techniques to reduce the amount of silt running into the lake were taught to both women and men. Both were also asked to monitor the lake's water quality to determine if conservation efforts were working. Both men and women showed no interest in monitoring until project planners learned that the women were more interested in health issues. They adjusted the program to teach women about the effect that clean water has on the health of the family. Project staff expanded the water inspection to include the monitoring for *E. coli* bacteria.

With these changes, women began to participate in efforts to reduce the silt runoff into the lake. They also became involved in other environmental activities and their enthusiasm for managing the community's natural resources helped engage the men in soil conservation efforts (USAID, 1998).

3. Forest Protection Project led by a Non-Government Organisation – Cambodia

The AMIC Workshop proceedings (2001) cited the case of Mr. Keo Son of Cambodia. As a member of the Forest Protection Association established in his district, he spearheaded a project with the support of Mlup Baitong (Green Shade) and this has been running for two years.

The Forest Protection Association has two objectives: 1) to protect the forests, animals, and fish; and 2) to take care of the saplings. Mr. Keo Son thinks that with good management, natural resources will remain an important asset for both present and future generations. The men's role within the association is to prevent traders from buying and selling trees or destroying things. The women, meanwhile, organised the women's movement to help protect the environment.

The sustainability of the project is ensured by the planting of trees. The partner, Mlup Baitong, provides the seeds and saplings for reforestation. The main threat to the sustainability of the programme is deforestation by illegal loggers who use guns to threaten the people. The advantage of having women on the committee is that women "persevere". However, some of the women admitted to not having understood clearly the objectives of the programme, as well as to their disinterest in participating in the project.

4. Advocacy Work Initated by Women and a Non-Governmental Organisation – Malaysia

Lastly, the AMIC proceedings (2001) highlighted Ms. Wang Lay Kim's story about the advocacy work initiated by women and a non-governmental organisation in Malaysia. The lobbying efforts were addressed against a proposed power project – the Bakun Hydro-Electric Power Project. The project was earmarked to be built on the Balui River in Sarawak and was expected upon completion to provide a generating capacity of 24,000 megawatts.

Like any other big infrastructure project, the power project necessitated the resettlement of some indigenous people. Also, the Bakun dam was evaluated by a 2000 Bloomberg report to be Southeast Asia's largest white elephant and would take a century to pay for itself.

Independent NGOs, specifically women's NGOs, rallied in support of the plight of those affected by the Bakun project. In collaboration with Pusat Komas, the indigenous women produced a video memorandum to appeal to the authorities not to destroy their land and heritage. The video was used as an instrument to lobby for changes and allowed the indigenous women to express their concerns. The campaigns were held in Kuala Lumpur to raise public awareness of how core-

51

periphery development plans have affected the environment and lives of ordinary people in the name of development. The success of this project as assessed by the author lies in the empowerment of indigenous women to speak out.

The forms of women participation in environmental protection include: 1) becoming aware of household environmental problems, health issues which are caused by environmental problems, and appropriate, ecologically-sustainable technology; 2) becoming actively involved in environmental protection and conservation activities like cleaning their surroundings, practising proper garbage management, and planting trees; and 3) women producing a video memorandum to appeal to the authorities not to destroy their land and heritage.

Other examples of how women can actively participate in environmental protection are as follows:

- Women concerned about environmental damage can voice their concerns on issues ranging from dumping toxic waste into landfill sites and waterways, to overpackaging, and from uranium mining to nuclear testing. In the last few years, as more women have recognised life-threatening consequences of environmental negligence and have acted to promote lasting change, these voices have increased in number. The world is now witnessing a crescendo of women's protest (Women in Action, 1991b).

- Women's groups are also organising themselves to integrate women fully into the political process, so they can take full part in policy decisions affecting their lives, such as policies on land and water use for agriculture; power; drinking water and energy supply; health and education services; and economic opportunities (State of World Population 2001).

- Women as consumers can play an important part in awareness raising and influencing the powerful business sector. They can refuse to buy goods that are damaging to the environment and recycle others (NCRFW, 1995).

The mini-cases and the other examples highlight the fact that women's organisations and networks play an increasingly important role in advocacy and in specific actions to improve the environment. According to Maria Jose Guazzelli, a member of a Brazilian branch of Friends of the Earth, a non-governmental environment organisation, her experience is that it is usually women who have been the first to organise and lead ecological grassroots movements to press for change, perhaps because they are directly involved with family affairs. Also, in her own work, she saw clearly how environmental degradation and unsustainable development have severely affected women (Women in Action, 1991c).

For women communicators and other development practitioners, the following are strategies for involving women in environmental protection:

1. Strengthen women's groups by providing support to women already struggling to preserve their environment and women's networks at the grassroots level, and by researching and documenting the linkages between women's lives and their environment (Asian and Pacific Women's Resource and Action Series: Environment, 1992, as cited in NCRFW, 1995).

2. Involve women at all levels of the planning and implementation process to improve the environment, including the home and work environment. Integrate the knowledge and experience of grassroots women in management of ecosystem into projects, programmes, and policies for environmentally sustainable development (NCRFW, 1995).

3. Ask themselves certain questions such as "If, as has been noted, women are at a disadvantage because they lack status, what adjustments in natural resource management projects could offer women a role within local governing bodies?" In addition to mandating that women have a role, project planners can be sure women have equal access to the technical training and education necessary to play a role in local management (USAID, 1998).

4. Since women are economically disadvantaged, projects can focus on increasing or diversifying their income. This could mean developing project components that give women the opportunity to generate income either through direct employment or access to credit (USAID, 1998).

GUIDE TO DISCUSSION 5

Objectives	Discussion Questions
• Identify and explain the role of women in environmental protection in the four ASEAN mini-cases presented	Ask the participants to read the lesson entitled "The Role of Women in Environmental Protection and Strategies for Involving Women in Environmental Protection". Key Question: What are the roles of women in environmental protection? Suggested answers: ▪ Attend activities which make them aware of household environmental problems, health issues caused by environmental problems, and appropriate, ecologically-sustainable technology. ▪ Become actively involved in environmental protection and conservation activities like cleaning their surroundings, practicing proper garbage management, and planting trees. ▪ Voice concerns on various environmental issues through the use of various media
• Identify other potential roles of women in environmental protection	Key Question: What are the other potential roles of women in environmental protection? Suggested answers: ▪ Women's groups are organising to integrate women fully into the political process, so they can take their full part in policy decisions affecting their lives, including policies on: the use of land and water resources for agriculture; power; drinking water and energy supply; health and education services; and economic opportunities. ▪ Women as consumers can play an important part in awareness-raising and influencing the powerful business sector. They can refuse to buy goods that are damaging to the environment and recycle others.
• Identify strategies for involving women in environmental protection	Key Question: What are the strategies women communicators and development practitioners can utilise to involve women in environmental protection? Suggested answers: ▪ Strengthen women's groups. ▪ Involve all women at all levels of the planning and implementation process to improve the environment. ▪ Make sure women have equal access to the technical training and education necessary to play a role in local management. ▪ To enable women to be economically sufficient, develop project components that give women the opportunity to generate income either through direct employment or access to credit.

CASES

The following two cases will serve to enrich the participants' knowledge of the role of women in environmental protection. The first case deals with women's involvement in the protection of coastal resources and the second to the protection of upland resources.

CASE 1

Objectives

By the end of Case No. 1, the participants are expected to:

1. Explain the role of DENR-CEP in breaking down barriers and integrating women into the natural resource management process in Pangangan Island, Calape, Bohol;
2. Identify the roles performed by women in coastal resource management of the island; and
3. Determine the effects on coastal resource management of the CEP-GAD project.

Case 1:

Coastal Resource Management Through Women Empowerment: The Case of the CEP-GAD in Pangangan Island

by Dinah Pura T. Depositario

It's early dawn and fishermen are ready to take off for their destination to as far as Palawan and Borneo to join the commercial fishing industries. The women and children are gathered along the beach to bid their loved ones goodbye. The husbands and male members of the families above 18 years of age would soon be away from their families from six months to one year. The weather is fine and despite the cold chilly breeze, the family members from the different parts of the island woke up early. Gone are the laughter and gleeful interlude during the Christmas season. Soon those left behind will have to perform their multiple roles with no other breadwinner to lean on. Such is the traditional annual episode in Pangangan Island.

Until January 1994, illegal, destructive fishing methods such as dynamite and sodium cyanide and trawl fishing were prevalent on the island. These activities destroyed the coral reefs of the marine habitat. A 1992 rapid aquatic resources appraisal showed there was only about 10% live coral cover and 90% dead standing coral.

There was also illegal and excessive cutting of mangroves to give way to the conversion of some areas for fishpond or fishpond expansion. Mangroves were also cut to provide firewood, posts for fish corrals, and for building or other structural uses.

Aggravating the coastal management problems was the establishment and development of beach resorts on the island and the indiscriminate throwing of waste along the coasts. Generally, there was a low level of awareness about the extent of damage or the ill-effects of illegal fishing activities, mangrove destruction, and other malpractices.

The situation in Pangangan Island started transforming when in January 1994, it was chosen as the pilot site for the Coastal Environment Project (CEP) in Central Visayas by DENR CENRO Tagbilaran City. CEP aimed to conserve and develop the country's coastal resources through a community-based management approach.

CEP started its development efforts by first organising and mobilising eight people's organisations (POs) at a rate of one PO per barangay with a total membership of 387 households (54% of the island households).

Under the CEP, the following major projects were undertaken: coastal rehabilitation (i.e., coastal clean-up and mangrove plantation), inland development (fish sanctuary establishment), and infrastructure projects (i.e., watchtower and staff house).

The two fish sanctuaries are in barangays. Magtongtong and Lomboy and are 7.27 and 8.68 ha, respectively. To ensure the enforcement of sanctuary boundaries and regulations, municipal ordinances were instituted, for Magtongtong in December 1995 and for Lomboy in August 1996. Fishing and other extractive activities were absolutely forbidden inside the sanctuaries.

The watchtower, on the other hand, was constructed adjacent to the Magtongtong Fish Sanctuary about 500 m from the CEP field station on the mainland. DENR CEP shelled out a total of P 30,000 for the construction of the said tower. Due to insufficient funds, the Magtongtong Farmers and Fishermen's Association (MAFFA) assumed the completion of the construction with the support and voluntary services of its members.

CEP also initiated the formation of Bantay Dagat teams in each barangay. The fish wardens voluntarily conduct land and sea-borne patrols in shifts every night. Since the Bantay Dagat teams were trained, organised, and deputised, the number of illegal fishing violations decreased.

In August 17, 1998, the Gender and Development (GAD) programme was integrated into the Coastal Environment Program. A series of meetings with the regional and provincial DENR offices were held on how GAD could be addressed in the project. In the absence of data on gender, the GAD unit in the regional DENR office lobbied for the conduct of a gender analysis to transform the CEP into a "gender-responsive" development effort. An annual budget of P250,000 was allocated from the regional DENR GAD funds for the implementation of GAD alongside CEP in the island.

In 1997, the project conducted a gender analysis using the Participatory Rural Appraisal on Gender and Environment Concerns (PRAGEN) tools in 1997 upon which a community gender responsive plan was formulated. PRAGEN's processes encourage the involvement of women and men in community decisionmaking, organisation, and mobilisation. PRAGEN also enhances the design, implementation, monitoring and evaluation of development projects. Through this tool, the gender needs, issues, and problems of female and male beneficiaries and strategies to address these were identified.

During the formal launching of GAD, the purpose of the CEP-GAD program was presented to invited project beneficiaries and identified PO allies (GOs and NGOs). The results of the gender analysis conducted were presented. The meeting culminated with all the PO allies signing a Memorandum of Agreement in order to help implement the action plan. The CEP-GAD action plan that resulted from the gender analysis activity served as the basis for the mobilisation of resources and other forms of support from the PO allies and was also used during the gender sensitivity training (GST) sessions that were held in each of the eight barangays.

To ease pressure on the island's coastal resources, alternative livelihood projects were also initiated under CEP-GAD. The livelihood activities in the area were supportive of the major goal of CEP of coastal resources conservation and protection. These were: vegetable gardening, tree plantation (gmelina) and mango production, hog dispersal, consumer store/ "bigasan", lending investment, goat dispersal, peanut production,

Euchuema (seaweed) culture and fish pot or "bobo" fishing. Backyard gardening was promoted especially among the women to encourage them to provide nutritious and fresh vegetables to their families.

To further promote environmental awareness among the beneficiaries as well as to equally empower its female and male beneficiaries, a number of other training sessions/workshops were conducted under the CEP-GAD. Among the training sessions were: fish sanctuary management, solid waste management, and coconut midribs basket-making for livelihood; small-scale farming technologies for inland development; catering services planning and management, and training/seminars on the deputation of fish wardens for bantay dagat. Project management noted that the women's participation in the training programs in 1999 already increased to 53% of the total female PO members.

CEP-GAD became the moving force in terms of the participation of the island's constituents (the majority of whom are women) in the island's economic activities. There were women constituents of the island whose projects were provided financial and logistical assistance. The most successful women entrepreneurs were Dionisia Talatagod, who was engaged in vegetable and tree farming, and Lourdes Granaderos, Flordeliza Tupos, and Marites Mozo, who were all engaged in the shellcraft business.

The project has also strengthened the participation of women in economic activities by giving them access to services and resources which enabled them to engage in worthwhile community and business projects. Women were provided financial as well as logistical (i.e., seeds and seedlings, fertilisers, tools, etc.) assistance.

The CEP-GAD has also empowered the women on the island to be more socially and politically active. Through the officers' training and planning workshop, team building and indicative planning, gender sensitivity training and the gender responsive planning workshops and action planning, the women were made aware of their leadership potential which they could use in managing their people's organisations and communities.

The increasing leadership and participation of the women is very much reflected in the percentage of females in the eight people's organisations (POs). By the end of 1999, 32.5% of the board of directors were females; 60.4%, committee leaders; 35.5%, officers; and 53.6%, members.

The prominent women leaders of POs were Angelberta Garay (PO President of Barangay Talisay), Gertrudes Suba-an (PO President of Barangay Lawis) and Fely Carmona (PO President of Barangay Kahayag). Other women who played active roles in their barangays were Marites Mozo, wife of the barangay captain of Kinabag-an and the head of the women's association, Dionisia Talatagod, secretary of the Kinabag-an PO, and Judith Forones, member of the Lomboy PO.

The presence of women was also manifested in the local politics arena. The most notable female political figure in the island is Adelaida Garay who is the current barangay captain of Barangay Magtongtong. She is serving her first term which started in 1996. At that time, she had just come out of retirement, having turned 60. Prior to 1996, she had not been permanently residing on the island; however, her barangay co-constituents convinced her to go back to Pangangan.

The female barangay captain also plays the role of mentor to other women leaders such as the second counselor of Magtongtong, Fely Vallejo. She is happy that more and more women on the island are taking an active role in their island's political landscape.

Furthermore, women also played an important role as concerned citizens. There were some women who volunteered their services as fish wardens. They would go out with their male counterparts at night to apprehend violators.

As a result of the project's promotion of livelihood activities among the island's female constituents, the women's skills for self-assertion, self-worth and self-determination have increased. These factors – together with the women becoming more well-informed – have enabled them to make crucial decisions about such issues as personal matters, family, career, and business plans. Some women who were formerly home-oriented have now become more entrepreneurial and career-oriented. They also now have greater aspirations.

Furthermore, through the gender sensitivity and other training, the project has also created and developed gender awareness in the community especially on the value of women's current and potential contributions in the community. The training has promoted a common understanding of gender equality in the community.

During one GAD Sensitivity training (GST) session, men had expressed the insights that they had gained. The most notable of their personal thoughts were that: men and women should be treated as equals, that there were indeed unequal opportunities between men and women, and that there was less recognition of womens' achievements.

The imbibed ideas of gender equality and partnership between the sexes, especially on the part of the husbands, have consequently led to a redivision of labour among the Pangangan islanders, with more women fishing and more men doing the housework. This development has enabled the women to be more active in the CEP-GAD livelihood projects and in social and political activities.

Family relationships have also been enhanced by the sharing of responsibilities in managing the home and family enterprises. As aptly expressed by one woman GST participant, "the men dig, the women plant, and the youth water (the vegetables)."

For now, the men welcome the changes in the role of the island's women. They do not feel threatened nor intimidated at all by the increased participation of women in almost all arenas of life.

For the above reasons, the CEP-GAD project in Pangangan Island was awarded the Most Gender Sensitive Project of DENR, first in Region VII and then at the National Level during the 1998 GAD Service Awards.

Since the efforts initiated by the CEP-GAD in coordination with other government and nongovernment agencies, the natural resources of the area have been protected and further developed. As documented in a report on coastal resource management on the island by Kintanar (1999), after just two years of the existence of the marine sanctuaries, the Panganganons now report improvements in the size and quantity of their fish and shell catches. Large "ketong", or rabbitfish, are now regularly caught near the buffer zones of the sanctuaries. Likewise, the fish catch in the sanctuaries' vicinity has improved from an average of 2 to 3 kilos per fishing effort and as of May 1999, there has been a substantial improvement in the live coral cover inside the Magtongtong and Lomboy sanctuaries. Lastly, there has been a change in attitudes among Panganganons in the way they view their environment and their capability to manage it.

The greatest achievement of CEP-GAD however is that it has empowered the islanders to strive for continuous progress in all aspects of their lives. Even with the inevitable expected phase-out of the project, the Panganganons are one in vowing to still continue with what they have started. If only for this, then the CEP-GAD can be considered a resounding success.

GUIDE QUESTIONS FOR CASE NO. 1

1. How did the CEP break down barriers and integrate women into the natural resource management process?
2. Identify the roles performed by the women which directly or indirectly contributed to coastal resource management in Pangangan Island.
3. What were the environmental and social effects of the integration of gender concerns on coastal resource management in Pangangan Island?

SUGGESTED ANSWERS

1. CEP strengthened the eight people's organisations (POs) by inviting the members to attend gender sensitivity training, gender responsive planning workshops, and leadership and team-building-related training sessions.

   Furthermore, to promote environmental awareness among the beneficiaries as well as to equally empower its female and male beneficiaries, a number of environmental protection-related training sessions/workshops were conducted under the CEP-GAD.

   To ease pressure on the island's coastal resources, alternative livelihood projects were also initiated under CEP-GAD. There were also women constituents of the island whose projects were provided financial and logistical assistance.

   Through the gender sensitivity and other training, the project created and developed gender awareness in the community especially about the value of women's current and potential contributions in the community.

2. The roles performed by the women which directly or indirectly contributed to coastal resource management in Pangangan Island:
   - Attended gender sensitivity training, and other leadership and livelihood training
   - Participated in coastal clean-up and mangrove planting
   - Furthermore, women also played an important role as concerned citizens. There were some women who volunteered their services as

fish wardens, and staffed watchtowers and fish sanctuaries. They
would go out with their male counterparts at night to apprehend
violators.

- Undertook livelihood activities such as vegetable gardening, tree
plantation (gmelina) and mango production, hog dispersal, consumer
store/ "bigasan", lending investment, goat dispersal, peanut
production, Euchuema (seaweed) culture and fish pot or "bobo"
fishing
- Assumed active roles in the POs by becoming board of director
members, committee heads, and active members. At the barangay
level, one became a Barangay Captain and another a counselor and
took part in project design and implementation and policy decision
making related to environmental-related policies.

3. The CEP-GAD has empowered the women in the island to be more
socially and politically active. The women were made aware of their
leadership potential which they could utilise in managing their people's
organisations and communities. The increasing leadership and
participation role of the women is very much reflected in the percentage
of females in the eight POs. By the end of 1999, 32.5% of the board of
directors were females; 60.4%, committee leaders; 35.5%, officers; and
53.6%, members.

The imbibed ideas of gender equality and partnership between the sexes,
especially on the part of the husbands, have also consequently led to a
redivision of labour among the Pangangan islanders, with more women
doing fishing and more men doing housework. Thus, family relationships
have also been enhanced by the sharing of responsibilities in managing
the home and family enterprises.

Lastly, the natural resources of the area have been protected and further
developed. As documented in a report on coastal resource management
in the island by Kintanar (1999), after just two years of the existence of
the marine sanctuaries, the Panganganons now report improvements in
the size and quantity of their fish and shell catches. Large "ketong" or
rabbitfish are now regularly caught near the buffer zones of the
sanctuaries. Likewise, the fish catch in the sanctuaries' vicinity has
improved from an average of 2 to 3 kilos per fishing effort and as of
May 1999, there has been a substantial improvement in the live coral
cover inside the Magtongtong and Lomboy sanctuaries. Lastly, there
has been a change in attitudes among Panganganons in the way they
view their environment and their capability to manage it.

CASE 2

Objectives
By the end of Case No. 2, the participants are expected to:
1. Identify the factors which prompted Josefina Campo and the other women to take part in the forest management programme in Davao del Norte;
2. Identify the roles performed by women in the protection of their forest; and
3. Discuss Josefina Campo's and the other women's (including children) innate advantages which effectively facilitated their part in the community-based forest management programme.

Case 2:

Woman, Mother, Teacher, Warrior: The Case of Josefina Campo

by Antonio P. Contreras, Helen F. Dayo, and Ila Virginia C. Ongkiko

Her commitment to protect the forests surrounding her village sprung from her instinct of self-preservation. The Ormoc tragedy which had killed thousands, most of whom were from poor to middle-income families like her own, etched a threatening scenario in the mind of this widowed elementary school teacher. Disturbed by her own awareness of the rape and plunder of the forests surrounding her village, most of which was done by illegal cutters from her own class and place, combined with the dark and eerie foreboding dramatically expressed as incessant sounds of power-chainsaws punctuating the stillness of her nights, this woman summoned her courage and decided to confront the problem. Her concern for her life, the life and future of her daughter, and the fate of her community motivated her to do something. The reality that she faced became even more difficult with the knowledge that the poaching of timber from the forests was done by people, mostly men, for the same reasons of self-preservation – to put food on the table, send children to school, buy medicine for the sick in the family. For her, however, there were other alternatives less destructive than marching into the forest in the deep of the night armed with a chain saw.

Ironically, it is this instinct for self-preservation that has also caused her to take a position which later threatened her very own security. But Josefina Campo remains unwavering in her commitment to lead her

63

community in the protection of the remaining forests surrounding it. This woman, mother and teacher also became, by choice, a warrior for the environment.

Inday Campo, as she is lovingly referred to in her village, actually comes from a privileged position in her community. As a school teacher in Binogsayan, a sitio in Barangay Napnapan in the municipality of Pantukan in Davao del Norte, she occupies a respected place. This is probably one of the factors which has contributed to her success in mobilising her community. In 1993, she became a member of the Binogsayan Community Multipurpose Cooperative. Because of her leadership qualities, she was elected as board member, the lone woman among eight men. Despite this, she eventually became President of the Cooperative. Her presence on the board and her eventual ascendancy to its Presidency also brought with it an increased representation of women in this very important local decisionmaking body. In 1996, the membership of the board expanded to 15, even as the number of women members increased from 1 to 4.

It was during her term as leader that she actively linked with DENR and worked for the establishment of a community-based forest management project in her locality. She organised community volunteers to oversee patrolling of forests. This strategy for forest protection was effective to a point that it led to a confrontation between Inday and her volunteer patrol on one side and the illegal loggers on the other.

Binogsayan is basically a community composed of households relying mainly on rainfed agricultural systems for their livelihood. The marginal productivity of the land, and the increasing demand for capital has forced some of its members to look at the forest as a source of additional income. The forest protection efforts of the Cooperative have threatened the continuity of this activity, which understandably created tensions within the village. Inday Campo was in the middle of this, and had repeatedly received threats to her life. Probably being a woman is what saved her from physical harm, since it has been said that the legal poachers thought twice about harming her since it is culturally unacceptable for men to pick fights with women.

But it is not only the timber poachers who are affected by Inday's war with illegal forest activities; those working with her are affected as well. Forest protection work is largely a voluntary commitment without financial remuneration from DENR or the government. Since most of the forest protection volunteers are men, and considering that patrolling of the perimeters of the forest is done during evenings, the work undoubtedly took the time of these men away from their daily productive work on their farms. This led to a substantial reduction in the effective household income, which as it is, was already insufficient for the needs of the family. It is in this context that women spouses are forced to take up the slack. They hire out as farm labourers, sell snacks at the elementary school, and work on their farms while their husbands are sleeping, obviously tired from doing all-night forest patrol. Some women, particularly Inday herself, have also actively participated in the night patrols, often at the side of their husbands. Children were also actively involved in the crusade to protect the forest. They served as look-outs and runners, reporting to their fathers if they notice any evidence of illegal logging. Some of them also serve as informants, reporting to their fathers what other children of illegal loggers say.

Inday's commitment has caught the attention not only of her enemies but also of the government. Her experience and the case of Binogsayan were projected by the forest bureaucracy which was hungry for success stories. She became Exhibit 1, even a poster girl for the campaign of the government in support of community-based forest management associations in the country, as the only female member, albeit its chair, of the all-male board of directors. As such, she now interacts with national DENR officials.

But Inday always comes back to Binogsayan, not to rest on her laurels and boast her newly found place in the national arena, but to join her village as it wrestles with the problems besetting it.

In her deep reflections, she is aware of the continuing struggles. She also feels the frustration of the forest protection volunteers who sacrifice their time, nights, and even security, and forego potential income from farming. They are now becoming desolate over the lack of tangible and material government support to provide them with an alternative livelihood. She expresses her impatience about the slowness and ineffectiveness of government responses to their needs for livelihood support. As a woman, mother and teacher, she is well aware that putting food on the table and sending children to school are equally important as protecting the forests.

Again, her warrior instinct for self-preservation has told her she has to do something. But this time, her battlefield is no longer local but national.

GUIDE QUESTIONS FOR CASE NO. 2

1. Why did Josefina Campo and the other women take part in the forest management programme in Davao del Norte?
2. Describe the direct and indirect roles performed by the women and children in the protection of their forest.
3. What were the Josefina Campo's and the other women's (including children) innate advantages which facilitated their effectively taking part in the community-based forest management programme?

SUGGESTED ANSWERS

1. With the knowledge that deforestation can cause floods and other natural calamities, Josefina and the other women's commitment to protect the forests surrounding their village has sprung from their instinct of self-preservation. They are concerned for their lives, their children's future, and the fate of their community.
2. The direct roles performed by the women and children in the protection of their forest:
   - Some women actively participated in the night patrols, often at the side of their husbands
   - Children were also actively involved in the crusade to protect the forest
   - The children served as look-outs and runners, reporting to their fathers if they noticed any evidence of illegal logging
   - Some children also served as informants, reporting to their fathers what other children of illegal loggers said.

   On the other hand, women also played an indirect role in the protection of their forest. Most of the forest protection volunteers were men, and considering that patrolling of the perimeters of the forest was done during evenings, the work done during the evenings took the time of these men away from their daily productive work in their farms. This additional task led to a substantial reduction in the effective household income, which as it is, was already insufficient for the needs of the family. Thus the women spouses were forced to take up the slack. They hired themselves out as farm labourers, sold snacks at the elementary school, and worked on their farms while their husbands were sleeping, obviously tired from doing all-night forest patrol.

3. Josefina's and the other women's (including children) innate advantages which facilitated their effectively taking part in the community-based forest management programme were as follows:

- Being a woman protected them from physical harm, since the legal poachers thought twice about harming them as it is culturally unacceptable for men to pick fights with women.
- As the only female member, albeit the chair, of the all-male board of directors, Josefina became a poster girl for the campaign of the government in support of community-based forest management association in the country. She was able to interact with national DENR officials.

SYNTHESIS ACTIVITY

This activity can be done after all the subchapters have been discussed.

Focus Group Discussion and Role-Playing/ Skit Presentation (3.5 hours)

Women coming from similar zonal classifications (i.e., coastal areas, upland areas, agricultural lowland areas,) and countries should be grouped by the facilitator. A group size of eight is ideal. The objective of this activity is to make the participants assess the environmental status of their respective zonal classifications and countries and identify the current and potential role of women in environmental protection.

The participants will have a one-hour focus group discussion (led by the facilitator) on the following topics:

a) Environmental problems in their respective zones/countries
b) Current and potential role of women/organisations in protecting their environment

They will then be given 30 minutes to prepare for their role-play/ skit presentation which should focus on the current and potential roles of women in environmental protection. Each group will then be given 7-10 minutes to present their skit.

There will then be a 30-minute to one-hour open forum led by the facilitator to discuss the roles identified per zonal classification, solicit additional identified roles from the rest of the group, identify the assistance needed to enable the women to participate in environmental protection, and discuss the insights gained from the activity. The facilitator should summarise the highlights of the open forum.

SUMMARY

Ecofeminism is a term used to describe the "diverse range of women's efforts to save the earth and the recent development of feminism resulting from the new view of women and nature." This new view stresses that women and nature have a symbiotic relationship – that is, a healthy life is dependent upon a healthy environment. Thus, the concept of ecofeminism suggests that women have to play an active role in the protection of the environment.

The reasons women have to be concerned with the protection of the environment are:

1) They are users and necessarily, nurturers, of natural resources.
2) Their undertaking of daily and livelihood activities are affected by environmental degradation.
3) They are affected by adverse health impacts of environmental degradation and pollution.
4) They have the biggest stake in the natural resource base and the best knowledge of their problems and needs, whose solutions cannot be arrived at without them.
5) They play an important role in shaping societal values and attitudes towards the environment on the young.
6) They are directly affected by "environmental" activities.

Those designed to rehabilitate degraded areas, reduce pollution or conserve genetic variety.

The constraints to women's sustainable use of natural resourcesare:

1) National law or local customs often effectively deny women the right to secure title or inherit land, which deny them of access to other resources such as credit.
2) Agricultural extension services are heavily biased towards men.

3) Poverty, precarious land tenure and lack of expert support discourage women from investing in newer technologies or long-term strategies.

4) Pressures on limited land resources deplete nutrients and degrade soil.

5) Women suffer from well-meaning but inappropriate development activities.

6) Women's ideas are not valued and their initiatives do not carry as much weight as those of men.

The current roles of women in environmental protection include:

1) Attending activities which make them aware of household environmental problems, health issues caused by environmental problems, and appropriate, ecologically-sustainable technology

2) Becoming actively involved in environmental protection and conservation activities like cleaning their surroundings, practising proper garbage management, and planting trees

3) Voicing concerns on various environmental issues through various media.

Furthermore, the potential roles of women in environmental protection are as follows:

1) Women's groups can organise to integrate women fully into the political process, so they can take their full part in policy decisions affecting their lives, including policies on: the use of land and water resources for agriculture; power; drinking water and energy supply; health and education services; and economic opportunities

2) Women as consumers can play an important part in raising awareness and influencing the powerful business sector and can refuse to buy goods that are damaging to the environment and recycle others.

The strategies women communicators and development practitioners can use to involve women in environmental protection include:

1) Strengthening women's groups
2) Involving all women at all levels of the planning and implementation process to improve the environment
3) Making sure women have equal access to the technical training and education necessary to play a role in local management
4) Developing project components that give women the opportunity to generate income either through direct employment or access to credit to enable women to be economically sufficient.

FACILITATOR'S GUIDE

Note to the facilitator: Participants should be asked to read in advance the entire chapter on women and the environment.

TOPIC	OBJECTIVES	TEXT	ACTIVITY	DURATION AM
Overview	1. Explain the interrelationship between women and the environment 2. Discuss the status of women in developing countries 3. Identify the environmental issues common among ASEAN countries 4. Explain the impact of environmental degradation on women	Introduction	Discussion of Answers to Discussion 1	30 minutes
Women and Environment	1. Explain why nature has been traditionally given a feminine gender 2. Discuss the concept of ecofeminism 3. Discuss the implication of the concept of ecofeminism on the nature of women's role in the protection of the environment	What is ecofeminism?	Discussion of Answers to Discussion 2	45 minutes
Women and Environment	1. Explain why women should be involved in the protection of the environment 2. Explain why any crisis in the environment necessarily affects women more than anybody else within the community. 3. Appreciate why solutions to environmental problems cannot be arrived at without the involvement of women	Why should women be concerned with protecting the environment?	Discussion of Answers to Discussion 3	One hour

TOPIC	OBJECTIVES	TEXT	ACTIVITY	DURATION AM
Women and Environment	1. Discuss the constraints to women's sustainable use of natural resources	What are the constraints to women's sustainable use of natural resources?	Discussion of Answers to Discussion 4	30 minutes
Role of Women in Environmental Protection	1. Identify and explain the role of women in environmental protection in the 4 ASEAN mini-cases presented 2. Identify other potential roles of women in environmental protection 3. Discuss strategies for involving women in environmental protection	The Role of Women in Environmental Protection	Discussion of Answers to Discussion 5	45 minutes
Integrative Cases of Women's Role in Environmental Protection	Analyse cases illustrating the role of women in environmental protection	Introduction Women and the Environment The Role of Women in Environmental Protection	Discussion of Answers to Questions of 2 Cases	**PM** One hour
Synthesis Activity	1. Discuss and identify environmental problems in their zones and countries 2. Identify and present the current and potential roles of women/women organisations in protecting their environment	Introduction Women and the Environment The Role of Women in Environmental Protection	Focus Group Discussion and Role-Playing/Skit Presentation	3.5 hours

REFERENCES

Asian and Pacific Women's Resource and Action Series: Environment. 1992. Asian and Pacific Development Centre, Kuala Lumpur.

Baden, S. 1993. BRIDGE Report no. 11: **Practical Strategies for Involving Women as well as Men in Water and Sanitation Activities**, commissioned by SIDA. http://www.gdrc.org/gender/gender-and-envi.html

Beijing+5 United Nations General Assembly Special Session. Undated. **Status of Women**. http://www.swc-fc.gc.ca/publish/beijing5/environment-e.pdf

Chelala, Cesar. 2002. **Women Taking Charge to Save the Environment**. http://www.commondreams.orgviews 01/0512-01.htm

Contreras, Antonio P., Helen F. Dayo, and Ila Virginia C. Ongkiko. 2000. **Woman, Mother, Teacher, Warrior: The Case of Josefina Campo**, Unpublished Case. National Commission on the Role of Filipino Women (NCRFW)-CIDA.

Cruz, Marissa and Irma Paule. 2000. "Gender Analysis in Development Project: Application in the Coastal Environment Sector", a case study featured in the National Commission on the Role of Filipino Women and the Women's Studies Association of the Philippines publication

Davidson, Joan. 1993. **Women's Relationship with the Environment**. Focus on Gender, Vol. 1, No. 1.

Depositario, Dinah Pura T. 2000. **Coastal Resource Management Through Women Empowerment: The Case of the CEP-GAD in Pangangan Island**, case based on the unpublished case entitled "Pangangan Women : Hope of the Island (A Case Study on the Gender Dimensions of DENR (CEP-GAD) Intervention in Pangangan Island, Calape, Bohol)", co-authored with Dr. Pura T. Depositario, National Commission on the Role of Filipino Women (NCRFW)-CIDA.

Dethrasavong, Chandavanh. 2001. **Country Report on Women in Lao PDR and Sustainable Development**, paper presented during the "Workshop on: Capacity Building of Women Communicators to Promote Environmental Awareness and Conservation", organised by the Asian Media Information and Communication Centre (AMIC), 5-9 November 2001, Bangkok.

Food and Agriculture Organization (Gender Unit). Undated. **Gender and Food Security**. gdrc.org/gender/1pager-004.html

Hopey, Don. 2000. **Environment Troubles Worse for Women than Men**. http://www.post-gazette.com/headlines20000608 IssueEight4.asp

Illo, Jeanne Frances I. 1997. **Women in the Philippines.** ADB Country Briefing Paper.

Joekes, Susan. Undated. **Do Environmental Projects Promote Gender Equity?** in environmental policy and gender issues. http://www.gdrc.org/gender/gender-and-envi.html

Kim, Wang Lay. 2001. **Research Report : Malaysia,** paper presented during the "Workshop on: Capacity Building of Women Communicators to Promote Environmental Awareness and Conservation", organised by the Asian Media Information and Communication Centre (AMIC), 5-9 November, 2001, Bangkok.

Kintanar, Anthony. 1999. **Beyond the Mangrove Path: Coastal Resource Management in Pangangan.**

Joekes, Susan. Undated. **Do Environmental Projects Promote Gender Equity?** in environmental policy and gender issues. http://www.gdrc.org/gender/gender-and-envi.html

Kim, Wang Lay. 2001. **Research Report : Malaysia,** paper presented during the "Workshop on: Capacity Building of Women Communicators to Promote Environmental Awareness and Conservation", organized by the Asian Media Information and Communication Centre (AMIC), November 5-9 2001, Bangkok.

Kintanar, Anthony. 1999. **Beyond the Mangrove Path: Coastal Resource Management in Pangangan.**

Martin-Brown, Joan. 1993. "The Rationale: Why Women and the Environment?" in **the Greenbook: A Manual to Support Organizing a National Assembly of Women and the Environment,** Global Regional Assemblies of Women and the Environment, UNEP.

Martinez, Luz Maria. 2000. **Mainstreaming Gender into National Food Security Policies: Why Food Security is Still a Concern for Women in the 21ˢᵗ Century.** Women in Action. March.

Moscoso, Mildred O. 2001. **Bringing Maria Back to her Mountain: Tapping Filipino Women's Potential for Environmental Communication Through Community Media,** paper presented during the "Workshop on: Capacity Building of Women Communicators to Promote Environmental Awareness and Conservation", organised by the Asian Media Information and Communication Centre (AMIC), 5 - 9 November 2001, Bangkok.

Nary, Hang and Ngann Thanak. 2001. **Cambodia Case – Cambodian Women: Their Role in Environmental Awareness and Conservation,** report prepared for the "Workshop on: Capacity Building of Women Communicators to Promote Environmental Awareness and Conservation", organised by the Asian Media Information and Communication Centre (AMIC), 5 - 9 November 2001, Bangkok.

Nary, Hang and Ngann Thanak and Luy Rasmey and Yin Sundarinet. 2001. **Country Report and Research Paper: Cambodia**, paper presented during the Workshop on: Capacity Building of Women Communicators to Promote Environmental Awareness and Conservation", organised by the Asian Media Information and Communication Centre (AMIC), 5-9 November 2001, Bangkok.

NCRFW. 1995. **Primer on Women and the Environment**. NCRFW.

Puente, Sonia G. Undated. **Women are Caretakers of the Environment**. http://www.metimes.com/issue45/commu/03environment.htm.

Second ASEAN State of the Environment Report. 2000. http://www.eapap.unep.org/reports/aseansoe

The State of World Population 2001. **Women and the Environment**. http://www.unfpa.org/swp/2001/english/ch04.html.

United States Agency for International Development (USAID). 1998. **Women and the Environment: The Role of Gender in Effective Natural Resource Management**, a news letter published by the Office of Women in Development Winter, 1997-1998.

WEDO. 1999. **Women's Health and the Environment**. http://www.gdrc.org/gender/1pager-002.html.

Women in Action. 1991a. **Malaysia: After the Malacca Water Crisis**.

Women in Action. 1991b. **Ecofeminism**.

Women in Action. 1991c. **Interview with a Brazilian Agriculturist**.

Women's Empowerment, Population and the Environment Factsheet: Global Population and Environment. Undated. http://www.sierraclub.org/population/factsheets/women.asp

Zimmerman, Michael E., J. Baird Callicott, George Sessions, Karen J. Warren, and John Clark (Eds.). 1993. **Environmental Philosophy: From Animal Rights to Radical Ecology**. Englewood Cliffs, NJ: Prentice-Hall, pp. 253-267. http://www2.pfeiffer.edu/~Iridenercourses/ecowarrn.html

CHAPTER **4**

Communication Planning

MILDRED O. MOSCOSO

OBJECTIVES
After this chapter, participants should be able to:

1. Explain the value of developing a communication plan for environmental communication;
2. Discuss the significance of the "convergence" communication model to environmental communication planning;
3. Enumerate the different steps to communication planning; and
4. Develop a communication campaign.

INTRODUCTION

Having considered the environmental scenario we are in, as well as the value of communicating for the environment and what we can do as women to alleviate the problems of our environment, the next step would be to look at how we can communicate for the environment as effectively and efficiently as possible. This is where planning and developing a good communication strategy for the environment comes in.

In this module, we will look into the reasons why a communication plan is necessary in environmental communication, consider a communication model which can be a basis for this type of communication, and follow a framework that can be used in developing an effective and efficient communication plan for the environment.

LESSON 1. THE VALUE OF A GOOD COMMUNICATION STRATEGY

For the first lesson, let us consider what a good communication strategy can do for environmental projects. One of the best ways to show the value of a good communication strategy would be to give an example of how one was utilised to help solve an actual environmental problem. The story of the solid waste management project of the local government of Los Baños, Laguna, Philippines is a case in point.

The Case of Los Baños, Laguna's Solid Waste Management Project

Solid waste management has been a major environmental concern in the Philippines for years now. Not only are urban areas affected, but even rural areas on the verge of rapid urbanisation and growth. One such area is Los Baños, a university town with the title of special science and nature city, located in the province of Laguna on the major island of Luzon in the Philippines. In fact, this was one of the first problems dealt with by the new municipal leadership that assumed office after the elections in May 2001.

Some of the complaints of the residents addressed by the new municipal leadership included erratic garbage collection schedules and the disturbing presence of the open town dumpsite on the otherwise serene Mt. Makiling (one of the Philippines' legendary mountains which occupies some areas of Los Baños and a nearby town in the province of Batangas).

These problems have beset former leaders of the town's local government. Nevertheless, the current chief local executive, Mayor Ceasar Perez, along with his town councilors and advisers, was more aggressive in confronting the solid waste management problem head on. He made it part of the mission of his local government to "install an environmentally sound solid waste management system with composting as the centerpiece". Varied activities were conducted for this purpose. More importantly, various sectors and stakeholders were mobilised to help solve the problem. Needless to say, communication played a key role in the whole process.

With the help of his town councilors, a new municipal ordinance was passed. Municipal Ordinance 2001-08 prohibits anyone from littering inside public vehicles, streets, and other public places of the town. Anyone caught will be fined P300 for the first offense, P500 for the second offense, P700 for the third offense, and P1,000 for the fourth offense or imprisonment for a maximum of six months. A group to enforce the ordinance was formed and named, "Task Force *Kalinisan*" (Task Force Cleanliness). This new ordinance was also announced over a local radio station and shown over the local cable TV channel.

Not only were local media utilised but so were the more traditional means of communicating, such as the use of public address systems. These public address systems were mounted on jeepneys (public utility vehicles) that went on motorcade all over the town. Messages heard over the public address systems persuaded the townsfolk to segregate their wastes into biodegradable and nonbiodegradable wastes.

Another major element of the mayor's strategy was to utilise interpersonal communication channels, this being a preferred method among the townsfolk of Los Baños. Every Saturday since he took office, the mayor met with the leaders of each *barangay* (village) to find out their problems and grievances, with solid waste being one of these troubles.

He also networked with other concerned sectors, like the Los Baños Science Community Foundation, Inc. (LBSC) , an organised group of research and development institutions in Los Baños, to help solve the problem. One of LBSC's long-term activities is to help the municipal government plan for and develop alternatives to the open dumpsite in Mt. Makiling. This being a long and ardous process, LBSC continues to conduct other activities that have a more immediate effect on solid waste management. One of these is to "adopt" certain barangays who are then taught the rigours of waste segregation.

Part of the campaign was the production and distribution of communication materials to help raise people's awareness and motivation to participate in the town project. Simple leaflets were distributed among the residents. These leaflets informed the people of the municipal ordinance with its accompanying penalty for offenders, the newly organised schedule of garbage collection in different villages of the town, as well as how to segregate wastes and the benefits of such practice. T-shirts with the message: *"Los Banos ito: Dapat walang kalat!"* (This is Los Banos: No one should litter here!) also served as an innovative giveaway to the townsfolk.

Mayor Perez's strategy seemed to have paid off. On the mayor's 100th day in office, a total of 40 violators of the municipal ordinance were apprehended and penalised. And according to the Office of the Municipal Planning and Development Coordinator, the good news was that the people were "proud of the results of this campaign. Never before have the people seen a much cleaner and orderly public market; most of the roads are kept clean that not even a cigarette butt or candy wrapper could be seen; and drainage canals are now continuously being declogged and cleaned...a more reliable, regular garbage collection scheme has been installed...a pilot project on composting of biodegradable wastes was started and is now in progress..." (from unpublished report, "Los Banos with Mayor Ceasar P. Perez at the Helm: The First 100 Days, 2001).

Upon analysis, we can see that the mayor used various communication strategies to improve the state of solid waste management of the town. He used: interpersonal communication channels; networking

QUESTIONS FOR DISCUSSION

1. What communication strategies did the local government of Los Banos employ to improve the state of solid waste management of the town?
2. Identify an environmental problem in your community and list the communication strategies you would use to help solve it.
3. Explain why you chose the communication strategies you listed.

with other concerned sectors; listening to complaints and suggestions of residents and advisers; local media through announcements over a local radio station and features aired on the community cable TV programme; other forms of community media such as the public address systems mounted on *jeepneys*; and printed messages on T-shirts as giveaways. He also employed other culturally appropriate communication strategies such as dialogue with different barangay leaders and residents.

Imagine if the mayor's vision of "an environmentally sound solid waste management system with composting as the centerpiece" and the Municipal Ordinance 2001-08 had not been communicated through these different channels to the people of Los Baños and if the mayor had not used his strong interpersonal communication skills to mobilise the other concerned sectors: the solid waste management situation of the town would not look as promising.

This true story highlights the value of an effective communication strategy. Particularly, for environmental awareness and conservation, a well-planned communication strategy is essential in order to achieve such environmental goals.

LESSON 2. THE CONVERGENCE MODEL OF COMMUNICATION

Let us now look at an appropriate communication model we can use as a basis for the kind of communication plan we want to develop.

Traditional IEC Programmes

Specific communication strategies, like conventional or traditional Information Education and Communication (IEC) programmes, are able to achieve definite cognitive, attitudinal, or behavioural objectives. These may be objectives such as throwing trash in designated places or practising waste segregation.

Having said this, however, it is important to note that "meaningful environmental awareness goes way, way deeper than this. Environmental consciousness is a function of a society's collective cosmology, worldview, and values, hardly things one can change with a news release, a cluttered poster, or a 30 second TV ad (Flor, 1993)."

This means that if we want true environmental consciousness to take root, we need to go beyond traditional IEC programmes which are often media-centric, source-oriented, and unsustained over time. It is also imperative that we consider culture, which has often been neglected in undertakings that concern nature (Flor and Matulac, 1994). Thus, this module espouses planning for a communication strategy or programme that is less media-centric, considers the source and the receiver as equals, is sustainable over time and emphasises the culture of the people to be reached.

Kincaid's Convergence Model of Communication

Central to this way of thinking is the Convergence Model of Communication. Developed by Dr. Laurence Kincaid, this model "depicts the relationship between Participant A and Participant B in a communicative interaction. There is a cyclical process of moving towards greater mutual understanding based on the giving and receiving of information. Several cycles of information exchange occur before mutual understanding is reached…." (Macqual and Windahl, 1993). The cycle develops as follows:

FIGURE 4.1 KINCAID'S COMMUNICATION MODEL

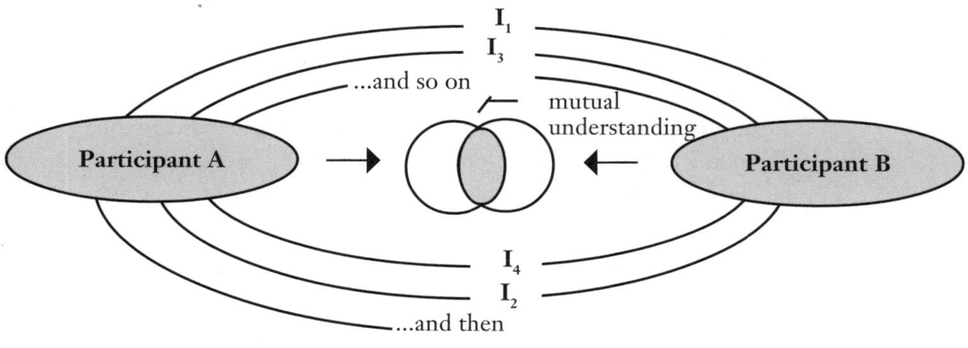

Participant A shares information (I_1) with participant B, who perceives, interprets, and responds (I_2). These phases are repeated until there is no further increase in understanding. The degree of understanding reached is represented in the figure by the shaded area where A and B overlap (Macqual and Windahl, 1993). This is convergence, where mutual understanding is reached between A and B. As the model implies, the primary purpose or function of the communication process is mutual understanding.

On the other hand, a unilinear model is often used to represent communication. The most common unilinear model is Berlo's SMCR model where the source sends the message to the receiver through a channel.

FIGURE 4.2 BERLO'S SMCR MODEL

S	M	C	R
Communication Skills	Code Content	Seeing Hearing	Communication Skills
Knowledge	Treatment	Touching	Knowledge
Attitude		Tasting	Attitude
Socio Cultural Background		Smelling	Socio Cultural Background

Let's look at both of the models and consider why the convergence model is preferred over unilinear models in terms of environmental communication.

When applied to environmental IEC programmes, the convergence framework is more "holistic and less analytical (i.e., breaking down the whole into parts and isolating these parts from one another). "Hence, it is not insensitive to the cultural contexts of the communication act." (Flor and Matulac, 1994). Moreover, according to Macqual and Windahl (1993), "The model is especially suitable for many situations in developing countries, where culture and power gaps between senders and receivers have to be bridged and this can only be achieved by gradual increases of trust and mutual awareness." Inherent in the model is the degree of trust and openness required to achieve mutual understanding.

Thus, considering that this chapter espouses planning for a communication strategy or programme that is less media-centric, considers the source and the receiver as equals, is sustainable over time and emphasises the culture of the people to be reached, then the Kincaid's convergence model of communication serves as an appropriate basis for our communication planning.

TABLE 4.1 COMPARISON OF BERLO'S SMCR MODEL WITH KINCAID'S CONVERGENCE MODEL OF COMMUNICATION

Berlo's SMCR Model	Kincaid's Convergence Model
Linear, one-way communication	Cyclical and interactive
Source-oriented. The message only comes from one end: the source.	No distinctions are made between the source and the receiver nor the information passed between them as either message or feedback. In other words, the participants in the communication process are regarded as equals (Flor and Matulac, 1994).
Based on dependency rather than on the relationship of those who communicate and their fundamental interdependency (Flor and Matulac, 1994).	Focuses on the relationship of the participants of the communication process and their interdependency.
	Emphasises mutual understanding and consensus

LESSON 3. THE STEPS TO COMMUNICATION PLANNING

After the previous lessons, we are now ready to look at communication planning and the different steps it entails.

Communication Planning

By definition, communication planning is the creation, allocation and/ or use of communication resources to achieve socially valued communication goals... (Middleton and Wedemeyer, undated). Communication planning seeks to organise resources (things, people, money) into actions, which when carried out, will lead to expected results.

Thus, a communication plan is essential in achieving the communication goals of any programme or project. These communication goals may be concerned with increasing knowledge (e.g., to increase women farmers' knowledge about the ill effects of using too much pesticide on their crops), changing attitudes (e.g., to make women farmers feel positive about the use of cultural practices to rid their farms of insect pests), or developing a skill or practice (e.g., to get women farmers to use cultural practices, instead of chemical pesticides, to get rid of insect pests on their crops).

This chapter on communication planning is mostly based on the framework developed by the Johns Hopkins University (JHU) in Baltimore, Maryland in the United States for the design, implementation, monitoring and evaluation of JHU health projects. This is called the P process (JHU, 1997). Although the "P process" was designed for health projects, its steps and principles can very well fit into the communication planning of programmes and projects in other sectors.

FIGURE 4.3 THE COMMUNICATION PLANNING PROCESS

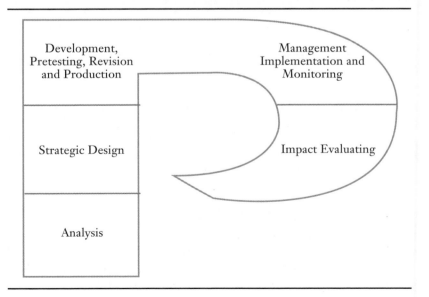

THE COMMUNICATION PLANNING PROCESS

The assumption is that an environmental issue or problem has already been identified for which the communication plan is being developed. Of course, concerned sectors should have participated in the process of identifying the problem. Or a communication programme for an environmental issue may already be in place. In any case, a communication plan is needed for either the communication campaign or the communication programme. The following are the steps in developing the plan:

ANALYSIS

The first step in the communication process is analysis. Whatever the problem and/or the objectives of the programme or project, communication analysis helps identify what is needed for communication to help achieve those objectives (Piotrow, et al., 1997).

The following is some important information needed for the communication analysis:

1. Audience Analysis

Your audience is the people you want to reach with your message; they are the ones whose behaviours must change in order for the campaign objectives to be achieved.

"Know thy audience" is the very first communication tenet we teach our students in development communication. Knowing your audience is a major step towards achieving mutual understanding, for which the convergence model of communication aims.

Whereas the conventional SMCR model puts the receiver (the audience) at the end of a one-way communication flow, the convergence approach reverses it. Communication is seen as a two-way dialogue involving equal parties who are both source and receiver (Piotrow, et al, 1997).

Knowledge about your audience is essential in any communication plan because what you know about them will be a major basis for developing your communication plan. Some questions to answer in audience analysis:

- Whose behaviour must change for programme objectives to be achieved (primary audience)?

- What are the characteristics of your primary audience?
- Who can influence the primary audience?
  (These people are considered your secondary audiences.)
- What are the characteristics of the secondary audience?
- How do different people perceive the environmental problem or issue?
- What are their knowledge, attitudes, and practices related to environmental awareness and conservation or about the specific environmental issue you are developing the communication plan for?
- How do people communicate about it?
- What communication channels do they prefer to use?

You may gather your information through interviews, surveys and/ or focus group discussions with representatives from your primary audience of the community you will be working on. Secondary information sources may also be useful, such as socio-demographic records and statistics, but these should only supplement information you have gathered from primary sources or from the people themselves.

As you go through this manual, you will discover that audience analysis is essential not only in the more general process of planning a communication campaign but also in the more specific design and development of different communication materials.

The Asian Pacific Women's Resource and Action Series: Environment (1992) mentions the Water Purification Project in Indonesia, which is a good example of how crucial knowledge about the audience is when planning a communication campaign. The project is discussed in the box below:

The seed of the **Moringa Oleifera** tree, a fast-acting agent, can be used to provide purified water for domestic purposes. **Moringa** seeds inhibit the growth of bacteria and fungi and do not create the risk of toxicity since it is a food as well.

Dian Desa, a grassroots organisation that introduces appropriate technology in the rural sector of Indonesia, conducted a survey to assess villagers' perceptions about water. Results showed that few villagers realised the danger of consuming polluted water. The first step then was to introduce health education in the villages to make villagers aware of the dangers of consuming dirty water.

The villagers were then introduced to the treatment of water with **Moringa Oleifera** seeds known as **kleor** to the Javanese people. So far, the villagers have accepted the technique and are enthusiastic about practising it. A nursery for the seeds has been set up to support dissemination nationally.

Knowledge about the audience helped the Dian Desa to be more effective in their campaign. They found out that it was the women's perception about the use of contaminated water that needed to be corrected first before they could teach the women to use the Moringa seeds in treating contaminated water. If they had not known this, then the Dian Desa might have taught the women to treat contaminated water with Moringa seeds and sadly found out that the women would not use this technology since they did not find it valuable. After all, they did not consider contaminated water to be dangerous.

ACTIVITY 4.1 GETTING TO KONW YOUR AUDIENCE

Objectives

After the activity, the participants should be able to:
1. Analyse the characteristics of a specific segment of a primary audience; and
2. Suggest communication strategies that they can employ based on the characteristics of the audience.

Procedure
1. Ask the participants to choose an environmental issue they would like to work on.
2. Ask them to identify a specific group of people as their primary audience for a communication campaign about their chosen environmental issue. They should be able to identify a very specific group that the participants would have some knowledge about (e.g., married women farmers with children from Gombong Village in Central Java, Indonesia.)

3. Divide the participants into groups. Assign each group to describe a particular aspect of your primary audience. For instance, assign Group 1 to describe the value system of the particular audience; Group 2 to describe the socio-economic status of the group, Group 3 to describe the way they communicate, and so on. (This would depend on the number of groups they have formed.)

4. Give each group a sheet of paper and markers. This is where they will write their descriptions of the aspect they've been assigned.

5. Give them about 30 minutes to discuss and write down their descriptions on the sheet.

6. Gather all the groups into a plenary and ask a representative from each group to report to everyone the result of their group work.

7. Give the others time to react, to question, or to validate the information each group reports.

8. Once all the groups have reported, ask the plenary to offer suggestions on what communication strategies can be utilised based on the identified characteristics of the audience. Facilitate the discussion.

9. Set aside the sheets or put them on display in the training venue. These will be used as reference for a subsequent exercise.

2. Policies and Programmes

This analysis identifies government policies and programmes that can impede or assist communication programmes (Piotrow, et al., 1997). This helps identify the opportunities and threats in the environment of the campaign so that the communication plan can effectively surmount obstacles and utilise available opportunities to help achieve the programme objectives.

Some questions to answer in policies and programmes analysis:

- What are the national and local policies, politics, and guidelines concerning a specific environmental issue would you like to work on?
- Who are the policymakers and opinion leaders?
- What programmes and services exist?
- How do private and public organisations work together?

If for example, your organisation wants to develop a campaign against the use of toxic pesticides in the farmlands in your village, then you must first find out if there are local policies or even national legislation relating to the use of these pesticides. You might then discover that there is no adequate legislation against the use of these toxic chemicals in agricultural lands so you can decide to make the legislators your secondary audience (SA) in the campaign. They become your SA because you want them to write laws against toxic pesticide use. After all, a campaign to get local farmers not to use these chemicals would not be as effective if there were no laws to back it up.

3. Organisations

A review of existing organisations shows which of them can best carry out an effective communication programme and how different organisations can collaborate to work for a common cause. (Piotrow, et al., 1997)

Some questions to answer in organisation analysis:

- What are the key organisations – government or non-government, private/commercial, peasant organisations – already active in environmental conservation and preservation or on the specific environmental issue you want to work on?
- Which organisations can implement or help carry out a communication plan or programme?
- Which organisations are willing but not yet capable of carrying out a communication plan?
- What would they need in order to be equipped to communicate for the environment?
- How do public and private organisations work together?
- What type of collaboration between organisations is needed?

When working together with other organisations, complementing each other and building on each other's strengths results in a more effective campaign.

I remember a collaborative project we did for an agricultural community in a village called Pinagdanglayan in the province of Quezon, Philippines. We were a team of communication specialists working for a communication project, the Development Support Communication for Selected Agricultural Technology Transfer Projects in Region 4 (DSC project). This was funded by the United Nations Development Program (UNDP) and the Philippine Council for Agriculture, Forestry, and Natural Resources Research and Development (PCARRD). The project provided communication support for the promotion of appropriate agricultural technologies needed in the community.

Other organisations were working in the area, too. One was the International Potato Center (CIP) and the other was the Farming Systems and Soil Research Institute (FSSRI) of the University of the Philippines Los Baños.

During consultations with the community, we learned that the people had a problem with soil erosion and depletion of soil nutrients. The residents of the village were mostly farming families and planted rootcrops, specifically sweet potato. The majority of them had farmland in sloping areas since most of the farms were on the foothills of a mountain.

Our team and those of the two other organisations, decided to work together since we believed that we were working toward a similar goal: to help the farmers of Pinagdanglayan to become productive while improving their soil fertility and stopping soil erosion. The campaign focused on the promotion of environment-friendly technologies like the use of a bio-organic fertiliser, and SALT (Sloping Agricultural Land Technology).

The team from FSSRI taught the farmers how to use these technologies through farmer training. CIP, on the other hand, sourced out the bio-organic fertiliser and provided funds for the farmers' wives to sell the bio-organic fertilisers in their area. We, the DSC team, on the other hand, provided communication support for the campaign by conducting classes (school-on-the-air or SOA) about SALT and other soil-saving, environment-friendly technologies aired over their makeshift local radio station. The resource persons we invited for the SOA were both from CIP and FSSRI. We also developed leaflets and even conducted song-writing contests to promote these technologies among the farmers of the village.

Unfortunately, our project funds were not enough to allow us to stay in the community longer to see the impact of this campaign. The other two organisations were able to stay and from their feedback we learned that the farmers are now more aware of these environment-friendly technologies and have in fact, established farms where these technologies are being practised.

Looking back, I realise that our collaboration with the other organisations was truly a wise move. It was not always easy working with others but together we were able to do more for the community and were even able to give them a range of services that we would not have been able to do had we worked individually. Thus, when it comes to saving the environment, it's true what they say, two heads (or organisations, for that matter) are always better than one.

4. Communication Resources

This analysis identifies the most appropriate and cost-effective channels available to reach primary and secondary audiences (Piotrow, et al., 1997). These channels can be the following:

- interpersonal channels, such as:
  - face-to-face dialogue or consultations
  - forums
  - barangay or village, meetings,
- mass media, such as:
  - television
  - radio
  - national newspapers
- community media, such as:
  - local cable TV programmes,
  - local radio stations,
  - community newspapers
  - newsletters
- folk media, such as:
  - community theatre, folk dramas
  - community celebrations
  - local songs and dances

Communication channels are not limited to these. T-shirts or hats with printed messages, speeches or even placards can also be used. They can be as varied as the imagination and creativity of those who use them. But in the end, what is important is that the channel used is the most effective and appropriate for the specific audience.

Some questions to answer in communication resources analysis:

- What are the best communication channels to reach the primary and secondary audiences?
- Who controls access to these channels?
- What laws or regulations govern these channels?

When trying to answer the first question, consider which dimensions (those in parentheses) of the channel is most important to your specific campaign for the environment. Not all these dimensions would have the same value to your campaign. Butknowing how these channels fare in terms of these dimensions will help you make the right choice when choosing which channels to use. Answer the following questions:

- Which channels do the primary and secondary audiences consider credible or believable (channel credibility)?
- Which channels will give the audience an opportunity to give feedback (channel feedback)?
- Which channels provide opportunity for the audience to be involved or participate in the communication process (channel involvement or participation)?
- Which channels are available to the audiences (channel availability)?
- Which channels have the ability to preserve a message (channel permanency)?
- Which channels have potential for covering an extensive geographical area with speed and timeliness (channel multiplicative power)?

FIGURE 4.4 GUIDE ON USE OF COMMUNICATION CHANNELS

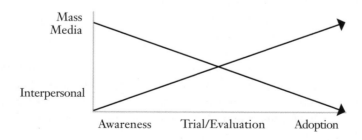

- Which channels have the potential for supplementing the communication work of another channel (channel complementarity)?

At this point, it is important to note that mass media plus interpersonal communication are most appropriately used at different points in your communication campaign. The figure below shows this.

Mass media are most effective at the beginning of a communication programme, when awareness is being established. Interpersonal communication channels, on the other hand, are most effective during the adoption phase of the campaign. This is important information to help you identify which media or channels you should invest in at definite point in your communication campaign.

5. Wrapping Up the Analysis

A good communication analysis takes both time and skill to produce but in the long run, it pays off. It provides strategic guidance, valuable baseline information, a timetable for action, and a basis for future advocacy.

For the analysis to be this useful, the data collected must first be summarised, then written into a report. The written report must outline the implications for the program or campaign and make recommendations for audiences, messages, materials, activities, and communication channels, which become the communication programme strategy (Piotrow, et al., 1997).

STRATEGIC DESIGN

After the initial analysis, developing a strategic design is the next step in communication planning. A strategic design is crucial in any communication programme or project, whether large or small as all future activities depend on it (Piotrow, et al., 1997). The following are the steps to developing a strategic design:

1. Setting Objectives

Before setting objectives, go back to the information you have gathered about your audiences. What are their current knowledge, attitudes, and practices about the specific environmental issue you are working on?

S Specific	Defining what is to be accomplished in terms of specific steps to behavioural change among specific, well-defined audiences
M Measurable	Quantifying the objectives by indicating a numerical or percentage change expected
A Appropriate	Defining intended changes that are culturally and locally acceptable
R Realistic	Avoiding objectives that are beyond the scope of available resources, contrary to relevant experience, or unrelated to communication efforts
T Timebound	Identifying the time frame in which changes should be achieved

Let this information be your guide in coming up with the campaign or programme objectives. It is also important to consider the culture of the people. The changes that you want as expressed in your objectives should be culturally appropriate for your audience.

Communication objectives should be "SMART". An example of a SMART objective:

The communication campaign for waste management in Village X aims that by the end of 2003, families where husbands and wives have been trained on composting and who dig and use compost pits in their backyards would have increased from 5% to 30%.

The general objective of the campaign for waste management in Village X is considered SMART because it has a specific primary audience: the families in village X whose husbands and wives have been trained in composting. It is measurable because it indicates a percent change (from 5% to 30%) expected and because it made the presence of compost pits in the backyards an indicator of behaviour change. It is timebound because it indicates a specific timeframe within which the campaign is expected to achieve this general objective (from now until the end of 2003). For it to be realistic and appropriate, the concerned sectors – the homeowners – in Village X should have also been involved in setting this objective. These concerned sectors would know best what is culturally appropriate for them.

Note that this is a general objective of a communication campaign. During the discussion on the production of communication materials for the campaign, you will also learn to write specific learning objectives for each. This will be discussed in more detail in the appropriate modules.

2. Positioning

Originally, positioning or creating a "niche" is a concept from the world of advertising. In strategic design, the concept has been borrowed to mean presenting an issue, service, or product in such a way that it stands out from other comparable or competing issues, services, or products and is appealing and persuasive (Piotrow, et al., 1997). Simply put, it means making the product or service you are promoting appear in a very positive light, persuading the audience to choose to use it (if it's a technology or service you are promoting) or to choose to do it (if it's a practice). Positioning creates unique images and terms associated with the product or idea your campaign is promoting.

Advertising commercial items are good examples of how products are positioned. For example, Levi's jeans are positioned as durable and "cool". Hewlett-Packard computer printers are positioned as state-of-the-art and reliable (Piotrow, et al., 1997).

Let's move on to examples related to the environment. Lately, television commercials of the Shell Oil Company shown over international cable channels show how socially responsible the company is. Mini-profiles of people who work for them are shown. As part of their duties at work, these people make sure that the environment is not depleted even if the company continues to produce oil. The TV commercials end with the statement, "They don't work against the oil company. They are the oil company". This is a good way to position this oil company. It is shown as a socially responsible and environmentally aware corporation which continues to produce oil but at the same time sees to it that the environment is not harmed.

Compare this with a campaign against the use of toxic pesticides and herbicides in the Asia Pacific Region. The Pesticide Action Network International (PAN) started an educational campaign. This campaign, named," Dirty Dozen", targeted the 12 most hazardous pesticides commonly used in the Third World. The campaign aimed to seek changes in legislation regarding these dangerous but commonly available pesticides (APDC, 1992).

Their use of the term "Dirty Dozen" connotes something negative, something bad. This was how PAN positioned these 12 most hazardous pesticides commonly used in the Third World. They wanted people to stop using them and the legislators to create adequate legislation regarding these toxic chemicals.

The latter example shows that positioning can also use negative imagery in order to achieve the campaign's objectives. The "Dirty Dozen" campaign made the issue of using these toxic chemicals stand out and was able to send a persuasive message to stop their use.

3. Strategising to Achieve Objectives

In a journey, once a destination has been identified, a map is essential in order to reach the identified destination. Like a journey, a communication programme needs a map to reach its objectives. This map is the strategic design.

FIGURE 4.5 GANTT CHART OF ACTIVITIES IN A COMMUNICATION PROGRAMME

Activities	Jan-Mar 2002	Apr-Jun 2002	July-Sept 2002	Oct-Dec 2002	Jan-Mar 2003	Apr-Jun 2003	Jan-Mar 2004	Apr-Jun 2004
Situation Analysis	------	------						
Training of communication officers/staff			-----					
Campaign Preparations			-----	-----				
Campaign Proper					-----	-----	------	
Expansion							------	
Evaluation								------

Once objectives, audiences, and positioning are established, the strategic design must provide a guide to what actions to take. The design must indicate the activities, channels, and schedules that will most likely lead to the desired destination (Piotrow, et al., 1997).

The preceding figure specifies the activities that should be undertaken and when they should be done in a specific communication programme.

Some important considerations in developing the strategic design:

- A communication programme can be implemented in phases, depending on the availability of services, training, and supplies or the readiness of the audience (Piotrow, et al., 1997).
- A good strategy always employs a multichannel, mutually-reinforcing approach appropriate to the audience and prevailing conditions. Communication can be divided into broad channels: *interpersonal*, including family and friends; *group*, including mobilisation of community organisations; *mass media*, including print and broadcast (Piotrow, et al, 1997); and *community media*, including folk dramas, community radio programs and community newspapers, song writing contests, puppet shows, etc.

Different channels have different strengths and limitations. Thus, using channels that complement each other is more effective than using a single channel. However, a single channel can serve as the leader to advance the message.

For example, in Wang Lay Kim's Research Report on the status of women and environment in Malaysia (AMIC, 2001), she cites how a video memorandum was used as a leader to advance the indigenous women's message to appeal to authorities not to destroy their land and heritage by building the Bakun Dam on their land. The video was used as an instrument to lobby for changes and allow the indigenous women to express their concerns. But the campaign did not end with the video. The media stepped in to support the indigenous people. Demonstrations and rallies were also conducted for this purpose by independent women's NGOs.

In your campaign, you may choose one channel or one strategy to serve as your leader. Your choice will depend on what channel or what strategy will be most effective for your primary audience. For instance, you may start with a letter-writing campaign to your national dailies or community newspapers about the environmental issue you are working on. Then supplement this with other strategies such as training sessions or forums for concerned sectors, whichever is appropriate for your audience and the prevailing conditions. A table showing the main advantages and disadvantages of some common channels you can use is found in the appendix.

• For the communication strategy to be persuasive, people and institutions who are credible to the primary and secondary audiences should be mobilised.

Many TV commercials have international stars as spokespersons in promoting environmental ideas, such as saving endangered animal species. These commercials are shown over international cable channels. By virtue of being international stars, they are easily recognised and have high credibility as well as influence on the viewers, making them natural choices for the role of spokespersons.

You may do the same for your campaign. You may choose community leaders or opinion leaders at your project sites to serve as spokespersons. It is also important to choose the people who have actually practiced the idea that you are promoting. For example, if you are doing an educational campaign for the use of alternative ways to combat crop pests rather than using pesticides, then your spokesperson should naturally be someone who uses these alternative methods himself or herself.

4. Identifying Implementing Organisations

Most communication planning (and action) involves a number of organisations which are expected to work together in order to accomplish goals (Middleton and Wedemeyer, undated). It is therefore very important to identify which organisations will help you implement the communication project or campaign.

The major criteria for choosing major implementing organisations are the following (Piotrow, et al., 1997):

a. Competence – Does the organisation have experience with similar activities? How skilled are its technical and management staff?
b. Commitment – Does the organisation support the environmental issue you are promoting? Does it believe in the role of communication in achieving the goals of the communication project or campaign?
c. Coverage – Is the organisation able to reach the primary and secondary audiences?

d.   Clout – Does the organisation have contacts and access among policymakers and influential people? Does it have political support for its work?

e.   Continuity – How long has the organisation been in operation? Does the organisation have an institutional base and resources for sustainability in the long run?

5. Planning for Documentation and Evaluation

Evaluation should be planned at the start of a programme. The purpose of evaluation is to measure the process and the impact of a programme against the objectives established in the strategic design in order to contribute to decisionmaking. Decisionmaking means applying the findings of an evaluation to improve ongoing or future programmes. This requires methods for collecting information and assessing the changes specified in the objectives (Piotrow, et al., 1997).

There are three kinds of evaluation:

*   Formative Evaluation – the evaluation is done before the communication intervention starts, e.g., baseline surveys on the knowledge, attitudes and practices (KAP) of the primary audience.
*   Process Evaluation – process refers to what takes place as the programme is implemented. This is where monitoring comes in.
*   Impact Evaluation – this is conducted after the communication intervention is through. Impact refers to programme outcomes.

Findings from each of these kinds of evaluation will serve as inputs for decisionmaking about the communication project. Thus, each should be planned for and made part of the strategic design, allotting adequate time and funds for both monitoring and evaluation.

DEVELOPMENT, PRETESTING, REVISION, AND PRODUCTION

Development and production of communication materials is discussed in more detail in the following chapters on preparation and production of media resources.

99

Nevertheless, here are some important points to consider in developing, pretesting, and producing communication materials:

- Message development should be collaborative and participative (Piotrow, et al., 1997). Aside from the communication professionals and the technical people, the intended audience should also be given a chance to participate in the development of the materials. This can be done by talking with them and finding out what they think about the product, programme, project, or service that the communication campaign is promoting. The audience should be able to express their thoughts in their own words. This then becomes input for the development of the communication materials.
- Participation of representatives from the intended audiences in pretesting helps ensure that the materials will speak effectively to actual audiences. Pretesting is asking selected members of the intended audience what they think about the messages and materials. Ideally, a pretest elicits comments on every feature of the communication material that might limit or enhance effectiveness (Piotrow, et al., 1997).
- Revising based on the results of the pretest may take time and money but helps to avoid the even greater costs of ineffective materials (Piotrow, et al., 1997).

MANAGEMENT, IMPLEMENTATION, AND MONITORING

Implementation, the fourth step the P Process, is where everything comes together. After months of analysis, design, materials development, pretesting, revision and production, the communication campaign begins. Implementing a campaign, a project, or a programme is a complex, challenging task. Managers and their staffs must keep dozens of interrelated and overlapping activities moving forward on schedule (Piotrow, et al., 1997).

Here are some important reminders for the effective management, implementation, and monitoring of the communication programme (Piotrow, et al., 1997):

- Identification of the lead agency and clear lines of responsibility for each phase of the project enables everyone to focus on achieving the communication objectives.

  The lead agency takes major responsibility for the management of the programme, project, or campaign. Thus, based on preliminary analysis and with the agreement of the government and non-governent organisations involved, a lead agency or organisation must be clearly identified.

  Likewise, the responsibilities of all other agencies or organisations involved must also be clearly identified. These should be spelled out in a work plan.

- Activities at the community level depend on strong local support. Community activities should be an integral part in the overall strategic design. These activities involve participation from the community. These may include folk dramas, puppet shows, video or radio forums, village meetings, and others. For these to be successful, strong support from the local government is needed. Thus, advocating to the local government for the environmental issue should also be part of the campaign.

- Training a core of people who will communicate for the campaign is important. Training sessions such as this will ensure that the people who are part of the team working for the campaign are equipped with communication skills needed for the communication project.

  It will also ensure that you all have the same conceptual frameworks and the same stand about the specific environmental issue you are working on. Training serves as a way to level off with these people.

- Dissemination of materials is a separate activity, requiring a specific plan and budget.

  Proper distribution of communication materials is essential to the success of your campaign for the environment. If the print or video materials are not delivered on time, then it is like producing radio or TV materials and not being able to broadcast it.

- A campaign launch is an opportunity for maximum public, press, and political attention. The launching of the campaign should be planned well. This is an opportune time to get as much attention possible for the environmental issue for which you are campaigning.

  The right people should be present in the campaign. Political leaders, celebrities, and local stars who are supporters of the issue should be present. Their presence will ensure the presence of media and combination ensures much media coverage. This, in turn, will create greater awareness about the issue. Finally, all this attention will certainly help your campaign.

- Regular and accurate monitoring helps ensure that outputs are produced and distributed as planned. Such monitoring also reveals if there are problems in any aspect of the project implementation. This immediate reporting will then ensure timely and appropriate responses.

IMPACT EVALUATION

Eventually, at the close of the programme, evaluation assesses impact on the intended audience or the entire population by measuring and analysing changes specified by the original objectives (Piotrow, et al., 1997). It measures how much of a knowledge increase your audience experienced, how many of their attitudes towards the environmental issue have changed and what behaviour changed because of their exposure to the campaign.

Ultimately, evaluation findings disseminated both within a programme and externally, provide the basis for decisionmaking to correct deficiencies, build on programme successes, and plan for continuity (Piotrow, et al., 1997).

The following are some important considerations in the impact evaluation phase of the communication programme (Piotrow, et al., 1997):

- The one-group, before-after design with sample surveys of the population of interest is an example of an impact evaluation method appropriate to evaluate a communication programme implemented for an entire population. In this design, a representative sample of that population is surveyed before and after the programme. Differences between "before" and "after" findings measure how much change occurred during the interval and whether people who were exposed to the programme changed more than those who were not exposed.
- Evaluations can benefit from asking audience members for their own opinions about the impact of the communication intervention or programme. However, most evaluation researchers do not give

much value to this type of data because it is based merely on opinion and can be somewhat biased. Nevertheless, the opinion of the participant is worthwhile and especially valuable as a complement to other types of evidence.

- Some of these problems with opinions being biased can be eliminated or reduced by a careful wording of questions. Open-ended questions that do not lead the respondent or indicate thedesired answer are better than closed or precoded questions that do.

Example:
Open-ended question: What did you do after listening to the radio plug on recycling of nonbiodegradable wastes?

Close-ended question: Did you bring your used plastic bottles and other nonbiodegradable wastes to the junkshop after listening to the radio plug on recycling of nonbiodegradable wastes?

____Yes ____ No

- Evaluation results should be communicated, understood, appreciated, and applied by the intended audiences.

What we did in past communication projects was to validate the information we gathered from evaluation results with the primary audience. In our case, this meant presenting the information during a village meeting attended by the farming families who served as primary audience in our communication project.

A written evaluation report would also prove useful to the primary audience, particularly if it is a community.

PLANNING FOR CONTINUITY

Now that we have gone through the whole P process for developing strategic communication programmes, you should consider continuity or sustainability of the initial communication project or campaign for the environment that you have designed. After all, the environmental issues we are faced with are not unidimensional but multifaceted. Thus, a single campaign with a single message needs to be reinforced by other similar messages in order to help make necessary changes in people's knowledge, attitudes, and practices. Besides, developing true environmental consciousness among people hardly happens with just one campaign.

Piotrow, et al (1997) also enumerates the reasons about why continuity is important:

- Repetition is a fundamental part of learning.
- The communication programme may have many different audiences to be reached.
- Different people move through the steps of behaviour change at different speeds, and therefore a single, one-time message will not influence an entire audience, even if everyone is exposed to it.
- People's circumstances and needs change over the years.
- Continuity allows programmes to expand, scaling up from pilot projects to regional or national efforts.
- Continuity creates opportunities for sustainability, by permitting programme managers to seek additional support for programmes and events that proved popular.
- With continuity, programme managers can apply the lessons learned from the past to improve and expand future efforts.

As in the beginning of the initial communication project, plans for follow-on communication programmes should begin with a review of analysis of current policies, programmes, audiences, and options to see how they have changed over the life of the initial project (Piotrow, et. al., 1997). Communication projects can then be redesigned to respond to these changes, whether these are opportunities or obstacles.

Continuity or expansion can take different forms: increasing the volume of current activities, expanding from urban and peri-urban to rural areas, moving into other geographic regions, or adding new programme elements (Piotrow, et. al., 1997).

After learning these lessons in developing a good communication plan for the environment and looking at tips to consider for continuity of the communication project you have planned, I think you are now ready to exercise your mental muscle through this activity.

104

ACTIVITY 4.2 DEVELOPING A COMMUNICATION PLAN

OBJECTIVES
After this activity, the participants should be able to:
1. Come up with an analysis for a communication campaign on a specific environmental issue in their community/ies; and
2. Develop a communication plan for the chosen environmental issue.

PROCEDURE
1. Divide the participants into groups.
2. Each group should choose an environmental issue in their community/ies that they would like to work on.
3. They may choose to work on the previous primary audience that they have chosen.
4. They should be able to come up with a reasonably comprehensive analysis (based on the available information they have and the limited time they have to do it). This should include analyses on the following: audience, policies and programs, organisations, and communication resources.
5. Based on the analysis, each group should be able to develop a strategic design for their campaign. The following information should be included: communication objectives for the campaign; positioning of the "idea" or practice they are campaigning for (or against, as the case may be); channels to use; and activities to conduct for the duration of the campaign.
6. They should be given the whole afternoon to work on this activity. Then at the end of the day, they should be given 15 minutes each to present to the plenary their analyses and strategic designs for their campaigns.
7. Open the plenary for questions and suggestions to improve their work. Facilitate the discussion.

SUMMARY

As we come towards the end of the chapter, let us look at the important points we should remember about communication planning.

A communication plan is necessary in order to have an effective and efficient communication programme, project or campaign for the environment. The communication planning process promoted by the module is based on the convergence model of communication. This model espouses planning for a communication strategy or programme that is less media-centric, considers source and receiver as equals, is sustainable over time, and emphasises the culture of the people to be reached.

The framework that this chapter followed in creating a communication plan for the environment is called the P process. This framework was developed for health projects by the Johns Hopkins University in Baltimore, Maryland, in the United States. Nevertheless, the steps and principles in the P process are applicable for any communication programme, project, or campaign.

The P process follows these steps: (1) analysis; (2) strategic design; (3) development, pretesting and production of communication materials; (4) management, implementation and monitoring of the communication programme, project or campaign; (5) Impact evaluation; and (6) planning for continuity.

Now that you're through with this chapter, you are now ready to look at how to develop and produce media resources that you can use for your campaign for the environment. This is what the succeeding modules are about.

FACILITATOR'S GUIDE

OBJECTIVE	TOPIC	TEXT	ACTIVITY	DURATION
Explain the value of developing a communication plan for environmental communication	The value of a good communication plan for environmental communication	Lesson 1. The value of a good communication strategy	Lecture/ Discussion	1 hour
		The case of Los Baños, Laguna's solid waste management project	Case analysis and discussion	
Discuss the significance of the "convergence" communication model to communication planning for environmental communication	The convergence model and environmental communication	Lesson 2. The Convergence Model of Communication	Lecture/ Discussion	1 hour
		Traditional IEC Programmes		
		Kincaid's Convergence Model of Communication		
Enumerate the different steps to communication planning	The steps to communication planning	Lesson 3. The Steps to Communication Planning	Lecture/ Discussion	2 hours
		Activity 4.1. Getting to know your audience	Group Work and Plenary Discussion	
Develop a communication campaign plan	Developing a communication campaign plan for the environment	Activity 4.2. Developing a communication plan	Group Work and Plenary Discussion	4 hours

APPENDIX

MEDIA	MAIN ADVANTAGE	MAIN DISADVANTAGE	COMMENT
Video Forum	Can be used to: • Introduce new ideas to selected audiences • Micro-teach • Introduce complicated concepts and technical issues in a series of presentations • record field operations and use them later • teach skills Can be handled by farmers and community leaders Can become part of a library for teaching and adult education classes	Expensive Breakdown in hardware is common and expensive Hardware is required (i.e., monitor and playback equipment)	Forums require oning attention from professional organisers. They are most successful in small group learning. Group discussion leaders (after or before video is shown) must be carefully selected and trained. It is most efficient when used in combination with print materials at the end of the discussion. It should be used to teach special skills, for structured instruction, and as a tool to generate participation among a rural community.
Films	Use of sight and sound attract audience attention. Can make great emotional appeal to large audiences	Good films are rare Equipment is costly to buy and maintain Requires skill in running film projector	Best if combined with discussion groups. Audience must be encouraged to evaluate film. Use film to stimulate discussion. Can record and play commentary.

APPENDIX (con't)

MEDIA	MAIN ADVANTAGE	MAIN DISADVANTAGE	COMMENT
Filmstrips	Much cheaper and easier to work with than films Easily made from local photographs Encourage discussion	Usually vusual medium only (no audio) Not as dramatic as motion pictures Could be expensive Difficult to jump from one frame to another	Strip can be cut up and individual pictures mounted as 2" slides to allow arrangement and selection.
Slides	Have all the advantages of film strips plus more flexibility Can be used in a series to illustrate a concept	Could be expensive Difficult to have them on all subjects to be taught	Should be used after careful preparation of logical sequence and good commentary.
Flannel-board	Can be portable and mobile Can be prepared by expert in advance Little skill required in actual operation Can be used to make presentation more dynamic	Can be used only for what it is prepared Cannot adapt to changing interest of group More elaborate than equipment Difficult to keep up-to-date	Very useful but only for prepared talks Should be used to show step-by-step process Flannel material must be stored properly for future use. Flannel graphs should be numbered according to order in presentation

109

APPENDIX (con't)

MEDIA	MAIN ADVANTAGE	MAIN DISADVANTAGE	COMMENT
Bulletin board	Striking, graphic, informative, flexible, replaces local newspapers Keeps community up-to-date with information	Requires preparation and attention to community needs	Should be combined with maps, talks and photographs. Very suitable for posting articles, announcements, and development news in the community.
Maps. Charts, Diagrams	Visual appeal Should simplify details. Permit leisurely study Can develop sequence on display boards	May mislead by over-simplicity Create transport and storage problems	Should be made especially for groups. May need careful explanation first. Could be used as summary of information. Symbols and layout should be familiar to the audience.
Blackboard	Flexible tool Easy to make and use Can be very attractive if used properly Use of colored chalk can add to visual appeal. Can be portable	Requires some manipulation skill (which can be quickly acquired) Requires teaching skills to make best use	Should be essential in every group. Very useful for schematic summaries, talk, discussion. Audience can participate. Small blackboards can be portable. Writing should be clear and organised.

APPENDIX (con't)

MEDIA	MAIN ADVANTAGE	MAIN DISADVANTAGE	COMMENT
Publications and loose leaflets	Excellent for in-depth presentation of issues and technical information Can cover more than one topic Easy reference and can be directed to specific audiences Can be illustrated and made attractive Can support other media for education purposes	Expensive Can only be effective if well designed and produced Poorly printed publications may be less expensive but not readable Require special editing, design, and production skills Distribution can be difficult and expensive	Should be used to support special campaigns, such as literacy and adult education. Most useful if topics are covered in series of publications. Could be used successfully in group discussions and as backup for public meetings. Can be used for in-service training of field staff and to keep up morale (i.e., if field staff are widely dispersed).

REFERENCES

BLAKE, R.H. and E.O. Haroldsen. 1974. **A Taxonomy of Concepts in Communication.**

FLOR, A.G. and I.V. Contado-Ongkiko. 1998. **Devcom 202: Development Communication Concepts and Approaches.** University of the Philippines Open University

FLOR, A.G. and E. D. Gomez. 1993. **Environmental Communication: Considerations in Curriculum and Delivery Systems Development.** University of the Philippines Los Baños.

FLOR, A.G. and L.A. Matulac. 1994. **Cultural Dimensions of Environmental Information, Education and Communication in the Philippines.** Environment and Resource Management Project (ERMP) Philippines.

KIM, W. L. 1991. **Research Report : Malaysia.** Paper presented in the AMIC-sponsored workshop, "Capacity Building of Women Communicators to Promote Environmental Awareness and Conservation," 5-9 November 2001, Bangkok, Singapore.

MIDDLETON, J. and D.J. Wedemeyer, undated. **Methods of Communication Planning. UNESCO.**

PIOTROW, P.T., D.L. Kincaid, J.G. Rimon III and W. Rinehart. 1997. **Health Communication: Lessons from Family Planning and Reproductive Health.** Praeger. Connecticut, London.

Office of the Municipal Planning and Development Coordinator, 2001. **Los Baños with Mayor Caesar P. Perez at the Helm: The First 100 Days.** Unpublished Report.

Interview with Mr. Leo Pantua. 2002. Executive Assistant for Operations, Office of the Mayor, Los Baños.

MACQUAL, D. and S. Windahl. 1993. **Communication Models for the Study of Mass Communications.** Second edition. Longman: London and New York

Asian and Pacific Development Center (APDC). 1992. **Asian and Pacific Women's Resource and Action Series: Environment.** APDC: Kuala Lumpur, Malaysia.

CHAPTER 5

Preparation and Production of Media Resources: Print Media

MA. ROVILLA C. SUDAPRASERT

OBJECTIVES
At the end of this chapter, the participants should be able to:

1. Define print media/materials;
2. Enumerate and describe the different types of print media/materials;
3. Explain the uses of print media/materials as applied in community/development work and environmental communication; and
4. Discuss the process of designing and producing print media/materials.

INTRODUCTION

Mass media, such as radio and television, have been successfully used in some areas. Traditional folk media, including puppet shows, theatre and songs are also valuable. However, while these techniques can augment and reinforce interpersonal communication, none of them can replace the interactive learning possibilities afforded by face-to-face communication. Nevertheless, carefully designed print materials can be used to support the interaction between trainers and trainees as well as people within the community (http://www.vsap.uq. edu.au/ruralpoultry/PATH%20manual.doc, May 9, 2002). In this context, these materials may be called "print support materials." Furthermore, print materials can also used to disseminate timely and relevant information that can serve as catalyst for change and development.

This chapter offers guidelines for developing print media/materials that can be used for environmental awareness, conservation, and preservation. It discusses the potentials and limitations of the print media, and some techniques in producing print materials for environmental communication purposes.

Although the chapter contains some technical aspects of production, it is hoped that you, as the trainer, will be able to develop techniques which would rely heavily on the involvement of the audience for whom the materials are intended (the target audience).

Make sure that as informational print materials are prepared – from the initial identification of need through the development of messages and the production of the piece itself – repeated interaction with representatives of the target audience is undertaken to ensure that the materials produced are accurate, well understood, and responsive to the audience's needs and concerns. Women leaders and advocates of environmental conservation and preservation should also be involved in the materials' development process to ensure that the final product meets their criteria and to give them a sense of "ownership" of the materials, thus increasing the likelihood that they will use the materials and will encourage others to do so (http:/www.vsap.uq.edu. au/ruralpoultry/PATH%20manual.doc, May 9, 2002).

LESSON 1. NATURE OF PRINT MEDIA MATERIALS

Print materials present general information of interest to a specific group of people or to the general public. They are written in informal and everyday language. The information in print materials comes from experiments or based on observations or experiences of the author. Thus, women's groups can consider using one print material or combination of different types to communicate issues regarding the environment (Lustria, 2000).

Print materials or publications (as they are often called) provide the most abstract type of learning among the communication media because using them requires mastery of printed verbal symbols, or in short, reading skills. These are also often used by readers individually, eliciting thought and reflection on one's own. As such, most publications can cover material more comprehensively and more in depth than the other kinds of media (Cadiz, 1991).

Print materials are basically printed on paper. They come in many forms. Newspapers, leaflets, brochures, flyers and even posters are examples of print materials. This implies that a women's group can choose from a variety of materials and decide on a particular medium or a use combination of these materials to communicate environmental issues.

Aside from coming in different forms, print materials are easy to store. After using them, they can be filed or put together so that they can be used as reference in the future. A women's group may also put up a small library in their areas so that others can have access to them.

Using print materials does not require any special equipment. One does not need to know how to operate the computer to be able to read the newsletter or view a poster. They are easy to handle and can be brought anywhere, thus, women can still use these materials even when they have to travel from one place to another.

However, there are also some limitations to print materials.

First, people who cannot read cannot use them. Although visual in nature, print materials mainly use text or letters in presenting ideas or information. So if the user has limited reading skills, print materials will not be of much help to him or her. Such an audience may prefer radio or television over print materials since these media do not require them to read to be able to understand the message.

Print materials lack personal touch. Since the user is exposed to printed words or letters on paper, there is limited "interaction" with another person. Some people may then prefer to listen to the radio because of the lively, conversational tone of the announcer. Others would enjoy watching television because of the sound and moving images. Therefore, there is the feeling of personal contact with other individuals while the radio or the television is being used. This, however, cannot be experienced through print materials, since no sound or moving images can be observed in using it.

Print materials cannot give immediate feedback on their own when readers have questions. However, if the print material is being used by an extension worker or a trainer, these people may supply the information that is lacking in the material.

LESSON 2. TYPES OF PRINT MEDIA/MATERIALS

There are many different types of print materials, however, are selected types of materials which are "low-cost and can easily be produced by women's groups in communicating environmental awareness and conservation issues" (Cadiz, 1991).

Comics

Comics are publications which are very visual, since most pages contain illustrations and sometimes, even pictures. They are mainly used for entertainment. As such, they are useful in teaching values and attitudes. However, they may also contain messages to increase awareness and understanding about certain social issues, such as the environment, for instance. Comics use illustrations to tell a story. They have dialogues among the characters through speech bubbles. An important guide in writing comics is to use dialogue and pictures in revealing information in the story.

Flyer

Flyers are loose papers containing information about an important issue or subject matter, person, things, activities, or events. These may be called "mini posters" as they look like posters that have been miniaturised so they can easily be given or handed to people.

Leaflet

Leaflets provide details about an information in varying degrees. They provide enough practical information that users need so that they can correctly apply the new idea or information. In general, they aim to urge, tell, advise, instruct, warn, inform, or explain. More often, a leaflet contains very little text and is highly illustrated. It may range from one to four pages, comes in different sizes and shapes, and can be folded in various ways.

Newsletter/Newspaper

A newsletter serves as a house organ that facilitates cooperation among members or subgroups in an organisation, such as a research and extension program, and as a means of informing clients about developments within it. A varied range of topics may be published in a newsletter, serving as some kind of miniature newspaper with specific coverage and audience. A newsletter commonly contains news reports or information that appeals to its readers, such as current activities of people in a group, achievements, and commendations.

Poster

Posters are popularly used in advertising and in campaigns and are mass media by nature. They lend well to making announcements or creating awareness about different issues for varied audiences. Posters must elicit some action to be effective, often through prescriptive or thought-provoking messages. Because messages are presented in capsule form, their visual and printed messages must arrest and hold enough attention and interest.

Posters are primarily used outdoors. But they can also be posted under a roof or shade for protection it from the sun and rain.

LESSON 3.USES OF PRINT MEDIA/MATERIALS

There are many advantages of using print materials in informing, educating, and communicating concepts not only about environmental awareness, conservation, and preservation, but about important development issue, in general.

Print materials are most commonly used to inform a particular group or audience about certain information. Comics, for instance, have been proven to be an effective print material in many countries. Japan and many European countries use comics to teach history and culture. The Italian Jesuits in China use it to teach the Bible. In Hongkong, teenagers are warned about AIDS with the help of comic strips. The Malaysian Medical Association uses comics to promote its anti-smoking drive. Thailand uses comics to educate people in the rural areas. UNESCO and UNICEF rely on the appeal of comics to help them teach everything from breastfeeding to the rights of human workers (AMIC-Philippines, 1995).

Another print material, the newspaper, was proven to be effective in persuading two states in Malaysia to declare an 87,000 ha forest area as a state forest reserve. The Star, the daily newspaper of Malaysia, publicised the need for such protection by running a year-long scientific expedition in the heart of the forest and invited scientists and the public alike to visit the base camp. As a result, almost 1,000 people begun to appreciate the forest, turning them into proponents of forest conservation.

In the Philippines, a newspaper was used to build a community. A detailed presentation of this case on the newspaper as a community print media is discussed at the last part of this module (Maslog, et.al., 1997)

In cases where print materials are going to be used for training or extension purposes, they become excellent tools to reinforce messages presented verbally during lectures and presentations, or even in interpersonal contacts with people in the community. These can also serve as reference materials in case the lecturer or resource person forgets any important message during the discussion.

Print materials are good sources of information on topics related to the environment, and some readers do not usually stop at just being informed. Women, especially like to share their new knowledge, thus, print materials provide a means for transmitting standardised information to an audience beyond the initial recipient, since clients often share their print materials with friends, relatives, or neighbors.

Based on studies conducted, print materials improve user comprehension. It is said that people think in terms of visuals, and print materials are basically visual in nature. The text used in presenting the information, as well as the pictures, illustrations, and other visual cues that are seen and read add to the user's understanding of the subject matter being presented. It was proven that those who used print materials in learning a new practice understood, remembered, and applied the skills better compared to those who just received verbal instructions. Thus, print materials increase users' understanding and retention of new knowledge and skills.

Through print materials, rumours and wrong information may also be corrected. These can likewise serve as a venue for community members to voice their opinions and comments, and present the plans, activities, and accomplishments of a group within the community or the community itself. Information presented through print materials can encourage and inspire people within a community to know about relevant issues that can help them move on as they continuously strive to achieve development in their own areas.

In general, print materials are easy to produce. Once equipped with the basic skills and knowledge, women's groups or communities can put up their own newsletter, for instance. It is also easy to design posters or flyers if they know the basic design principles. They can use all of these for environmental communication purposes. Thus, print materials are usually appropriate for local production and can be tailored for specific audiences (http://www.vsap.uq. edu.au/ruralpoultry/PATH%20 manual.doc, May 9, 2002).

LESSON 4. DESIGN AND PRODUCTION OF PRINT MEDIA/MATERIALS

Print materials may vary in forms or types, but all of them undergo the same process of design and production. I will discuss here the general process of design and production that applies to all print materials, then go to the specific principles and practical tips that should be used for each material.

The 4P-E-R Process of Designing and Producing Print Materials

4P-E-R is a mnemonic device that I use to remember the process of design and production. It stand for Plan, Prepare, Produce, Present, Evaluate, and Revise. Thus, the 4Ps, the E and the R. Graphically, I would illustrate the process this way:

**FIGURE 5.1. THE PRINT MATERIALS DESIGN
AND PRODUCTION PROCESS**

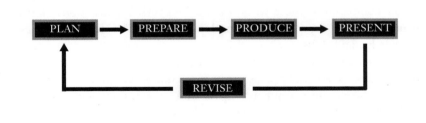

The process of designing and producing print materials may sound complicated at first. But you will learn that the concepts discussed here are really very practical things that are taken for granted most of the time. Let's discuss each step one by one.

PLAN

The first P refers to planning. The first purpose of planning is to determine whether the problem can be addressed through communication. In particular, consider if women can make use of print materials, such as a poster or comics, to communicate environmental concerns. If so, the planning stage provides the foundation for the entire environmental communication process.

Planning to produce a print material requires some consideration:

• Determine the need, problems, or constraints that the print material/s will help meet or solve.
• Analyse learner or audience characteristics.
• Set the objectives.
• Plan how the material/s will be evaluated.
• Analyse resource requirements against availability.
• Prepare the production plan.

Let us discuss each step in the planning process:

Determine the need, problems, or constraints that the print material/s will help meet or solve

Before deciding to produce the material, determine if it is really needed in the first place. Are you really sure that print materials will help solve problems regarding the environment? In what way will these support the environmental communication process?

Make an analysis of the situation in which the print materials will be used, including the messages to be conveyed, and the strategies to be used. The table on the next page presents a list of guide questions that will help you determine the role of print materials in the process of communicating environmental issues (Cadiz, 1991).

Analyse learner or audience characteristics

The next step is to analyse characteristics of the intended audience. Doing this will help you plan the objectives, the content, and the presentation of the message that you want to communicate through print materials.

Analyse their needs and problems. Consider their background. Make sure that they will be able to use the material by determining if they know how to read. Otherwise, the print materials will be useless. Find out their knowledge level and attitudes towards the message. Do they see the conservation of environment as important, or do they not care at all? Knowing about these matters can help you decide on the information that you need to include in the materials, and how you are going to present them.

Consider also their visual literacy. Since print materials are not all text, how will the audience interpret symbols and illustrations that may be included in the material? What kinds of drawings and visual cues would be offensive or acceptable to them?

It is important that the print material should be interpreted correctly by its intended audience. Thus, the visual cues and representations used should be familiar to the audience, that is, the cues and symbols must be found within the culture and environment of the audience.

121

GUIDE QUESTION	ROLE OF PRINT MATERIALS
1. Is the concept of environmental awareness, conservation, preservation, communication new or unfamiliar to the intended audience?	Enhance understanding with minimum verbal explanation.
2. Is the topic too general, technical, or abstract such that misunderstandings may occur if words or verbal communication alone is used?	Enhance understanding with minimum verbal explanation.
3. Is the level of literacy or educational attainment of the audience relatively low, such that verbal instructions would be difficult to follow?	Enhance understanding with minimum verbal explanation.
4. Does the message need to be repeated in various forms to ensure that the audience remembers it?	Reinforce spoken/written words to enhance retention
5. Do values/attitudes need to be internalised?	Stimulate thought and discussion so that members of the group can arrive at conclusions based on their own deductions.
6. Is the audience non-communicative and their active participation important?	Stimulate thought and discussion so that members of the group can arrive at conclusions based on their own deductions; these may serve as take-off points for discussion.
7. Does the message pertain to a skill or procedure that is not easy to follow?	Enhance understanding and recall of steps.

Other things which you should consider for analysis are listed here, though not discussed thoroughly (http://www.vsap.uq.edu.au/ruralpoultry/PATH%20 manual.doc. , May 9, 2002):
- Age, sex, ethnicity, places of work, and residence
- Communication behaviours
- Related knowledge, attitudes, and behaviours
- Media preferences and habits

Set the objectives

The next step is to set your objectives in using the print materials in relation to communicating environmental issues. In general, setting objectives means proposing answers to the identified needs and problems calling for the use of print materials. Write the objectives in terms of the intended outcome that can be observed in the audience's behaviour. In short, the objectives should tell what the intended audience should be able to do after using the print material/s.

Furthermore, objectives describe the intermediate steps that must be reached to accomplish the broader goals. Therefore, communication objectives should be:

- Specific
- Attainable
- Prioritised to direct the allocation of resources
- Measurable to assess progress towards the goal
- Timely

Finally, objectives should be realistic. You don't want your materials to be considered a "failure" because you set unrealistic expectations. Therefore, set your objectives considering again the characteristics of the intended audience.

Plan how the material will be evaluated

Next, make an evaluation plan. Evaluation must be done to determine how effective the print materials are. This must be planned early enough so that evaluation requirements and tasks may be counted in the budget, work schedule, and work assignments.

In evaluating the print materials, consider two things: 1) their ability to elicit desired responses (attainment of objectives) from their audience, and 2) their treatment or execution. One method of evaluation is called pretesting. It is done by eliciting feedback to either a prototype or a preliminary version of the material from respondents representing the intended audience.

Pretesting may help improve the prototype or draft version of the materials even before it will be reproduced and utilised. This extra effort will help correct errors even before a large sum of money is invested in its reproduction.

Analyse resource requirements against availability

When you have decided on a specific print material or a combination of them, start analysing the resource requirements against the available resources. A thorough resource analysis yields not only a list of needs but also a realistic budget for the production of the material/s.

Before doing a thorough analysis, check first if the print material/s already exist/s. If the available material/s will serve your purpose, then think of how you're going to use it for a specific activity.

Sometimes, however, available materials would still need modifications to suit your particular needs. Or maybe, a new material is needed to support existing ones. Then you have to draw up specifications for the new print material, because this will guide you in listing the resources required for the activity.

The resources will include talent and effort, art and photographic supplies and paraphernalia, funds, and time to prepare the needed materials. In listing these, do not forget to include their quantities and specifications, such as size, color, and quality. Make sure also that these materials are readily accessible.

The availability of resources will later affect the design of the material. For example, limited supplies and funds may force you to produce a single-page cartoonised, black and white leaflet, rather than a full-color six-page comic to tell a story about a mother's desire to promote a clean and healthy community. Thus, the treatment for each material may differ, but they could impart the same message. Such a limitation is an opportunity for you to innovate and come up with materials that are community-based.

Prepare production plan

The final step in the planning process is to prepare the production plan. The production plans consists of the budget, the work schedule, and the list of assignments for the members of the production team, or the people who will be involved in the production of the print material. The plan does not have to be complicated if the project is simple enough.

ACTIVITY 5.1

Objectives

At the end of this activity, the participants should be able to:

1. Identify a print material or set of print materials to produce and determine the need for producing such material/s;
2. Identify the intended audience for the print materials and describe their characteristics;
3. Enumerate the objectives that the visual materials will help accomplish;
4. Describe how the material/s will be evaluated; and
5. Prepare production plan.

Materials

- Pen/marker
- Paper

Procedure

1. Divide the participants into working groups with 5 to 6 members. However, if the number of participants is large, there can be more members in a group.
2. Explain the mechanics of the activity. Tell the participants that they should be able to plan for the production of the print material they decide to work on.
3. Give the groups half an hour to discuss their plan. They should undergo the following steps:
   - Determine the need, problems, or constraints that the print material/s will help meet or solve
   - Analyse learner or audience characteristics
   - Set the objectives
   - Plan how the material/s will be evaluated
   - Analyse resource requirements against availability
   - Prepare production plan
4. They can draw up a table or a matrix to summarise their discussion.
5. Allow another half hour for group presentations. The groups can give their comments and/or recommendations during the presentation.
6. Synthesise the activity and tell the participants that you will proceed to the next part of the training.

Prepare

The second P in the design and production process is preparation. Preparation also refers to the message design and treatment of the print materials. What is common among the different print materials is that they are all written using text or letters.

In writing the text for your print material, make sure that you make it immediately clear to your readers why you are making such material, and what you want them to be able to do once they have read or used the material.

People usually have their own reasons for using a print material. Some want to be entertained, others want to be informed or educated. But unless something interests them, they will not attempt to read it.

When deciding on a particular format for a print material, ask these questions:

‣ Will this kind of print material attract readers and sustain their interest?
‣ Will the information be relevant, comprehensive, and accurate?
‣ If this material is needed, will the message be clear immediately?
‣ Will it be a useful guide for understanding complex ideas?
‣ Will it provide for smooth flow of information?
‣ Will it have an ending that reinforces the message?

In general, therefore, print materials should be written and presented this way:

It should have an INTRODUCTION that will immediately catch the attention of the readers and give a basic idea of what the whole piece is about.

It should have a BODY or EXPOSITION that should supply all the important information needed to understand the message. It should be written in a logical manner. Make sure also that it is easy to read and has good transitions.

There should be an ENDING that reinforces the message by either summarising the important points, giving a conclusion, making recommendations or a combination of these ways.

ACTIVITY 5.2

Objectives

At the end of this activity, the participants should be able to:

1. Define visual design;
2. Enumerate the visual design elements;
3. Discuss the tips or pointers in applying the elements in visual design;
4. Explain the principles of visual design as applied to print materials; and
5. Make a rough design of a print material (e.g., poster) based on the materials available.

Materials

- Cutouts of text/letters, pictures/illustrations/drawings depicting environment and women issues
- Pen/marker
- Paper
- Glue or paste
- Colouring material (e.g. crayons, craypas, paints and brushes)

Procedure

1. Divide the participants into working groups.
2. Give each group a set of cut-out materials.
3. Ask them to design a print material (e.g., poster) using the cut-out materials. They can decide on a particular layout and paste them on the paper. They can also add colour and some text. They can work for 30 minutes on this activity.
4. Ask them to present their design to the group. They should be able to identify the target audience of their materials and the specific objectives they want to attain. Let them explain what their considerations are in making the design of the print material. The rest of the group can also give their comments.
5. Synthesise the activity. Point out the elements of visual design and the do's and don'ts in designing print materials. Focus on this as the discussion on designing print materials is being conducted.

Designing the Print Material

Aside from content, print materials must also look attractive and presentable. This can be achieved by "designing" them, that is, employing visual design principles using text, graphics or illustrations, colour, and layout.

Proper design of your print materials will make sure that they will easily be noticed, easy to understand and readily remembered.

There are four basic elements of visual design that you must consider when you start thinking of the design for your print materials.

Let's take up the elements of visual design.

Text or Lettering

This is the headline or text which carries the main message or reinforces the message carried by the visual.

Functions of Text or Lettering

In general, the text gives more information regarding the topic. It does this by explaining and expounding on the important concepts. When used together with illustrations, the text calls attention to some parts of the picture and helps emphasise some of its aspects. Lastly, the text also contributes to the mood of the "story" or information in a printed material.

The most important characteristic of text or lettering is its LEGIBILITY.

Legibility is affected by the following:

1. Style or Typefonts

    - block, gothic, san serif
    - roman or serif
    - **old english**
    - *script*
    - decorative or modern

    Among these, block letters are the easiest to read.

128

2. Use of capital and lowercase letters

STOP   ILLEGAL   LOGGING!

This is useful and appropriate for headlines.

The most dangerous place for a baby to be today is in the
MOTHER'S WOMB.

This becomes useful if you want to give emphasis to a concept.

3. Spacing

M E C H A N I C A L

This kind uses even spacing between the letters and may not always appear legible.

OPTICAL

The spacing here is based on the shape of letter and is considered to be more legible.

The key is to compensate for extra outer spaces of some letters by positioning them a bit closer to other letters. Thus, for letters T, A, V, X, which carry more space in outer position, the letters are placed closer together. The same goes for letters H, M, N, B, which also occupy more outer space. However, for letters such as H, M, N, W which are similar in shape, the spaces should be a little farther from each other.

4. Thickness

light   **medium**   **bold**

5. Width

normal   **expanded**   condensed

6. Colour and contrast

DARK   *LIGHT*

Viewing Distance vs Size of Letters

If you want to determine how big your letters should be in bigger print materials such as posters, consider the following guides.

VIEWING DISTANCE	MINIMUM SIZE OF LETTER
64 ft.	2 inches
32 ft.	11 inches
16 ft.	1 inch
8 ft.	1 inch

To make sure that your text will be easily seen, read, and understood, follow these tips:

1. Avoid fancy or too thin letters.
2. Use simple letter style; be consistent with style.
3. Combine big and small letters.
4. Use relatively shorter lines, at most seven words in a headline or slogan.
5. Select appropriate letter style that will suit the message.
6. Use contrast/boldness to make letters more legible.

The way you have written the text will also affect the legibility of your print material. In using words and structuring sentences, keep in mind the following guidelines:

1. Keep words to a minimum. Do not overload your materials with too much textual information.
2. Present correct or accurate information.
3. Use correct word syntax (e.g., spelling, punctuation, word usage).
4. Put together words in an engaging manner. Use a slogan or a verse, but make phrasing original.
5. Use simple and correct language.

Illustrations or Graphics

In determining the graphics or illustrations that you will include in the print material, you must undergo the process of visualization.

The visualisation process consists of the following steps:

1. It starts with an idea.
2. A picture/image is created or visualised to represent the idea.
3. Elements of the picture/image are arranged to produce a layout which follows the composition design principles.
4. Sketches and/or prototypes are developed and created as outputs.

Levels of Visualisation

Visualisation can be done in three levels:

1. **Representational**
   This requires use of realistic visuals to show your idea or support it. Realistic visuals can be real objects or photographs. For print materials, photos are commonly used. However, other options include illustrations showing people, scenes, and objects that are close to reality.

2. **Symbolical**
   This requires use of visuals with learned meanings. Realistic visuals can also be used, but they areusually used to symbolise another concept. For example, a lady in a gown with long hair is often used to symbolise Mother Nature.

3. **Abstract**
   This includes visuals understandable to a specific group. These visuals are usually subject to different interpretations. Examples of these are logos, and abstract paintings. For instance, the three circular arrows representing the concept of recycling may not be clear to people who are not familiar with environmental concepts, but avid environmentalists would easily know what it stands for.

Forms of Illustrations

If you do not want to use photos as visuals for your print materials, use illustrations instead. There are different forms of illustration you can choose from based on your objectives and target audience.

These are the different forms of illustrations:

Stick figures	Cartoons	Humanised

• Simple line drawings to show facial expressions, positions, motions, or actions. Stick figures usually lack details.	• Also referred to as pictorials. They use satire, and caricature exaggeration to tell a story about a person, group, or situation.	• Inanimate objects are made to look like humans. Human features, such as eyes, nose, arms, or feet are added.

Realistic	Semi-realistic	Stylised

• Closest to reality, though highly pictorial, they show details of the things they represent. • Popularly used in comic books, illustrated manuals, and textbooks.	• Almost similar to realistic illustrations, but with less details. • In between cartoonised and realistic illustrations.	• Considered abstract in nature because of the useof irregular lines and shapes • Commonly used for logos and symbols

However, if you have to include photos in your print materials, it is important for you to describe the subjects or scenes you need. Photos, and other types of visuals, are described according to types of shots and types of angles.

Types of Shots

- Long Shot (LS) – used to establish the scene and the different objects that are found in it; serves to set the mood, locations, and relationships among the various elements in the scene; it shows the subject, its background, and foreground. Showing a long shot of a person is also called a full body shot.
- Medium Shot (MS) – focuses on a character in action with a shot from the waist up; used to show bodily movements and interaction with some elements in the scene.
- Close Up (CU) – used to achieve dramatic emphasis by revealing details in the subject; used to isolate a single element; attention is focused on the subject.

On the other hand, changing angles provides variety as well as drama in your shots.

Types of Angles

- Straight or Normal Angle (NA) – this gives a normal view of the scene; gives stability to your picture.
- High Angle – give the impression of height where the view is looking down from a high place; make subject appear small, inferior, or powerless.
- Low Angle – gives a view from a low plane looking up; makes subject appear larger giving the impression of gigantism and superiority.

Illustrations/graphics/visuals can be produced using the following:

1. **Photographs**
   If you know how to take pictures, then you can take photographs to include in your print materials. Make sure, though, that you are familiar with shooting good photos.

2. **Cut-outs**

If appropriate, you can also do some cut-outs from newspapers or magazines and paste these in your print materials. This may be done in for materials such as posters. Another option is to use letter cut-outs instead of writing text manually.

3. **Stencils**

This is also called silk screen printing or serigraphic printing. It is good for the self-reproduction of print materials which may be done either in one-color or multi-color. Screen printing makes use of silk as screen, which results in smooth printing on paper.

You can also use thin stainless brass or bronze plates and transparent acetate as stencil with or without screen. Without the screen, cut-out designs can be sprayed with aerosol spray paint in pressurised canisters or dabbed with foam soaked in acrylic paint.

4. **Rubber or woodcut**

You need a carving tool to be able to make visuals out of rubber or woodcut. The process involves cutting out your design on wood or rubber, then transferring it on to paper using a rubber roller. If the size of the image area is too big for a rubber roller, a press machine is used to cover the entire design.

5. **Tracing and copying**

These two are the easiest techniques in transferring illustrations to your working sheet. But you may encounter problems when it comes to the size you want of the final image. Nowadays, you can reduce or enlarge originals to the desired size by having it photocopied. However, it might help you to know some basic traditional techniques:

- *Grid method*

   Also called the square method, it makes use of squares to copy the illustration.

   1) Divide the picture into square grids.
   2) On a blank sheet, make the same number of squares; use larger squares to enlarge and smaller squares to reduce the original illustration.
   3) All features on the copy sheet must correspond with that of the original.

- *Pantograph method*

   It uses the pantograph, a device made of wood or aluminum that can be bought in local stores.

1) Place the pencil at the corner of the copy sheet and adjust the original until it centers exactly under the stylus.
2) Move the stylus carefully over the outline of the original drawing, guiding it with your left hand, and your right hand guiding the pencil.

- *Projection method*
  It uses a slide or overhead projector, to copy images from a slide or overhead transparency.
  1) Paste paper on the wall.
  2) Load the slide into the carousel or place the transparency on the stage.
  3) Project the image on the wall where the paper is posted.
  4) Trace the image projected onto the paper.

6. **Computer-generated**
   With the advent of computers, visuals can now be chosen and pasted on an empty layout sheet. It can also be drawn and modified using a graphics software, such as Photo Paint, Corel or PhotoShop.

Colour

Colour is an important visual element simply because it adds "life" to the print material. In general, colour can perform the following functions:

- Provide attention
- Heighten the realism
- Emphasise focal point in a message
- Aid in recognition or identity
- Add aesthetic appeal
- Add meaning to a message

Guidelines in Using Colours

1. Limit colors to a maximum of five hues.
2. Choose colours with positive associations for positive parts of your message, and color with negative associations for negative parts of your message.
3. Group related elements by placing these over a common background colour.

135

4. Use warm colours (red, orange, yellow) to signify a call-to-action or a needed response.
5. Use cool colours (green, blue, violet) to signify status quo or for background information.
6. Use colour change (such as increasing the intensity of a colour) to indicate progressive change or sequence.
7. Use a colour that will contrast with other colours if you want to emphasise a particular part of your visual. Opposite colours on the colour wheel will contrast with each other.
8. Use colours in harmony with each other if you want to relate parts of a visual or achieve colour harmony. Usually adjoining colours on the colour wheel are harmonious to each other. For example, yellow is harmonious to green and orange and red is harmonious to orange and violet. Contrasting colours can be made from each other by adding a third colour or a non-colour (usually white).

TABLE 5.1 BEST AND WORST COLOUR COMBINATIONS

BACKGROUND COLOUR	BEST COLOUR FOR LINES/TEXT/DESIGN AREAS	WORST COLOUR FOR LINES/TEXT/ DESIGN AREAS
Red	Yellow, White, Black	Magenta, Cyan, Blue, Green
Orange	Red, Blue, Black	Yellow, White
Yellow	Red, Blue, Black	White, Cyan
Green	Black, Blue, Red	Cyan, Magenta, Yellow
Blue	White, Yellow, Cyan	Green, Black
Cyan	Blue, Black, Red	Green, Yellow, White
Magenta	Black, White, Yellow, Blue	Green, Red, Cyan
Black	White, Yellow	Blue, Red, Magenta
White	Blue, Black, Red	Yellow, Cyan

Layout Or Composition

After determining the specifications for your text, illustrations, and colours, the next task is to put these all together. You will then have to consider the type of layout for your print materials. In general, these are the different types of layout:

1. **Symmetrical layout**

   Vertically divide the space into two then distribute he elements evenly on both sides or put them in the middle. You'll come up with a balanced layout, with one side being a mirror image of the other side.

   You can also arrange the elements diagonally and have a more dynamic and moving layout.

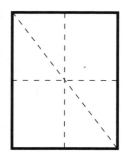

2. **Assymetrical layout**

   Divide the space vertically and horizontally. Having these two axes will allow you to arrange the elements in a variety of ways.

   You can also consider proportions. Look at how the axes can be placed in proportion to each other:

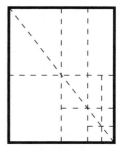

Decide where you want to put the elements based on these proportions. Here are some examples:

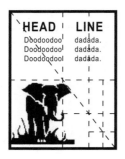
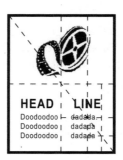
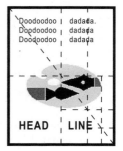

3. **Two-thirds, One-third layout**

   Divide the space in B, 2 proportion horizontally and vertically. Place the visual elements accordingly. These illustrations can help you in laying out your page.

4. **Rule of thirds**

Divide the space into three parts horizontally and vertically. Look at the points where the lines intersect. These are the areas where you can place the visual elements.

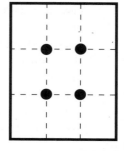

Most of these layouts, except for symmetrical, aims to eliminate "dead center", since putting elements at the center makes the visual dull and static. To avoid "dead centered" layouts, try using assymetrical, B 2 layouts or rule of thirds to make your visual materials more attractive, dynamic, and pleasing.

Principles of Visual Design

When making decisions on the design of your print materials, consider the five major principles of visual design which maybe remembered the word CUBES. CUBES stands for Contrast, Unity, Balance, Emphasis, and Simplicity.

Contrast

- Use contrasting values or colour, a particular texture of paper or unusual shapes.
- This creates an overall effect which will make the visual materials stand out favourably among others and avoids monotony in the shape and arrangement of visual elements.

Unity

- Create a sense of "oneness" by relating or grouping visual elements and words to achieve a unified composition.

- Avoid splitting the visual material into sections which stand independent of one another.
- Use the "overlapping" technique, "borders", "fencing in" or repetition of shape or colour.

Balance
- Arrange the visual elements to achieve a pleasing distribution of weight within the layout.
- This can be done by using symmetrical and asymmetrical layout.

Emphasis
Since not all parts of the layout can be equal in importance, decide which parts are the most important and emphasise them with colour, size, shape, texture, and others.

- Take note of eye movement.
- Use numbers, bullets, arrows and other directing devices.

Simplicity
- Eliminate unnecessary details and use simple background.

"KISS" Your Print Materials

The key to having a well-written print material is to "KISS" it. "KISS" means Keep It Short and Simple. Whatever message you intend to communicate through a leaflet, flyer, comics, or poster, it will be effective if it is attractive, readily understood, and remembered by your intended audience. Following the principles of clear and effective writing will assure you of a material that is simple and easy to understand.

But print materials do not just use text or letters. Visuals are also included on the printed pages. They are used to support the text and reinforce the message. Some print materials are even very visual, like comics, which mainly use illustrations to tell the story. Applying some visual design principles will help you produce attractive and clear visuals.

By combining these two – clear and effective writing and visual design – in the production of your print materials, will help you achieve

your objectives and will ensure that you will come up with simple yet
effective print materials that can be used to promote environmental
awareness and conservation.

ACTIVITY 5.3

Objectives

At the end of this activity, the participants should be able to:

1. Apply the principles of visual design; and
2. Re-design the visual material following the visual design principles.

Materials

- Cut-outs of text/letters, pictures/illustrations, and
  drawings depicting environment and women issues
- Pen/marker
- Paper
- Glue or paste
- Colouring material (e.g., crayons, craypas, paints and brushes)

Procedure

1. Based on the discussion on designing print materials, ask the
   participants to look at their original design of the print material
   (e.g., poster).
2. Let them review and discuss the revisions they should incorporate
   in the design of the material.
3. Let them apply the changes in the design.
4. Ask them to present the re-designed material to the group and
   relate the lessons they learned.
5. Synthesise the group presentations and proceed to the next topic.

PRODUCE

We are already in the third P of the design and production process. The
third P refers to production. In this part of the module, each print
material will be discussed, focusing on its basic production considerations

and techniques. The print materials highlighted here are considered low cost materials and can be easily produced to communicate environmental issues and concerns. A range of print materials is presented to give women a choice on the print media that is most appropriate to use in their particular situation.

Comics

Originally, comics aimed to entertain people, particularly children, who are easily attracted to colourful paper with lots of cartoons or illustrations. They are written with humour and usually present something funny. They are easy to read because of their audio-visual nature, the audio referring to the text or dialogues and the visuals to the illustrations. However, at present, comics are being used not only to entertain, but also to inform and persuade people. That is why even during elections, candidates will tell their life story and their platforms through comics. This is because they know people in the rural areas are fond of reading comics. This is also one reason why comics are being used to promote developmental messages (Matulac, 1992).

Much of what is done in comics production is the writing up of the script. Once the script is done, it is given to the artist or illustrator so that the script will be executed or drawn. To illustrate, comics production is done this way:

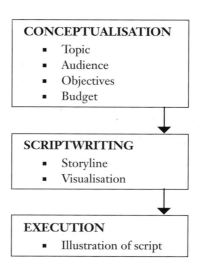

Think of the Concept

When you plan to produce comics to communicate issues regarding the environment, first think of who will be reading it. In this particular case, the comics may be intended for women, but could also include other of audiences who could be associated with women, like their husbands or their children. Find out why you think comics is the most or one of the most appropriate print materials for them. Consider their backgrounds, their interests, their problems. Determining these would help you decide on the topics that could be communicated through comics.

What are the specific things that you would like your audience to do after reading the comics? Make sure that these behaviours can be observed and are measurable. Your objectives will indicate the changes that you would like to elicit from your audience's behaviour. For example, they may not be aware that there is a women's group that strongly opposes illegal logging. When the audience is able to read the story from the comics, then they will be able to know that such a group exists and may even go out of their way to find out more about the group and support their activities, too.

Decide on how you will be able to produce and reproduce your comics by analysing your supplies and resources. If you will write the script, do you know an artist who can do the illustrations for you? Or can you do the illustrations yourself? It might be interesting to tap people from the community who are interested to write the script and do the illustrations. In this case, the story in the comics, as well as its production, is based on community experience. How will it be reproduced? Will you bring it to the printing press, or just have it photocopied in black and white? You may have marvelous plans for the production of your comics, but if your budget is not enough, you might settle for the cheapest, but most innovative way of producing it.

Write the script

When writing the script for comics, always "think in terms of visuals". Transform words into pictures and organise them, such that you come up with a story.

Start with a plot. In the scriptwriting process, this is technically called a treatment. Think of how the story and the characters will be introduced; how it will be elaborated and presented using dialogues and illustrations; and how the story will end.

Think of the storyline. What will be the specific events in the story? Visualise these so it will be easy to describe in the script, and clear to the artist/illustrator who will execute the scenes described in the script. In general, the storyline serves as a guide for writing the illustration guide (IG), the dialogues, and captions.

Decide on the title. The script should have a title that will indicate the main idea of the story. Titles are usually short and interesting and should encourage the readers to go on read and finish the story. Think of catchy titles that will attract your readers' attention. Also, consider titles that are based on accepted norms, and will not sound offensive when written or read.

Divide your storyline into frames. Remember that comics are read frame by frame, and it is the task of the scriptwriter to think of the important chunks of information that will be included in each frame of the comics script. Usually, one complete comics story is made up of 18 - 21 frames.

Determine how many pages the comics will have. This will also indicate the limit of your frame numbers. In general, comics commonly have four pages with prints on both sides. Each page consists of 4 - 6 frames.

Visualise the frames. Each frame usually has a dialogue, a caption, and an illustration. There are also variations, such that one frame would only have the dialogue. Sometimes, it will only have the caption. Other times, it will just have the illustration. You, as the scriptwriter, have the freedom to decide on the treatment for each frame.

It is also wise to try different types of layout or arrangement of the frames for each page. Make sure, however, that your layout will not confusing. Consider the reader's direction or way of reading and decide on a layout that will be comfortable and clear for the readers.

Write the caption. As mentioned, not all the frames necessarily have captions. Captions are written only for emphasis. Thus, there are different reasons why you should use captions in your comics script. One, if you cannot convey a mood by illustrating it, then use a caption. It might better to describe the scene through words rather than illustrate it. Next, if you want to introduce a new character, use a caption. Words will be more useful in giving the background of the new character instead of illustrating it. Lastly, when there is change in setting of either time or locale, it is more convenient to use a caption, rather than visualise the passage of time or change of locale. However, when writing the caption, use minimal words, as much as possible. Make your sentences short and straight to the point. Make sure also that the caption will not take up much space in your frames.

Express the dialogues. This could be the most exciting part of your comics script because through the dialogues, the two-dimensional characters drawn on the printed page become alive. The story revolves around the exchange of ideas between or among the characters, and making the comics more exciting to read. Dialogues, however, should be written as briefly as possible. It is difficult to read a dialogue that is very long, isn't it? It should be direct and to the point, the same way a caption should be. It could be written using a combination of any local dialect and English. Consider how people converse in day-to-day living, and that's how the dialogue should sound or be read in comics.

Describe the illustrations. The comic is not complete without the drawings or illustrations. The life, actually, of the comics is the illustration. Without it, comics would not be called comics. The comics script should have an illustration guide that describes the specific directions for the artist while he or she draws the illustrations. The types of shot, angle, and description of the scene is included in the illustration guide. The expression of the characters should be described in detail and accurately, so that even of the artist has his or her own drawing style, the concept of the scriptwriter will not be "lost".

In general, the standard size for comics is 7 x 10 inches, although varying the size is not really prohibited. The illustrations take more space within the printed page, and the actual working area of the artist is 6 x 8 inches. An allowance is given for the sides and for writing the page numbers.

Draw the illustrations

Once the comic script is written and finalised, there is really no problem for the artist –illustrator in executing the visuals. He would just refer to the script and consider the specific directions contained in it. That is why it is important to make the comics script clear and complete. In terms of procedure, an artist I know makes use of a technical pen in making the illustrations. Likewise, he uses poster paint and a brush to add colour to the material. He does illustrations manually or "freehand". On the other hand, artists who are computer literate might opt to use computer software to make the illustrations. They would use a pen mouse (as mouse shaped like a pen) for drawing, and edit the illustrations using an image editing software, such as Adobe PhotoShop.

Regardless of the method the artist uses, what is important is the final product. The comic, with its entertaining nature, should be able to capture the interest of the audience. It should be able to impart inspiring stories so that people will be made aware that saving the environment should be one of our major concerns now.

Both the scriptwriter and the artist should know the "language" of comics, so that it would be easy to "tell the story" using its signs or symbols. In general, the writer should follow these "rules" when writing and illustrating the dialogues or narration of the story in comics.

- The tail of the "balloon" points to the speaker.
- A telephone voice has a zigzag shape with an arrow going into the telephone.
- Little icicles underneath the balloon means the words or thoughts are to be taken as cold, cruel, or filled with hatred.
- Smoke puff icicles instead of a tail pointing to the character mean the contents are thoughts or dreams rather than spoken words
- The balloon's tail pointing outside the cartoon frame indicates the speaker is "off screen".
- Use of a close-up or larger frame is effective specially in showing details.
- Sound effects are shown by repeated letters that try to spell out the sound.
- The boldness of the letters indicates the volume of the speakers' voice.
- Speed lines indicate movement and sometimes are used to hide violence.
- A split panel can be used to indicate passage of time without having to write "and several hours later".
- Usually eight frames can fit on a page, but important scenes have a bigger panel.

- The drawings go from left to right, top to bottom. Interest is added by using different angles. Close-ups are important because they show details (Amic-Philippines, 1995).

Flyer

The flyer is perhaps the easiest and the least expensive print material to produce since it is usually just a loose leaf. Nevertheless, certain production tips should be considered to be able to produce a flyer that can effectively convey environmental issues.

Use these simple tips as guidelines when designing and producing flyers:

- **Make your message interesting.** Use a slogan that will easily capture the attention of the reader. Remember that the flyer should be able to tell the message in less than a minute, so if your text is written simply, clearly, but with interest, the reader will most probably not throw the loose leaf away.
- **Establish a center of attention.** Decide which idea or image is most important on the page and make it the single most dominant visual element by playing up its size, position, or density.
- **Use photographs to tell your story.** Show the benefit or the result of taking care of the environment by using a photograph. Photos showing the consequences of destroying the environment can be depicted. Women's groups' activities can also be printed to show what they are doing to help conserve the environment. You can shoot your own photos or borrow from your friends. If the resources are limited, flyers with photos can be reproduced through photocopying.
- **Use a delicate hand.** If you are just learning how to design your own flyer, you may have the tendency to "overdo" it. You might make your text so big or too bold, and it may not look good on a loose leaf. Make sure you keep your layout simple. Limit yourself to two typefaces to minimize the visual confusion. Use illustrations that build on your message. You can go back to our discussion on visual design to see how these could be done. Remember, the simpler the design, the better.
- **Organise your page with boxes and borders.** These visual cues can help the readers focus on your main point as well as the

146

supporting facts or details. You can also include several different levels of information on a single page by enclosing separate material in a box or border.

Illustration is more than ornamentation. At a minimum, a picture or graphic image should grab attention and draw your reader into the message. At its best, it will express something words can't. So remember to choose your pictures carefully. Consider the changes in shots and angles, as well as the different types of illustration when deciding on the visual for your flyer. Make your picture tell the story.

Leaflet

A leaflet is a single sheet of paper containing highly illustrated information on one topic. Unlike the flyer which is a single, loose page, the leaflet uses paper, usually 8 X 11 inches, that is folded in a number of ways.

Consider these tips or guidelines in producing leaflets:

Determine the "appearance" of your leaflet

First, identify the type of fold you will use. It is important to know the type of fold so that you can decide on how much information you are going to put in your leaflet and how you are going to organise it.

Some common types of folds are the following:

- Single fold – the sheet is folded once vertically or horizontally across the middle.
- Right-angle fold – folded like the common greeting card; first in half, then again but this time right angles to the first fold.
- Concertina or accordion – folded like a fan or accordion
- Gate fold – the leaflet is divided into four panels with the two end panels folded towards each other, resembling a gate when opened.
- Parallel fold – the sheet is first folded in half, then this again folded in half parallel to the first fold.

FIGURE 5.2 TYPES OF FOLDS

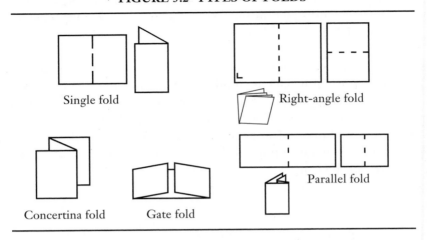

Single fold

Right-angle fold

Concertina fold

Gate fold

Parallel fold

Decide on the information to be put on each page or panel

The leaflet can be likened to a series of pages or panels joined together. Each page or panel should be able to stand on its own. The pages or panels and what it should contain are discussed here:

- **Cover.** Your reader will look at the cover first, so make sure you pay special attention to it. Make it attractive, with eye-catching visuals and an interesting title.
- **First Panel.** This should give reader information about how the leaflet can help him/her. Don't give information that won't interest the reader.
- **Later panels.** These should give the rest of the important information and should be highly illustrated to maintain the reader's interest. Write the text in simple, non-technical language and make certain if contains interesting information that your   reader can relate to.
- **Last Panel.** This usually contains references to where readers can get more information about the topic and a list of credits and acknowledgements.

Write the text for your leaflet

Before writing the text, plan how you would want the leaflet to look. Think about its form, size, shape, color, and illustrations.

Write an outline and make sure ideas are logically arranged. In writing your text, present ideas in short, easy parts – condense the information from paragraphs to sentences to phrases then finally to points. Use words that are familiar to the readers with a personalise or direct approach. Break long paragraphs into several short ones. Enumerate items to break materials into short, easy parts. You can also use subheads to break monotony. End the text by summarising the information with a concise statement.

Decide on your title
When thinking of a title for your leaflet, consider that it should be one which would help catch the attention of the reader and explain the contents of the leaflet. Make the title brief, containing only a few words. Divide a long title into a main title and a subtitle. Sometimes, too short titles can be misleading. Expanding it by adding a subtitle may help. Also, make your title interesting, but put action in it by using verbs instead of nouns. Use everyday, simple words. Don't be too technical. If you cannot avoid using technical terms, be sure to explain them simply and clearly.

Consider the following ways of stating your title:

* Statement
  e.g., Solid Waste Management for a Clean Environment
* Question
  e.g., Is There Hope For The Trees?
* How-to
  e.g., How To Make Compost Out Of Garbage
* Command/Suggestion
  e.g., Make a Difference, Plant a Tree Now!

Design your leaflet
To show a "consistent look" for a set of leaflets, use the same typefaces, type sizes, and type styles for headlines and body copy. Photos should also have the same style and format. Be consistent in putting margins, borders, and graphic accents.

Design the cover
The cover should carry only one simple message, i.e., what is the print

material all about? To make the cover more interesting, use an attractive illustration and when appropriate, show people in action. Be sure that the message of the illustration is clear. Illustrations are usually placed lower half of the cover. Suit the color of the cover to the subject of the publication. Use a big font size for the title.

Take a last look at your leaflet to see if the basic requirements of a leaflet are complete

First, check if the front cover headline summarises the primary benefit of the project offered or the information being disseminated. Make sure that all facts and figures needed to encourage a positive decision or a desired action or behaviour change are written. Finally, there should be a prominently displayed, clear, reader-response instructions, which include names, addresses, and telephone numbers.

Newsletter/Newspaper

Newspapers and newsletters may seem difficult to produce but if women's groups recognise the importance of these print materials and how they can help promote environmental conservation, it may offset the difficulty associated with producing such materials.

Newspapers and newsletters are two print materials very different in format. Newspapers are larger and are also referred to as spread sheets. Newsletters usually have a smaller format but can come in tabloid sizes. They also focus on news or information recognised to be valuable to a particular group or community. Nevertheless, whatever the format is, these two print materials contain the same information, i.e., news.

Here are some simple guidelines on how to produce newspapers and newsletters:

Know what news is

Decide what information you will put in the newspaper or newsletter. It is generally accepted that for information to be described as news, it must be of interest to a number of people. News means something we did not know before or something we knew very little about before we read about it in the paper. For information to be described as news, it must be new, important, interesting, dramatic, or exciting. The news must be important to someone. It is written to make some difference in our lives and the lives of the people we know. News has to be interesting. It must grab the attention of the readers. It must make them take notice and want to know more about the subject. The information described must be something exciting, shocking, or surprising.

Identify the elements of news
To be able to write a good news article, people, events, and places should be looked at as having the following elements:

- **Timeliness.** The issue or event must be current, or the story should contain new information about an issue that has already been reported.
- **Prominence.** People are newsworthy but famous people are even more so. We are more likely to pay attention to news about world leaders and celebrities. We are also interested in local persons if they are prominent personalities in the community.
- **Geographical.** An event can be interesting if it happens in your own community. If there is a big fire in a distant town for instance, we may not be interested, but if there is a forest fire in our own community, that is news.
- **Cultural.** If the event is about people who have customs and lifestyles similar to our own, we will find that interesting. Australians would find stories from Great Britain and the United States interesting because they have the same culture. Asians would be more likely to understand stories about fellow Asians.
- **Personal.** Stories that deal with our basic needs – clothing, food, shelter, affection, recognition – will always interest us. News about items that affect us directly like tax increases, medical cures, implications of a heat wave, or shortage of water supply in our town, will be of interest. A nuclear war will be big news no matter where the story comes from because our lives might be threatened by the event.
- **Topical.** Some issues are topical. They are talked about for a while. Gambling, for instance, may be talked about for a few weeks then disappear from public attention. This will be replaced by another issue like elections, graft and corruptions or drugs. While the issue is hot, stories about it will be newsworthy. It is

151

the media covering the issue that keeps news, who make the story more newsworthy. Once the media stops talking about it, the issue often dies or fades away.

- **Human Interest.** The subject can range from pathetic to humorous. Some of the more predictable characters in human interest stories are children, animals, reunited relatives, or someone celebrating a 100th birthday.

Identify the members of the editorial staff and know their functions

- **Editor.** The editor is responsible for what is printed in the paper. He or she has the final say about what news is printed and how it is presented on each page. The editor takes care of setting the deadlines for the tasks to be completed. It is the editor's responsibility to make sure nothing offensive or untruthful gets into the paper.
- **Sub-editors.** The sub-editors carry out decisions made by the editor, they write the headlines from the news stories and captions for the photos. They have to see to it that the facts in the stories are accurate. They correct mistakes in grammar, punctuation and spelling. If a news story is too long for the space given to it on a page, the sub-editor should either shorten the story or re-write it. This group works closely with the layout sub-editors.
- **Layout sub-editors.** The layout sub-editors decide on two things. First, they identify the size of paper to be used. The most convenient is either A4 or foolscap. These can be copied on any duplicating machine or photocopier. Second, they agree on the number of pages. For a first attempt, four pages is the ideal target. Layout sub-editors also decide where each news story will be placed on a page. They insert headlines with a marker. They are responsible for the cartoons, sketches, crossword puzzles, and other non-news items. They are also responsible for the design of the advertisements.
- **Reporters.** Finally, the reporters look for the news stories, research the details and then write a rough draft to be shown to the sub-editors, before writing up the final story. The group should be prepared to move around, contacting people, asking a lot of questions.

Write the News Article

Newspaper articles are selected according to some unwritten rules. First comes the information (or "content") and then its organisation. The way in which the information is organised affects our interpretations. Thus, newspaper stories must be written in such a way that they are easily understood. They should appeal to many people of many ages and backgrounds. If the language is too complicated, people will feel they must exert too much effort to read the paper.

Consider these tips in writing:

*   Think of some questions which will have to be answered if the news story is to be complete and accurate.
*   Find out who has the information needed and where it can be found.
*   Write the story as soon as possible.
*   Be accurate by checking the facts.
*   Be fair and neutral by including both sides of the story.
*   Be specific. Give full names, people's titles, time, dates, day of the week, name of places, etc.
*   Use photographs or drawings, if possible. They will make the story more interesting and appealing.
*   Edit the writing and remove all unnecessary words.
*   Submit the news stories at the agreed time.

Decide in Which Part of the Newspaper or Newsletter Your Article Belongs

*   **Front page.** The front page is where you will find the most important news stories of the day. New pages contain a selection of news stories from the locality and from around the world. News feature pages include articles that explain or give the background to the more important news stories.
*   **Editorial.** The editorial contains the editor's opinion on news stories. General feature pages include articles that entertain the reader like fashion, cookery, hints and tips, crossword puzzles and comic strips. The articles on these pages are usually of a non-news variety.
*   **Sport page.** The sports page gives you the latest sports news.
*   **Business and finance.** The business and finance section gives you detailed accounts of news about money, business, commerce and industry.

- **Classified advertisements.** Classified advertisements list vehicles and houses for sale or for rent, job vacancies, etc. under different headings.
- **Box/display advertisements.** Box/display advertisements are full or part-page advertisements marked out in boxes.
- **Entertainment page.** The entertainment page is where you will usually find the schedule of movies, radio and TV programmes, as well as stories about film stars and celebrities.

Decide on the Page Layout

This entails knowing the different elements that you can put in a page or in one spreadsheet. Basically, the way the headlines and articles are arranged is the page layout. But there are other parts of the newspaper/newsletter layout which you have to consider such as:

- **Masthead.** The masthead at the top of the front page not only identifies the name of the paper, but also distinguishes the title from the other newspapers. Many of them have logos (symbols) which help readers to readily identify the paper.
- **Headlines.** Words and phrases printed on large type over each story in a newspaper are called headlines and usually indicate what are the most important stories for the day. When there is a very important news story, the editor will run a very large headline across the page. This is called a banner headline. When the stories are of equal importance, the same size of letters are used.
- **Columns.** Newspapers are divided into columns. In the past, news stories would have run straight up and down the columns. Pages of news were often difficult to read and sometimes resembled a jigsaw puzzle. Today, newspapers still use columns to present the news, but the pages are divided into boxes of different sizes and shapes. This way, the pages are easier to read.
- **Photographs.** Photographs in a newspaper help illustrate a news story by showing the person or events involved. The photos capture the tension and drama of the event, the emotions of the participants, the atmosphere. Good photos can also capture the unusual, the unexpected, or off-beat. Sometimes, it is the photos

154

in the newspapers that will attract the reader's attention more than the article itself. Newspaper photos are always accompanied by a caption. A caption is a small group of words which helps to explain what the picture is all about.

- **Cartoons.** Most newspapers use political cartoons to express opinions about important topics. Sometimes the cartoon can be more effective than the article that presents the same opinion.

If you are just starting to learn how to do a layout, take note of these tips in laying out pages:

- Use a pencil to draw an inch border around the four sides of the page. This can be erased later.
- Draw a box for the newspaper title.
- Draw a column line down the center page.
- Mark in spaces for illustrations.

Have Your Paper Printed and Reproduced

You can bring your layout to a printing press where you could have the master copy printed and reproduced. Otherwise, if the paper can be put together either through the cut-and-paste method or by using a computer software or program that allows you to make a newsletter or do layout, a master can be produced and it can be run in a photocopying machine to produce many copies.

Poster

The poster is a method of communicating an idea, message, instruction, or information to a mainly mobile audience. It is used to do any of the following:

- Persuade, suggest, command;
- Alert, warn, draw attention to something;
- Dissuade, forbid; and
- Instruct, inform.

Posters may be placed in a busy street or on a crowded notice board, but they must have impact and catch the eye in order to be seen at all.

155

To achieve this, consider the following steps:

- **Think of a catchy and interesting slogan.** The wording of the slogan must be concise and straight to the point. A few, well chosen words are all that is necessary. Try not to have more than seven words in a slogan. A catchy phrase may be needed to stick in people's minds. Remember that the poster may be viewed at a speed, from a bus or car. Even someone walking in the street may not have time to take in more than a few words before passing on.
- **Design your slogan or verbal message.** The lettering or text should be clear, large, and evenly spaced. Too much space between lettering looks bitty and confusing, but too little space is hard to read. You can refer to the discussion on visual design to get more ideas on how to design the slogan or verbal message of your poster. Moreover, do not use too many capital letters; they are alright for one or two words, but if used for the whole passage it will hard to read. However, capital letters can be used in headings or slogans if it is not more than seven words. For information which may need a lot of text, like for explanation or discussion, a combination of capital and lower case letters should be used.
- **Determine the image or pictorial content/elements.** Usually, images such as photos or illustrations draw the attention of the viewer, so it must be carefully chosen to achieve the effect that a poster should have, that is, to persuade people to do something, or to stop them from doing something they are accustomed to. Bold shapes and outlines have more impact than fussy details, so aim for simplicity. This means that when you choose the type of illustration for your poster, line drawings are easier to understand than realistic drawings.
- **Make sure there is balance in your poster design.** Look at the verbal and pictorial components of your poster and see to it that they complement each other. Do the images strongly support the verbal message or vice-versa? Are these elements composed on the visual space in a way that is pleasing to the eye? Always determine which among the elements are the most important, the more important and the least important, then you

can decide how to arrange the verbal and visual components of your poster. For example, if the text is more important then the visual, place it on top and make it the biggest so that it will be noticed first. On the other hand, if the visual is more important than the text, put a big illustration in the middle so that it will the center of attention. There are, however, other ways you can arrange the text and images for your poster. You can experiment with these different layouts and pretest them, so that you can be assured that there is balance, either formal or informal, in your layout. You can go back to the discussion on visual design to get more ideas on how to do this. But in general, you have to balance the images and verbal message of your poster to form a pleasing effect.

• **Determine your colour combination.** Some colors stand out more than others, so make sure that the dominant colour will support the main message of your poster. Look at the background colours and see to it that these do not clash with your primary colour. Try to establish an order or priority, and see that important items of information are not dominated by competing bright colours all around them. As much as possible, do not use more than three colours, so that your poster will be easier to look at. Using too many colours may attract viewers but it does not ensure a clearer understanding of the poster's message.

PRESENT

The fourth P in the print materials design and production process refers to presentation of the materials. In this case, print materials are not really presented, but they are utilised instead. This is the essence of the whole design and production process, since print materials are basically designed and produced to be viewed and/or read by the intended audience.

EVALUATE

As a result of presenting the print materials and/or using them, solicit comments, reactions, and recommendations from the intended users. From this, determine what specific changes to improve the print materials may be. It is always useful to hear from the target audience because they are the ones who can determine the appropriate design for the print materials. If the design of the print material looks good enough for the intended users, then it could be an effective print material.

REVISE

The last letter of the 4PsER process refers to revision. After knowing the comments, suggestions, and recommendations of the intended users, the design of the print material could be revised to suit their specific needs. Undergoing this process means that available print materials are continuously being improved to help give relevant and accurate information that will aid in the promotion of environmental conservation, in particular, and in the development process, in general.

ACTIVITY 5.4

Objectives

At the end of this activity, the participants should be able to:

1. Identify a print material that they will design and produce;
2. Discuss the considerations of designing and producing a particular print material;
3. design the print material following the principles of clear and effective writing and visual design; and
4. produce the print material following the steps techniques/guidelines/ principles in the production of the specific print material they have chosen.

Materials

- Paper
- Pencil, pen, and other colouring materials
- Sheets of bond paper
- Glue/paste
- Scissors

- Typewriter or computer with MS Office Program
- Printer

Procedure

1. Based on the results of the group's discussion on Activity 5.1, let the participants finalise the planning considerations.

2. Ask them to design and produce the print material they have decided to create, following the principles on designing and producing print materials.

3. Give them half a day to work on this activity.

4. Let the groups present their output. Encourage the group to give their comments, suggestions, and recommendations regarding the materials presented.

5. Synthesise the main points and give a summary on the session on print media design and production.

SUMMARY

Print media/materials are basically printed on paper and cater to the sense of sight. These materials give information on certain relevant topics and issues, including environmental conservation issues. Some common print materials include comics, flyers, leaflets, newsletters, newspapers and posters. These are textual in nature since they use words to provide informations; however, visuals and other graphics are also incorporated to reinforce the messages. It is therefore important to apply the principles of clear and effective writing as well as visual design in producing print materials. If print materials are carefully planned, designed and produced, it could strongly support efforts of women's groups in communicating issues on environmental conservation and preservation.

FACILITATOR'S GUIDE

TOPIC	OBJECTIVE	CONTENT/ TEXT	ACTIVITY	DURATION
Lesson 1. Nature of Print Materials	1. Define print media/ materials;	• Definition of Print Materials • Common Characteristics of Print Materials	Lecture/ discussion	1 hour
Lesson 2. Types of Print Media Materials	2. Enumerate and describe the different types of print media/ materials;	• Comics • Flyer • Leaflet • Newsletter/ Newspaper • Poster	Lecture/ discussion	1 hour
Lesson 3. Uses of Print Media	3. Explain the uses of print media/materials as applied in community/ development work and environmental communication;	• Examples of situations where print medial/ materials are used • Case on "Ang Bandilyo: Building a Community"	Lecture/ discussion	1 hour
Lesson 4. Design and Production of Print Materials	4. Discuss the process of designing and producing print media/materials; and	The 4PsER Process • Plan • Prepare • Produce • Present • Evaluate • Revise	Lecture discussion Activity 5.1 Activity 5.2 Activity 5.3	3 hours (NOTE: Activities should be included here already.)
	5. Design and produce a simple print material.		Activity 5.4 (NOTE: An evaluation should follow after this activity.)	4 hours workshop

160

APPENDIX

ANG BANDILYO: BUILDING A COMMUNITY

FR. JAMES B. REUTER, S.J.

In the early 1970s, a group of journalists in Manila expressed professional concern that the press is the weakest of the mass media in the Philippines.

Under the leadership of Johnny Mercado, they held conferences to try to find a way of strengthening and developing the press. Their consensus was that the process had to begin at the bottom. What was needed, they decided, was a chain of grassroots news sheets printed in the local language. Obviously these could not be profit-oriented. In fact, these could not even be self-supporting. The problem was to find dedicated people willing to undertake such an unselfish enterprise. Instead of trying to build up a structure for this purpose, they looked around for some existing structure already engaged in mass media, with a national identity but existing at the grassroots level, which would be willing to publish rural "mimeo" (mimeographs), news sheets at a financial loss.

Inevitably, their attention fastened on the Catholic diocesan directors of mass media. They exist at the grassroots level but have a national identity in the National Office of Mass Media. The easiest access to these people was through the Philippine Federation of Catholic Broadcasters, since most of the directors of Catholic radio stations were diocesan directors of mass media. Moreover they held regular meetings in Manila, making it possible to talk to them in a group. Mr. Mercado therefore appealed to Father James Reuter, S.J., Executive Secretary of the National Office of Mass Media, and arranged to speak to the members of the Philippine Federation of Catholic Broadcasters at their next regular meeting.

This was done in early 1972, and, immediately, many diocesan directors of mass media agreed to publish weekly rural mimeo news sheets, subject to the approval of their respective bishops.

At that time, the prelature director of mass media for the Prelature of Malaybalay was Father Joseph I. Stoffel, S.J. He had already organised the Communications Media Center (C.M.C.) of the Prelature in three departments – Press, Cinema, and Radio. Besides the Press and Cinema facilities which he had built over a period of ten years, he had recently

161

built Radio Station DXBB which constituted the radio department of the C.M.C. Hence, adding a mimeo news sheet to the already operating functions of the C.M.C. was merely adding more of the same thing to an existing and functioning institution.

While fulfilling the objectives of the sponsoring journalists, the bishop of Malaybalay and his mass media director also had their own objective. This was to consolidate the Catholics of Bukidnon and form them into a Catholic community. A group of people who do not communicate with one another is not a community. To have a community, communication is essential; and to have communication, communications media are needed. The mimeo news sheet would reinforce the radio station as communications made to serve and develop the Catholic community.

Father Stoffel had called the radio station *Ang Bandilyo sa Bukidnon* to identify it with the ancient traditional mass medium of the Philippines, the *bandilyero* (town crier), who was used before the age of modern communications media. But the voice of the modern electronic *bandilyero* can be heard much farther, and by many more people, than that of the old-time *bandilyero*. This was why the radio station was given the call letters DXBB. It was but natural to give to the new rural mimeo news sheet the name *Ang Bandilyo.*

The first issue of *Ang Bandilyo* was dated July 15, 1973. This was after martial law had been declared, but the rural mimeo news sheets had been planned long before the declaration of martial law. Those involved were reluctant to abandon their well- laid plans merely because of the suppression of freedom of speech.

Actually, martial law created instant readership for *Ang Bandilyo*. With the military in control, and the resulting abuse of the military power, incidents were happening everywhere. Unreliable rumors were in constant circulation, and people were hungry for a reliable source of information on current events. This was supplied through Radio DXBB and *Ang Bandilyo*.

Through these media, people were telling the community what was happening to them. A community was being formed, and the members of the community were communicating with one another. The demand for *Ang Bandilyo* kept growing until the circulation had to be limited by the limits of financial resources.

The power of the press as a deterrent to crime soon became apparent. Wrongdoers were afraid of publicity; they created the word *gibandilyo* for the dreaded fate of those whose wrongdoing was held up to public scrutiny in the pages of *Ang Bandilyo*.

In 1975, Father Stoffel, at the age of 68, retired from the directorship of the Communications Media Center and was replaced by Father Agustin Nazareno, S.J. Under Father Nazareno's editorship, *Ang Bandilyo* scintillated with brilliant writing which the previous editor, not being a native Visayan or as facile with the language, could hardly achieve. *Ang Bandilyo* was read more avidly than ever and circulation soared. Unfortunately, this lead to its suppression.

Then Minister of National Defense, Juan Ponce Enrile, swamped with complaints of military misbehaviour throughout the country, urged the mass media to help fiscalise the military. Radio DXBB and *Ang Bandilyo* complied with Enrile's wishes, which made the Bukidnon Constabulary unhappy.

On November 18, 1976, a Philippine Constabulary (PC) team under Col. Olano raided Radio Station DXBB and shut it down, confiscating its files, some equipment, and sealing the studios. It was the intention of Col. Cesar Navarro, Provincial Commander of the Bukidnon Command, to silence the entire Communications Media Center, but he had written on the Arrest, Search and Seizure Order (ASSO) only "Radio Station DXBB" as the place to be raided. Col. Olano implemented the ASSO to the letter confining the raid to the radio station, and excluding the press and cinema departments. This permitted *Ang Bandilyo* to continue publishing after the raid. Col. Navarro was furious and expressed determination to remedy Col. Olano's interpretation of the ASSO which he considered too narrow.

This Col. Navarro did, two months later in a raid he himself conducted. This time, to avoid the mistake he had made before, he did not mention in the ASSO any particular place to be raided, thinking he gave himself a blanket ASSO authorisarion which would enable him to raid anywhere, not realising that such an ASSO is invalid.

A criminal charge was prepared against three priests (Frs. Nazareno, Poulin and Stoffel), one Sister (Sr. Rebecca, MCM), and 21 lay persons associated with the Communications Media Center. The charge was "inciting to sedition."

But the defendants were never brought to trial. During a period of two years, the military intelligence experts in Manila scrutinised the CMC files, and the Defense Department finally reported to Mr. Marcos that no evidence had been found to support the charge against the Catholic radio station. The Defense Department recommended that the cases be dropped and the radio station be allowed to resume operations. Mr. Marcos approved of dropping the cases but gave his personal order that it must not be permitted to resume operation.

In the meantime, Father Nazareno was succeeded by Father Gaudioso Sustento, and he was succeeded by Father William Yap in the CMC office. After Father Yap, the office was entrusted to seminarians.

During the incumbency of Fr. Yap in the CMC office, *Ang Bandilyo* nonetheless resumed publication. At one time, another raid on *Ang Bandilyo* was expected . Plainclothes intelligence operatives were noticed occupying the Murillo building across the street from the CMC, indicating that a raid was imminent. But they quietly vanished after a few days, and *Ang Bandilyo* has continued to come out every Sunday without molestation from the Philippine Constabulary.

From its very first issue on July 15, 1973 until the present, except for the period when it was illegally suppressed by the PC, *Ang Bandilyo* has never missed an issue, and every issue has been released at the scheduled time. This record is believed to be unique among the various rural mimeo news sheets.

Ang Bandilyo Production Process

Equipment. The **Ang Bandilyo** required minimal equipment. The main pieces were the mimeographing machine and the typewriter, plus accessories.

Staffing. The active staff of *Ang Bandilyo* was composed of three persons, namely, the editor whose main role was to solicit and edit news items and educational and informational materials for printing; the secretary-typist, who manned the office and to whom went all typing jobs; and the technical assistant, whose main task was to mimeograph and bundle the copies. He also saw to it that the copies were sent to the various subscribers.

News Gathering. The news items from the rural areas were initially gathered by reporters of radio station DXBB. This was the period before the closure of DXBB. At that time, DXBB reporters roamed around the prelature from parish to parish trying to pick up news worth announcing through the radio. The more important items would find their way into the pages of *Ang Bandilyo.*

With the closure of the radio station in November 1976, a new way of gathering information had to be devised. During the editorship of Fr. Gau Sustento, *alagads* (deacons) and catechists were requested to attend KUKANG seminars (the acronym stands for the first letters of Cebuano words meaning: Who, What, When, Where, How, and Why).

Equipped with the basics of news reporting, the *alagads* and catechists would then report to the main office whatever occurred in their repective barrios or sitios. The general populace in the rural areas were advised to report occurrences which they witnessed or heard in their immediate surroundings to the *alagads*, catechists, or the parish priests. These people in turn would relay the news items to the main office for publication.

So as not to jeopardise the safety of the sources of information, the names were never divulged, unless the source would expressly say so. However, in printing items that were sent in from the different parishes, there was always an indication that the particular item was signed (*pinirmahan*).

Distribution of Copies. Each parish or establishment told the central office the number of copies they would like to subscribe to. In spite of this, the number of copies sent could not meet the request. At the start, the copies were delivered by one person on a motorcycle. When the motorcycle became too costly to maintain, the drivers or conductors of local bus lines and jeepneys were requested to make the delivery. They would receive a minimal fee – the amount sufficient to buy a pack of cigarettes.

The delivery points were the parish *conventos*, which in most cases were very close to the parish church. Deliveries took place on Saturdays; by the next day (Sunday) people coming to Mass would get copies of the newsletter from the *convento*. *Alagads* coming from the *sitios* or barrios would normally take back two or three copies to their respective communities.

Normally, a copy passed from one reader to another. Copies were also tacked on the parish bulletin boards and remained there for some time. This was for the benefit of parishioners who were not able to get hold of a copy. In one particular barrio, where most of the residents belong to a tribal group not well-versed in the Cebuano dialect, the *alagads* would read and translate the contents of *Ang Bandilyo* into the tribal tongue.

This particular case was mentioned by a 25-year-old farmer of barrio Opis, in the municipality of San Fernando. He said, "even if only two (persons) can read the local dialect in our place, we try to explain what has been read to the other members of the community." This community happened to be one composed mainly of tribal Filipinos whose main concern was the encroachment of a certain logging firm and the "exploitations of Panaminism."

REFERENCES

AMIC-Philippines. 1995. **Media Education.** Asian Mass Communication Research and Information Centre, Singapore.

Audiovisual Media Planning and Production. Unpublished handout for DEVC 141. Institute of Development Communication, UP Los Baños.

Cadiz, M.C.H. 1991. **Educational Communication for Development: Basic Concepts, Theories and Know-How**. CA Publications Program, UP Los Baños.

Deza, A.B. 1995. **The Poster Handbook**. Asian Social Institute, Malate, Manila.

http://www.vsap.uq.edu.au/ruralpoultry/PATH%20manual.doc., May 9, 2002

International Rice Research Institute (IRRI). undated. **Designing and Producing Instructional Media and Materials**. IRRI, Los Baños.

Lustria, M.L.A., Sudaprasert, M.R.C. and Matela, A.B. 1998. **Preparation and Production of Development Communication Materials**. UP Open University, UP Los Baños.

Lustria, M.L.A. 2000. **Training on Identifying, Writing Up, Packaging and Communicating Good Health Practices**, CDC, UPLB and MSH.

Matulac, L.A. 1992. **Lecture Notes In Devc 102** (Writing For The Educational Communication Media), IDC, UP Los Baños.

Maslog, C.C. et al.1997. **Communication for People Power**. UNESCO-Tambuli Project, Quezon City.

Preparation and Production of Media Resources: Community Radio Broadcasts

MA. TERESITA B. OSALLA

OBJECTIVES
At the end of this chapter, the
participants are expected to be able to:

1. Describe the characteristics of community radio;
2. Enumerate and explain the steps in planning and producing a radio programme;
3. Explain the principles of writing for radio;
4. Write a short radio talk;
5. Conduct radio interviews;
6. Plan and write radio news;
7. Plan, write, and produce radio plugs on environmental topics/issues; and
8. Plan, write, and produce a radio magazine tackling an environmental issue.

INTRODUCTION

Considering the gravity of the environmental problems that the world is faced with, we need as many sectors and stakeholders to be aware, concerned, involved, and active in helping solve these problems. Radio can be utilized for this purpose. It has various characteristics that make it an ideal medium for environmental communication education, as well as advocacy.

Radio is a widespread communication medium whether in rural or urban communities. It is a common item in every household. More than being a companion medium, it also serves as the people's source of information, education, and entertainment. With radio, there is an assurance that environmental messages will reach the people.

Radio is easy to understand. It transcends the problem of illiteracy. Its messages can be understood and appreciated by a person who has little or no formal schooling. It brings information in the language of the listeners and in the form that suits them. There is then no reason why the target audiences will not understand discussions on various environmental topics as well as the calls for preserving the environment.

Radio is efficient and economical to use. Information is immediately disseminated to a large number of people in one broadcast. Spreading news, updates, notices, and various concerns about the environment is easy through radio.

Lastly, radio appeals to the emotion. Using some techniques in production, a radio message can be made dramatic or very emotional that could drive listeners to become sympathetic and concerned.

DEFINING COMMUNITY RADIO BROADCASTING

Community broadcasting seems to be the trend now. The establishment of community radio stations is happening in many countries. Some examples include more than 20 Tambuli community radio stations in remote areas of various provinces in the Philippines, Radio Sagarmatha in Nepal, Radio Maliana in East Timor, and another community radio station in Lospalos, East Timor.

What is behind this fascination with community broadcasting? How does community radio broadcasting differ from mainstream broadcasting?

The differences between community broadcasting and mainstream broadcasting lie in areas such as power/reach, objective, programmemes, target audience, and programmeme makers/producers.

Community radios are low-powered, ranging from 10 watts to five (5) kilowatts, compared to mainstream radios whose power is more than ten times greater than that of community radios. Community radios concentrate on a relatively smaller coverage area such as a barangay, a town, or a province.

The primary objective of community radio is to facilitate the development of the community that it serves. It is more concerned with improving the economic, cultural, and political conditions of the people rather than in gaining profits from broadcasting activities.

Programmes for community radios are planned and produced with specific objectives. Hence, they are purposive. The programmemes serve to motivate, to inform, to teach, and to encourage community members to take necessary actions. The contents of the programmes are relevant to the situations of the audiences. They are based on researches and surveys. They tackle the needs and issues of the community. They do not only feature local talent but involve them in programme production as well.

The audiences of community radios are well defined. They are the various sectors of the community such as the women, farmers, laborers, youth, children, transport groups, and others. Community radios cater to the underprivileged and marginalised.

The programme makers/producers are not necessarily holders of a degree in communication or in broadcasting. They could be the ordinary people in the community who have skills or who were trained in programme making.

Community radio broadcasting is reaching out to people, allowing the voice of the small ones to be heard, making the marginalised sectors of the society partners in development, and helping the concerned to be actively involved in analysing and solving their own problems.

BASIC STEPS IN PROGRAMME PLANNING AND PRODUCTION

This lesson is divided into two parts. The first part deals with programme planning for radio, while the second part discusses the activities involved during production of a programme.

PROGRAMME PLANNING

As with other developmental efforts, planning is a crucial stage in programme production. Programme planning is building the foundation of the programme. A good plan is usually what's behind a successful programme.

The following are the steps in planning a radio programme:

1. Know the Intended Audiences

Intended audience refers to the group of people to whom you are addressing your message. They usually share common characteristics, behaviour, feelings, or views in connection to an issue. They may also be located in a particular place or area, or members of a specific group.

Examples of target audiences are farmers involved in slash and burn farming, families living along river banks, vegetable growers using non-organic fertilisers, and fishermen practicing illegal fishing methods.

In planning a developmental radio programme, you should first know who would listen to it. Identify the particular group of people for whom your message is intended. Seek information about them, including the following:

- Their general predispositions:
  - Socio-cultural aspects (sex, religion, regional origin, language, etc.)
  - Level of intelligence/literacy
  - Education
  - General knowledge
  - Beliefs
  - Practices/habits
- Their situational predispositions:
  - Need for information
  - Existing knowledge about the subject
  - Attitude towards the topic
  - Attitude towards the source
  - Media habits (including preferences for day, time, and length of programme)

These characteristics of the intended audiences will serve as your guide as programme planner/producer, in choosing a topic for discussion, in emphasising a particular point or information, in selecting appropriate format or message presentation, and making decisions about the proper time for disseminating information.

For example, you can easily decide whether there is also a need to discuss the difference between biodegradable and non-biodegradable wastes when a local ordinance on solid wastes management is discussed; whether you must provide your audience with energy saving tips or you just have to motivate them to practice energy saving measures. Furthermore, it will be easier for you to choose whether to present a message as purely talk, dramatic, or musical; whether to air in the morning, in the afternoon, or in the evening; and whether to run the programme for 15 minutes, 30 minutes, or one hour.

As programme planner/producer, you will know your intended audience through the following:

1. Reviewing previous studies and surveys such as census documents, books, theses results, and opinion surveys;
2. Conducting assessment studies or specific research about the target audience;
3. Carrying out in-depth interviews with knowledgeable individuals who work with the intended audience, such as extension workers or researchers; and
4. doing focus-group interviews (i.e., interviewing a group of people who are representatives of the intended audience, with the use of a prepared list of questions about a topic).

2. Identify Programme Objectives

Programme objectives are statements of specific intentions as to what your audience must know, learn, or do after listening to the programme. Objectives may be stated either at the cognitive level, affective level, or the behavioural level.

Cognitive level. This expresses the gain in knowledge that you expect from the audience. Objectives in this level specifically refer to what you want your audience to know or learn after listening to the programme.

171

Examples:
- After listening to the programme, the audience is expected to be aware of the different illegal fishing methods.
- After listening to the programme, the audience is expected to be aware of the new ordinance on solid waste management.

Affective level. This tells what changes you would expect in the audience's attitudes after listening to the programme.

Examples:
- After listening to the programme, the audience is expected to disapprove of the use of illegal fishing methods.
- After listening to the programme, the audience is expected to be in favour of waste segregation.

Behavioural level. This states the definite actions you want your audience to do/take after listening to the programme.

Examples:
- After listening to the programme, the audience is expected to report to authorities those who practise illegal fishing methods.
- After listening to the programme, the audience is expected to separate the biodegradable wastes from the non-biodegradable wastes.

3. Determine and Allocate Resources

Manpower, supplies and materials, funds, and time are the essential resources in programme production. These must be properly allocated during the planning stage of the programme.

Manpower. Identify all agencies that must be involved and every individual that will compose the programme's production team such as producer, announcer, talent, researcher, writer, musical scorer, sound effects and other, technicians, etc. Clearly define the roles and/or responsibilities of everyone involved in the programme. Furthermore, name the specific person who will do a particular job.

Supplies and Materials. Supplies and materials include the hardware and software needed in the production of the programme. Hardware refers to equipment and facilities, while software refers to the materials that go into the programme. Microphones, tape recorders, tapes, and studio are hardware, whereas scripts, music, voice clips, and sound effects are software. See to it that all necessary supplies and materials are available and ready during programme production.

Funds. Have a good estimate of the budget that will be needed for producing the programme. Determine the cost of personal services, supplies and materials, and sundries such as communication expenses, and other services. Then, know how much is already available. When what is available is not sufficient, the programme planner/producer must identify means to generate the needed resources.

Time. Timetable and rundown sheets are useful tools for time management. A timetable is used to schedule programme activities, while a rundown sheet is used to allocate whatever time is available for airing a programme.

Examples of a timetable and a rundown sheet are as follows:

SAMPLE TIMETABLE

ACTIVITIES	Jan				Feb				Mar				Apr			
	1	2	3	4	1	2	3	4	1	2	3	4	1	2	3	4
1. Gathering of programme materials	▓	▓														
2. Preparing the programme outline			▓													
3. Scriptwriting				▓	▓											
4. Auditioning talent, music and sound effects						▓										
5. Voice taping							▓									
6. Mixing/producing the programme								▓	▓							
7. Pre-testing and revising the programme										▓						
8. Promoting the programme											▓					
9. Airing the programme													▓			

SAMPLE RUNDOWN SHEET

Programme	:	Eco Newscast
Date of Airing	:	28 June 2002 (Friday)
Time of Airing	:	7:00 - 7:30a.m.

RUNDOWN SHEET

Item No	Contents	Length
I	Standard Intro	1 min.
II	Host's greetings	1min.
III	Envirommental News	5 mins.
IV	Plugs	2 mins.
V	Ad lib	1 min.
VI	Feature	7 mins 30 secs.
VII	Station ID &Plug	2 mins.
VIII	Expert Interview	5 mins.
IX	Recap and Goodbyes	2 mins.
		3 mins.
	TOTAL:	29 mins 30 secs.

4. Select an Appropriate Format

Consider the preferences of the audience when selecting a programme format. Do they like pure information? Are they fond of listening to prominent people? What type of music do they enjoy listening to? How much time can they to devote listening to the programme?

Once what is acceptable to the audiences is ascertained, start designing the programme. The following are some options for a programme format:

Musical. This format, whose general aim is to entertain, entails filling up the airtime.

A musical programme can be *integrated* or *diverse*. An integrated music programme revolves around a definite theme. For example, the programme can feature music that tells about the beauty of nature, or conveys the importance of caring for the environment.

Diverse music programmes, on the other hand, contain a variety of music such as old and new songs, popular songs, etc.

174

Talk. This format entails relaying straight information to the audience. The announcer/broadcaster tackles a particular topic or issue. It does not use music or sound effects, just the announcer's voice. This makes the production of the programme very economical.

This format is also more acceptable for adult and sophisticated audiences who have knowledge and interest in the subject. Since this programme format lacks variety, the broadcaster must compensate by making it really informative, interesting, amusing, or a bit humorous.

Documentary. This format requires highlighting an important subject matter or issue. It aims to do any of the following:

1. Provide socially useful information;
2. Persuade the audience to take remedial action; and
3. Inspire or uplift.

Magazine. This format requires a variety of either related or unrelated items or segments to be linked together by narration, music, or sound effects. It consists of segments utilising various presentations such as interviews, feature, jingles, straight talk, etc. Moreover, since the programme can tackle a variety of subjects in one broadcast, it is very interesting for a wide radio audience.

Drama. This format tells a story through action and dialogue. The story can be based on an event or happening, a theme, or a character and the major elements are the plot, dialogue, and setting.

News. This format contains accounts of the latest happenings, locally or internationally. News serves to provide its audience with current, relevant, essential, and interesting information. News may be reports about accidents and conflicts, gatherings, news projects, government actions, nature, sports, and people.

A more detailed discussion on this topic can also be found in the succeeding parts of this chapter.

5. Identify the Priority Messages

Identify your priority messages based on audience's needs and programme objectives. Consider the following questions in selecting messages for broadcast:

1. Is the message useful? Does the message have advantages over the prevailing knowledge of the audience?
2. Is it timely? Isn't it too late or too early to influence specific actions? For example, coping with heat must be discussed during El Niño rather than during La Niña.
3. Is the information appropriate? Does it offer a solution to the problem? Will the audience be able to utilise such information? For example, do not discuss a technology that is not appropriate for local conditions.
4. Is the information simple? Will the audience easily understand the message?

PROGRAMME PRODUCTION

While programme planning involves conceptualising a programme and allocating resources for it, programme production is the implementation of the plans made regarding the programme. Here are the activities in programme production:

1. Gather Broadcast Materials

Broadcast materials may be gathered from the library, concerned agencies/institutions/organizations, or by doing informal visits to the barrios. You may also interview a subject matter specialist, or gather people's opinion on the topic.

2. Write Scripts

Writing for radio takes on a different form than that of writing for the print medium. Certain characteristics of the radio medium must be considered. Hence, there are principles that you must be follow. The principles of clear and effective radio writing are discussed as a separate chapter in this chapter.

3. Auditioning Talent, Music, and Sound Effects

Music, sound effects, and voice are the tools of radio. Prepare them before the production of the programme.

Consider the following guidelines in selecting talents, music, and sound effects.

Guidelines for Choosing Voice Talent

Choose a voice talent who possesses the following characteristics:
- His/her voice quality is appropriate for the character to be portrayed;
- He/she has no inhibitions and can freely act out the required role;
- He/she can deliver dialogues naturally without sounding as though reading from a script; and
- He/she can follow instructions from the director as well as those that are stated in the script.

Guidelines for Musical Scoring

Music can enhance a production. However, it should not be used excessively. Music must be used for a definite purpose such as:

- Bridge/transition from one scene to another;
- Sound effect;
- A stab/sting;
- A symbolic effect; and
- A background to a scene or narration.

The music that will be used must:

- Represent the mood and the content of the production;
- Be of the same instrumentation when used within one production; and
- Not be popular or too familiar.

Guidelines for Selecting and Using Sound Effects

Use sound effects only if:

- They can add realism and authenticity to the production;
- They can enhance the mood or atmosphere of a scene;
- They can make something clear; and
- The audience expects to hear the sound.

Be sure that the sound is clear and easily recognisable. It helps to achieve this by observing the proper volume of the sound effects.

Moreover, the audience identify the sound by referring to it in the dialogue or narration.

4. Taping, Mixing, and Dubbing

There are two steps in producing a radio programme – the taping of cold cuts, and the mixing.

Cold cut taping essentially concentrates on recording all dialogues only. Mixing, on the other hand, is adding the background music and the necessary sound effects to the cold cuts.

During mixing, observe if the volume level of the different sounds are balanced and are loud enough to be heard clearly. Make sure that the music is not drowning out the voice of the announcer, or that the volume level of the sound effects is not so soft that it is almost difficult to identify.

RADIO SCRIPTWRITING

The Radio Script

A script is a written document containing all dialogues, and directions for music, voicing, and sound effects that must go into a programme. It tells the announcer exactly what to say or do, when, and how to say it.

A script has certain importance, such as the following:

It ensures smooth programme continuity. The script provides an announcer with what to say, including how he must switch from one discussion to another one. Therefore, he/she will not be at a loss for words to say. The script also keeps the announcer within the topic. It prevents him from saying anything irrelevant. It likewise tells him/her to put in a particular information, plug, music, etc.

It ensures accuracy of information. The script eliminates unverified information. It facilitates the giving of facts such as names of persons, titles, figures, etc.

It helps in presenting information in an organised manner. A script allows the announcer to arrange his information in a logical order.

It aids in proper programme timing. A script keeps the announcer within the programme's time limit. He/she is able to choose to discuss only vital information which can be covered within the time available.

Types of Scripts

Not all programmes require a full script. However, scripts are very necessary for productions that are difficult to handle if they contain facts and details.

The following are examples of scripts that need to be prepared for radio broadcasts:

News Script

News require a full-blown script because accuracy and relevance of information is a prime requisite. An announcer must report the facts about the event and issues in the community, in the nation, and in the world, not give his/her interpretation of the significance of the events.

Interview Script

Although scripting an interview is being discouraged, sometimes this cannot be avoided especially when accuracy of statements must be ensured, or when the interviewee really prefers to have a script.

Public Service Announcements

Announcements usually come from people who are not part of the station. For example if the listeners wish to invite the public to certain affairs, or make announcements about their activities, the information is written for the announcer to read during his/her broadcast whenever there is still time to do so.

Some agencies or offices also send prepared media releases to the station, which the broadcaster will air as a form of public service.

Drama Scripts

Producing a radio drama is more meticulous than producing other types of radio programmes. It requires more creativity from the writer especially in translating scenes into sound pictures. The interplay of dialogues, sound effects, and music must be carefully studied or planned. A radio drama therefore, definitely requires a full-blown script.

Principles of Clear and Effective Writing for Radio

It is helpful to always think of radio as a sound medium. This mean everything must be translated into sound – from the emotions/feelings of the radio characters to their movement, expressions, personalities, etc. Indeed, writing for radio requires a different style compared to writing letters, reports, term papers, or lecture notes. The following are the principles of writing for radio:

1. **Write for the ear as well as for the eye.** Be concerned with how the script will sound and how it will look like on paper. Keep in mind that there are other people who may be involved in the production and have to read the script also. Thus, script must be easy to say, easy to read with the eyes, and easy to listen to.

2. **Use simple words and short sentences.**

3. **Avoid numbers or statistics.** If, however, it necessary to give figures, simplify them. For example, Instead of writing "7,995,851 casualties", write "nearly 8 million casualties".

4. **When using complex or long words is necessary, make them easier to read by separating the stem word from the prefix by inserting a hyphen.**
    Example:
    Write "re-installed" instead of "reinstalled"
    pre-requisites instead of "prerequisites"

5. **Avoid using the same or similar phrases several times in the same page.** There is a danger that the reader (voice talent) could accidentally skip over some lines of the script.
    Example:
    Environmental degradation is one of our biggest problems.
    Environmental degradation is happening worldwide.
    Environmental degradation is most serious in newly industrialising countries.

6. **Be informal.** Write as though you are talking to a person sitting in front of you. Be conversational and friendly. Write using the first and second person form – such as, we and us.

7. **Aim for clarity.** Use familiar words or those which are commonly used by the listeners and which are acceptable to them. Prefer words with clear, concise meaning.

8. **Repeat important points or messages.**

9. **Remove excess words that will just make the sentences long.**

Examples:

Past history	-	history
A round shape	-	round
The year of 2002	-	2002
In a dying condition	-	dying

10. **Use active verbs.** They create excitement and action, and make sentences short and alive.

11. Use words that will help readers form a definite picture of things in their minds.

12. **Cite examples or use statements that are related to the listeners' experiences.**

ACTIVITY 6.1

Objectives

In this activity, the participants are expected to be able to write a short radio talk.

Procedure

1. Ask the participants to write a 3-5 minute radio talk on any of the following topics:
   - The Waste Management System in our Community
   - My Role in Preserving the Environment
   - Why I Should Care for the Environment

2. Allow them to read their scripts aloud. Based on the principles of writing for radio, the class should be able to point out the good points of each script as well as suggest ways to improve it.

INTERVIEWING FOR RADIO

The Radio Interview

An interview is a question and answer situation, whose purpose can be to obtain answers, draw information, gather explanations, solicit ideas or opinions, and clarify issues.

An interview has the following characteristics that make it very useful in radio broadcasting:

It is easy to understand. The question and answer format facilitates and simplifies the discussion of a topic.

It is factual and believable. The presence of an interviewee, who is an authority on the topic, adds more credibility to a radio programme.

It is elaborate. A particular topic can be discussed fully in an interview because there is an authoritative source who can expound on the topic.

It is entertaining. Its being conversational makes it appealing to the audience.

Principles of Effective Interviewing

Deal with an interesting subject. Look for the most interesting angle of the topic. Consider what the audience wants to hear about the topic.

Have a clear objective. Be definite with the purpose of the interview. Keep that objective in mind until the end of the interview session.

Know the subject. Do research on the subject matter. Use the facts that you can gather in shaping the interview.

Choose the most suitable interviewee. Choose an interviewee who is not only a qualified expert in the field, but at the same time, somebody who will sound good on the air.

Planning the Interview

Choose a topic that is manageable within a given amount of time. Deal with a specific topic rather than a general one.

Know exactly the purpose of the interview. Identify the objective of the interview so that the discussion will be kept within that objective

Decide how the interview will appear in the programme/ production. Know whether the interview will appear as a lengthy discussion or as clips which will be inserted between narrations. Have an idea of how long an interview should be.

Preparing for the Interview

Be informed.
Gather enough background materials on the topic. Know the

guest very well, e.g., his/her background, position, attitudes, beliefs, accomplishments, expertise, etc. This will help the interviewer in determining the type of questions to ask the interviewee as well as in establishing his/her credentials at the start of the interview.

Be equipped.

• Draw an outline to ensure that the interview will proceed in a logical manner. List down some questions to start the interview and fill awkward gaps. Prepare the introduction and the conclusion of the interview. However, indicate a point in the prepared conclusion at which to ad-lib the summary of the important information revealed during the interview.

• Prepare the necessary equipment.

Coducting the Interview

Be friendly. Put the guest at ease and try to gain his/her trust in a pre-interview chat. Give him/her an idea about the coverage of the interview but avoid asking specific questions.

Be objective. Do not indicate surprise, pleasure, or disagreement at the interviewee's answer. But do not also just accept what he/she says. Ask further questions to bring out factual evidence.

Be attentive. Listen carefully to the interviewee and follow-up important statements with the appropriate questions. Sometimes, preplanned questions may be set aside when more interesting ones arise from the discussion. Also, summarise the conversation every now and then.

Be in control. Do not allow the guest to digress from the topic or wander from the point.

Be spontaneous. Make the interview sound like a natural conversation. Study the questions very well so that you will sound natural.

Be relaxed and casual. Remain calm so that the guest will not feel nervous. Let the guest enjoy the interview.

Avoid meaningless comments. Comments like, "Mmm", "Yes, I see", or "How interesting" do not help your interview at all except add to the sound your listener may hear.

GUIDELINES FOR ASKING QUESTIONS

1. Start with facts and questions that are easy before moving to personal matters.
2. Do not ask more than one question at a time.
3. Do not impress the interviewee about your knowledge on the topic.
4. Do not ask general questions.
5. Do not ask leading questions.
6. Do not ask questions answerable by "yes" or "no".
7. Do not refer to conversations held before airtime.
8. Avoid predictable and obvious questions
9. Be interesting by bringing out information that the audience wants and ask questions that listeners want to ask.
10. Keep your opinion to yourself.
11. Ask a question in the same manner that you want the guest to answer.

ACTIVITY 6.2

Objective

In this activity, the participants are expected to be able to plan and conduct expert interviews for radio.

Procedure

1. Group the participants into groups of three or more or depending on the size of the class.
2. Ask each group to think of an interesting environmental topic and identify a subject matter specialist for a five minute interview.
3. Give the participants enough time to plan, prepare, and conduct the interview.
4. Ask the whole class to listen to each recorded interview and allow them to point out what has been good and what could be improved in each interview. If time is lacking, you as training facilitator must evaluate each interview.
5. Discuss comments with the participants.

THE RADIO NEWS

What is News?

News is a piece of information about a significant and recent event that affects and interests the listeners.

- News has the following characteristics:
- It is new information. It is what happens now or what is about to happen. The audiences havenot yet heard of it.
- It is significant information to the audience and it affects many of them.
- It is true information.

News Sources

News is everywhere. They may be found in different places. Examples of news sources are the following:

- **Regular Sources:** hospitals, police departments, government agencies, community groups/organisations, political ministers, leaders in all major national and local activities, etc.
- **Personal Contacts:** the people in strategic places with whom a broadcaster can become friends.
- **Public Notices:** memoranda and advertisements.
- **Publications:** newspapers, newsletters, and local, national and international magazines.
- **National and international news agencies:**
  Reuters, AP, etc.

News Gathering Techniques

Most broadcast stations feature news. Some air purely news programmes, some give hourly reports, and some provide news only either in the morning or in the evening. Regardless of how frequent your station airs news, you must come up with sufficient amount of news for the broadcast. The following are some techniques of newsgathering:

Research

Review and analyse events that have taken place before. You may chance upon bits of information which can be joined together to produce a very interesting story or explain an existing event.

Go to the library. The library is a rich source of background information that can enrich your broadcast material.

Consult the specialists or scientists. They are the best source of information about a particular field. They can provide you with more background information that is not available elsewhere.

Go to research institutions. They are rich sources of news about technological advancements. However, the information available from them is highly technical, thus, has to be translated for radio.

Ask the ordinary people. They may provide some interesting stories. For example, the farmers can talk about how environment-friendly a particular new technology is.

Observation

Be curious and observant of the things that happen around you. What may appear too ordinary or trivial may lead to something unexpected. News reports may be based on your own observations. Describe what happened. Always crosscheck the facts and give your own points of view.

On-the-Spot Coverage

Attend special events and report directly to the station what is taking place there. Describe the ongoing activities and allow your listeners to hear parts of important speeches.

Interview

Get facts from authorities and concerned individuals about a particular event. Gather people's opinions and present them to the public.

How will you gather news? What information will you get? The following information is what you should look for:

- What happened?
- Why did it happen?
- When did it happen?
- Where did it happen?

186

- Who was involved?
- How did it happen?

Although you may be able to gather a lot of information, not all may be worth airing. You must be able to judge if the information is important and interesting enough to become news. You may consider the following when determining the newsworthiness of a story:

- **Importance.** Evaluate how many people are affected by the event and for how long.
- **Nearness or Proximity.** Will the audience be able to identify with what the news item tells? Remember that people are more interested with the things that happen near them or with those with which they are familiar.
- **Timeliness.** The more recently the event has happened, the more interesting it is for the people.
- **Prominence.** People want to hear about well-known personalities. The more a person is known to the audience, the more they want to hear about him/her, his/her viewpoints, and his/her activities.
- **Unusualness.** Things that are unusual or different are generally interesting for the listeners.
- **Human Interest.** People are interested in people. The listeners are always interested with stories that tell anything unusual or somethimg important happening to another person.

News Writing

The basic principles of writing for radio are the same principles that must be followed when writing news. However, here are a few more things to remember when writing your news story:

1. Be sure that the names of places and people are correct.
2. Be careful to give correct titles (e.g., Honourable, Doctor, Major).
3. Express names of famous persons and their relatives carefully to avoid confusion.
4. Avoid indiscriminate use of personal pronouns. Repeat the names of the persons in the story rather that using he, she, or they. Otherwise, there is a chance that the reference may be misunderstood.

5.   Avoid the words latter, former, and respectively.
6.   Change direct quotations from first person to third person.
7.   Avoid initials. Use initials only when they are so well-known that no ambiguity is possible.
8.   Do not give addresses in the story unless they are famous or necessary.

Tips on News Reporting

1.   Read the news aloud several times before the actual broadcast. This will help you become familiar with the sounds used in the script and give you enough practice in saying the words and names which may be difficult to pronounce.
2.   Sit comfortably so that you can project your voice well. Remember, your posture will affect your voice.
3.   Position yourself so that you can coordinate the elements of the newscast easily.
4.   When delivering the news, find a speed that is slow enough so the listeners will understand but fast enough so that your speech will not sound dull.
5.   Follow a speech pattern when reading news on air. Help the listeners identify when a news story begins and when it ends.

ACTIVITY 6.3

Objective
In this activity, the participants are expected to be able to gather, plan, and write news for radio.

Procedure
1. Let the participants identify the different news sources in their community.
2. Group the training participants into teams of two members.
3. Assign the teams to the different news sources that were identified.
4. Each team must be able to write two news stories (each one minute long) based on the data that they have gathered.
5. Evaluate each news script and discuss your comments to the respective writers.

PLANNING AND PRODUCTION OF DEVELOPMETAL RADIO PLUGS

What are Plugs?

Plugs are short message presentations, usually lasting about 30 seconds to one minute, inserted between programmes or programme segments. They are popularly known as "advertisements" since they are commonly used to endorse/advertise a product. However in development broadcasting, the objective of using spots/plugs can be any of the following:

1. To make the audience aware of certain events, happenings, or occasions (e.g., anniversary celebrations, contests, visit of an important personality, etc.);
2. To present ideas and viewpoints;
3. To provide useful information to the audience (e.g., about a particular project, community activity, radio programme, etc.); and
4. To stress the benefits of a product or an idea.

The following characteristics of plugs make them an effective approach in presenting development information/messages:

1. They last only for a few seconds, thus, they cannot bore the listeners;
2. They can be taped and aired repeatedly by the station to reinforce a message to the audience;
3. They can be produced to serve a particular objective/purpose;
4. They can be presented in various forms and moods to suit the interest of the audience; and
5. They are economical to produce.

Planning the Plug's Message

Since the time to deliver a message via a plug is very limited, it is better that the plug contains only one definite message. However, as writer, you should be able to give the most important details of the main message. In order to come up with a good message, know the following about the topic, idea, service, or product that you will write about:

189

- Its outstanding characteristics;
- Benefits for the audience;
- Advantages or features which may be highlighted;
- Advantages and/or disadvantages of similar competing products/ services; and
- Any slogan, phrase, logo, or concept that will be reinforced to the audience.

Scripting

Writing plugs is not just putting together some pieces of information. It is an art that requires your creativity so that you will be able to present messages in a clear, concise, and effective manner.

Scripting the plug involves choosing the most appropriate presentation, structuring and writing of the message.

Types of Presentation

Plugs may be presented in various forms. The most common forms are the straight-announced, dramatised, and the jingle.

The straight-announced plug is the simplest type of presentation. The message is just narrated by the announcer. However, an instrumental music may also be used as background to the narration to make the plug a bit lively.

In a dramatised plug, the message is presented through conversation or dialogue between characters. Usually, one character is presented as having a problem. The other character offers him a solution. Later, the problematic character will be convinced and become satisfied with the solution offered to him.

In a jingle, the message of the plug is presented in the form of a song.

Writers may also use a combination of the various treatments. For example, a dramatised plug may be combined with a jingle, or a straight announcement with a jingle.

Structuring the Plug

There are different ways of structuring the plug's message. However, the motivated sequence may be the simplest especially when you are a new writer. This structure of the plug will provide you with an idea of what to say and when to say a message.

The Motivated Sequence

Attention Step (What's that?)

The first step is to capture the attention of the audience. See to it that at the very start, your audience will be eagerly interested on what the plug has to say.

The following are the common attention-grabbing devices:

- **A startling statement.** This is a surprising or intriguing statement that may be based on facts or an opinion. However, the statement should not alienate your audience. You should carefully choose the words or phrases to use as they may have a negative connotation/ effect for the audience.
- **A rhetorical question.** This is a question that you expect the audience to answer to themselves, maybe subconsciously. The question should relate directly to the main message of the plug, must elicit a positive response, and must not alienate anyone.
- **Suspense.** This is a statement that brings your audience into a state of anxious expectancy.
- **Humour.** This requires using an amusing or funny statement/ illustration.

Other attention-getting techniques include references to a common problem, illustration of a problem, making a personal reference to the audience, or making provocative reference to a problem or solution.

FIGURE 6.1 THE MOTIVATED SEQUENCE STEP

ATTENTION

NEED

SATISFACTION

VISUALISATION

ACTION

Need Step (What for?)

After capturing the attention of your audience, show them the need for a solution to the problem that was posed in the attention step. Make them feel an overwhelming need for the idea/information/product.

You may base this step following any of the many needs of an individual:

- **Physiological needs.** The desire to meet basic requirements, such as food and shelter.
- **Safety needs.** The desire to be protected from physical and emotional harm.
- **Need for belonging and love.** The desire for family, friends, and group affiliation or to be accepted and/or be an acceptable member of society.
- **Esteem needs.** The desire to feel good about oneself and one's relationship with others.
- **Self-actualisation needs.** The desire to be the best possible person

Satisfaction Step (Tell me more)

This step must fulfill whatever need the earlier stages have created. Here you should be able to explain how the problem posed earlier may be solved. Show how the idea/information/service/ product can satisfy your audience's needs and/or what benefits they can derive from it.

Visualisation Step (What good is it for me?)

Help the audience visualise what will happen when they adopt the idea/information/service/product, what benefits they can expect, as well as the negative things that will happen if they refuse to use or buy the idea/service/information/product.

The following may be used as techniques: demonstration, testimonials, and by giving scientific explanation.

Action Step (How can I get it?)

This is the last stage/portion of the plug. Here, it is necessary to summarise or reinforce the main message of the plug. Next, call for action, probably by asking the audience to avail of the service, adopt the information, or act on something. Finally, tell the audience how they can avail of the information/service/product.

Writing the Message

The principles of clear and effective writing also apply when writing plugs. As writer, you must:

- Use conversational words;
- Be straight to the point;
- Use shorter words, phrases, and/or sentences;
- Use concrete words;
- Avoid tongue-twisters; and
- Avoid too much statistics/numbers.

Production

The production process involves voicing, musical scoring, and mixing. Remember the tips discussed earlier about selecting voice talents, music, and sound effects.

ACTIVITY 6.4

Objective
In this activity, the participants are expected to be able to plan and write radio plugs concerning environmental issues.

Procedure
1. Group the participants such that there are three to four members in a group.
2. Allow the groups to brainstorm on the environmental problems or issues faced by their community and identify which among the problems/issues need to be addressed immediately.
3. Ask them to write a one-minute plug on this problem/issue.

PLANNING AND PRODUCTION OF RADIO MAGAZINE PROGRAMMES

The Radio Magazine Programme

The word "magazine" comes from the Arabic term "makhzan" which means warehouse, or a place where a variety of things are kept. Similarly, a radio magazine programme is a production where many different kinds of materials all come together.

A radio magazine programmes differs from other kinds of radio production through the following characteristics:

1. It contains segments that tackle a variety of topics or subjects.
2. The segments utilise different presentation styles.
3. It involves different voice talents.
4. Music, narration, and sound effects tie the segments together.

Types of Magazine Programmes

A magazine programme can be any of the following types:

- **Variety Magazine.** This is a programme that tackles unrelated topics.
- **News Magazine.** This contains news items that are presented in different forms such as an interview, feature, trivia, dramatisation, etc.
- **Special Audience Magazine.** This programme designed for a specified group of audience.
- **Subject Magazine.** This programme discusses a particular subject matter.

Contents of the Magazine Programme

A single magazine programme may contain some, if not all, of the following parts or segments:

- Interview(s), probably with an expert about a topic, or with people on the street about their opinion on a topic/issue, or with a person about his/her experience.
- Short dramatization of information.
- Trivia (bits of information).
- Musical number maybe from records, CDs, or tapes, or rendered by local talent(s).
- News, short situationer reports, updates, or announcements.
- Feature story of an interesting topic.
- Audience participation, such as phone calls, letters, studio guests, or visitors.
- Plugs or Spots.

Planning and Producing a Magazine Programme

Here are the steps to planning and producing a magazine programme:

1. Identify the target audience.
   - For whom is the programme?
   - What are their needs and interests?
2. Specify programme objectives.
   - Be definite with what you expect from the listeners after they have been exposed to the programme/messages. Do you expect only knowledge gain or awareness of the issue/topic, or a change in behavior/practice?
3. Gather enough information about the topic. Do research.
4. Review the materials that you have gathered and select only those that are relevant to the objectives of the programme.
5. Prepare an outline/running order of the programme.
6. Determine the appropriate treatment/manner of presentation of each segment.
7. Approximate the length of each segment.
8. Write the scripts for the different segments and the continuity narration.
9. Prepare for taping/production.
   - Reserve the recording studio early and set an appointment with the technician
   - Prepare enough copies of the final script for the talents, technician, director, and other members of the production team
   - Audition music and sound effects
   - Select and rehearse the voice talents
10. Record the programme.
11. Listen to and evaluate the production.
12. Make the necessary revisions.
13. Air the radio magazine.

SUMMARY

Radio is one communication medium that can be used for effective environmental information, education, and communication.

Radio is accessible whether in urban or rural communities. Its messages are easy to understand. It can immediately disseminate information.

Some specific productions that may be utilised for environmental information, education, and communication are the radio news, interviews, plugs, and radio magazines.

News is a piece of information about a significant and recent event that affects and interests the listeners. It may be used to provide reports on the latest state of the environment or update the people about various environmental programmes, issues, and concerns.

A radio interview is an important means to obtain answers, draw information, gather explanations, solicit ideas or opinions, and clarify various environmental issues. People listen to interviews because they are simple, easy to understand, factual, believable, entertaining, and elaborate.

Plugs are short message presentations (about 30 seconds to one minute in length) that serve as breaks between programmes or programme segments. They may be used for making announcements about certain events, happenings, and occasions; to present ideas and viewpoints; to inform the audience about a particular project or a community activity; and to emphasise an idea.

The radio magazine, on the other hand, is a programme that contains different kinds of materials such as interviews, feature, plugs, trivia, and dramatisations. This production is appropriate for tackling varied topics and for a reaching diverse audience.

FACILITATOR'S GUIDE

SUBJECT MATTER	OBJECTIVE	TEXT	ACTIVITY	DURATION
Definition of Terms	To describe the characteristics of a community radio.	• Defining Community Radio Broadcasting	Lecture/ Discussion	1 hour
Basic Steps in Programme Planning and Production	To enumerate and explain the steps in planning and producing a radio programme.	• Programme Planning • Programme Production	Lecture/ Discussion	2 hours
Radio Scriptwriting	1. To explain the principles of writing for radio.	• Principles of Clear and Effective Scriptwriting for Radio	Lecture/ Discussion	1 hours
	2. To write a short radio talk.	• Activity	Exercise on writing a short radio talk	30 minutes
Interviewing for Radio	To conduct radio interviews.	• Principles of Effective Interviewing • Planning the Interview • Preparing for the Interview • Conducting the Interview • Guidelines for Asking Questions	Lecture/ Discussion Practicum Exercise on interviewing for radio (NOTE: The facilitator should be able to evaluate each interview and discuss the comments with the interviewer.)	1 hours 2 hours
The Radio News	To plan and write radio news.	• Radio News • News Sources • News Writing	Lecture/ Discussion Exercise & Evaluation (NOTE: Evaluation of radio news scripts must be done by the facilitator. Comments must be discussed with the writer.)	1 hour 2 hours

FACILITATOR'S GUIDE (con't)

SUBJECT MATTER	OBJECTIVE	TEXT	ACTIVITY	DURATION
Planning and Production of Developmental Radio Plugs	To plan and write radio plugs on environmental topics/issues.	What are Plugs Planning the Plugs Message Scripting Types of Presentation Structuring the Plug Writing the Message Production	Lecture/ Discussion Exercise on Writing Radio Plugs	2 hours 1 hour
Planning and Production of Radio Magazine	To plan and write a radio magazine tackling an environmental issue.	The Radio Magazine Types of Radio Magazine Contents of Radio Magazine Planning and Producing a Magazine Programme	Lecture/ Discussion Exercise on Writing a Radio Magazine (NOTE: The facilitator should ask the participants to bring broadcast materials, e.g., references.)	1 hour 2 hours

198

APPENDIX

WOMEN'S RADIO (PHILIPPINES) *

In 1989, the then Institute of Development Communication (now a college) conducted the action-research project on "Rural Women's Participation in Development Broadcasting in Selected Philippine Communities" or Women's Radio (Philippines). Funded by the International Development Research Center (IDRC), Women's Radio (Philippines) aimed to: a) study the nature and extent of rural women's participation in development broadcasting; b) ascertain the reasons for rural women's participation in development broadcasting; c) identify factors that could influence rural women's participation; d) determine if relationships between such factors and rural women's extent of participation; e) train rural women in community broadcasting and other related skills; f) pilot test participatory development radio programs produced by and for rural women; and g) determine the effects of rural women's participation.

In line with these objectives, the project was implemented in four phases: Survey/Research, Training, Pilot Testing, and Evaluation.

Baseline data was gathered during the Survey/Research phase. Results revealed that the the typical rural woman in Laguna, Philippines was relatively young, married, with children, had at least an elementary education, and had been a resident of her barangay for 30 years or less.

She interacted most with her husband and children, had little or no contact with extension workers, seldom joined
organisations for lack of time or interest, but was at least a member of a clique (group of three to five women). She seldom left her barangay except to go to market or to settle bills.

She failed to participate in community-related activities for lack of information regarding the activities, lack of time, and lack of inclination. Yet, she expressed a desire for a society with an equal distribution of power and wealth and a people who had more concern with their fellowmen.

Furthermore, she wanted a better life for herself but was uncertain about the realities of her existence. She had no confidence in voicing opinions. She expressed an interest in participating in the project's developmental radio programme.

Survey results helped the research team focus on two barangays for the Training Phase: Isla in Pangil, Laguna and Mayatba in Famy, Laguna.

Participants were selected with the help of their communities. They attended a 30-day training on community broadcasting, interpersonal communication, and leadership and community organizing at the Institute of Development Communication, University of the Philippines Los Baños (IDC-UPLB).

The training equipped them with broadcasting skills that they would need as rural broadcasters in their barangays. After the training, the women formed an association for each barangay and elected their officers.

During the Pilot Testing Phase, participants conducted listenership campaigns to ensure listenership of the participatory radio programmes that they would initiate. They also conducted monthly community assembly meetings at their barangays to flesh out courses of action regarding community projects and problems discussed in the radio programmes.

Thirty-four radio magazines produced in the Pilot-testing Phase of the project were aired over DZLB, the educational radio station of the University of the Philippines.

The Evaluation Phase determined the effects of the participatory radio programmes on the participants, their communtiies and families, and their listeners.

Listeners claimed they learned much from the programme regarding health and home management, farming, food production, livelihood, and moral values.

The majority favoured the women's participation in the programme. Even husbands and fathers of participants said they would allow their women to continue participation despite the time and money that was involved. Some men were willing to join the women on the programme.

When compared with a non-participatory radio program, the participatory program was perceived as being important in mobilizing women in a community.

One important effect of the radio programme was on the listeners' perception of rural women. They realised that women can be men's partners in community development and learned that women are as capable as men of being active in community activities.

Not surprisingly, the project team learned that the participatory radio programme had the most impact on its participants. Despite the hardships that they went through to produce a programme, their participation gave them an immeasurable feeling of self-worth, an idea that they could make things happen in their communities. They felt they had become more responsible members of their communities.

As a result of this project, the Mayatba women have started a swine-raising project while the Isla women have established a multi-purpose cooperative and engaged in soap making. Furthermore, the Isla women's vegetable garden provides their families with fresh vegetables. On the other hand, the Mayatba women find that their "Pook Luntian" (herbal garden) offers a source of herbal medicine for minor ailments.

Ultimately, participation in the project helped in developing the self-worth of the rural women participants. This in turn had an impact on their families, their friends, and their communities.

REFERENCES

Bertran, Jane T. 1978. **Communications Pretesting.** The Community and Family Study Center, The University of Chicago, USA.

Department of Development Communication. 1979. **A Manual on Radio Broadcasting.** UPLB, College, Laguna, Philippines

De Jong, Robert Brunwin. 1994. **Addressing Audiences in their Interest: A Paper on Methods and Techniques of Radio and Television Programming With a Message and Purpose.** Radio Netherlands International, Natherland.

De Jong, Robert Brunwin. 1994. **Public Information and the Use of Mass Media: A Reader in support of the Workshop on addressing Audiences in Their Interests.** Radio Netherlands International, Natherland.

Mody, Bella. 1991. **Designing Messages for Development Communication: An Audience Participation-Based Approach.** New Delhi, Newsnury. SAGE Publications, London.

Preparation and Production of Media Resources: Small Format Video and Cable TV Production

OLIVER CARLO T. CASTILLO

OBJECTIVES
At the end of this chapter, the participants should be able to:

1. List the potentials and limitations of small format video in development work;
2. Explain the video production process; and
3. Produce a simple video for cable TV broadcast.

INTRODUCTION

Video is a powerful tool in communicating environmental messages. It can even be more powerful if cable television is used to broadcast such videos. Compared to print and radio, video can graphically and audibly present people, places, events, and issues. Video has both sound and moving pictures which other media do not have.

In this chapter, we will study the nature of video and cable TV in order to see its power and limitations in communicating environmental messages. We will also take a look at several case studies about video, cable TV and women in development work. Then finally, we will go through the different phases of the video production process so you can produce your own videos at the end of this module/training.

THE NATURE OF VIDEO

Video is an audio-visual medium. It targets two of our senses – sight and hearing. It allows for pictures to be seen and sounds to be heard at the same time. Because of this, video, is effective in capturing an audience's attention better when compared to other media.

Video is also electronic in nature. This means it requires an electronic gadget – in this case, the camcorder, to record images of people, places, and events. It also uses a magnetic tape which records images and sounds electronically and allows for playback instantly. New images and sound can also be recorded over old. Compared to film, which is not an electronic media, video is cheaper and easier to produce. Film does not provide re-recording /re-use of material, and instant playback. Film has to be developed first before we can view what the cameraman has shot. The film development process itself is also expensive.

Three decades ago, video was a rare and expensive commodity. Only TV stations possessed video cameras and video tapes. But because of the advent of technology, video supplies and equipment have become smaller in size, and are now readily available and affordable to almost everybody. Video tapes with a width of less than one inch are called "small format" video tapes. Examples are the VHS, SVHS, VHSC, SVHSC, V8 and Hi-8 tapes.

Historical Development of Cable TV

One hundred years ago, nobody ever thought of television. Having a box which showed moving pictures was never in man's wildest imagination.

Today, as one looks around, technology has gone much, much farther. Practically every household in the Philippines has a television set. People of different walks of life can be hooked to the modern world around them through the wonders of television, otherwise known as the "boob tube."

Since, television was mass-produced, technology has advanced dramatically. For instance, gone are the days of the black-and-white screen. The remote control replaced the dial and push button controls. Television sets now come in different widths, as well as thickness.

One of the latest innovations in television technology is the development and popularisation of cable television. Instead of the traditional antenna that picks up signals in the airwaves, images are transmitted in electrical impulses through cables from the satellite dish to the TV unit in one's living room. Through this technology, more channels, including international channels, can now be accessed by television viewers. Cable TV has also improved the resolution of pictures because the cable eliminates atmospheric interference.

Close-circuit television or cable TV is less expensive than open-circuit telecasting. Generally speaking, cable TV does not require as extensive a production staff, and its programmes can be tailored to meet the needs and interests of a specific audience (Encyclopedia International, 1979).

Commercial use of cable TV in the Philippines began in the early 1990s. The cable TV industry first flourished in Iloilo City before hitting Metro Manila and Luzon. Today, almost every city and key municipality in the country has a cable TV network servicing its constituents (Lanuza, 2000).

Under the provisions set by the National Telecommunications Commission (NTC), every cable system provider operating in the country is compelled to have at least one channel reserved for the sole purpose of information dissemination to the subscribers within the area of jurisdiction of the cable system provider (Lagrimas et al., 2000).

Some municipalities and cities saw the potential of cable TV for creative community broadcasts. Community news and issues that national TV networks ignore or give low priority can now be given airtime. The most common community-related cable TV broadcasts shown on cable

TV channels are community advisories and public service announcements such as upcoming civic activities of community organisations.

Limitations of Cable TV

However, video production for cable TV has some drawbacks and limitations. First and foremost is cost. It is very expensive to produce videos compared to print materials and other low cost media. Several expensive pieces of equipment are needed, such as a video camera, tripod, lights, and an editing machine. Video production also requires great manpower. Many people are needed – scriptwriters, director, cameramen, production assistants, actors/actresses, and post-production people. The whole video production process itself is arduous and time consuming.

When the video is finally produced, bringing it to the intended audience can be another problem. Not everybody has cable TV. In the Philippines, only the upper middle class and the elite can afford a cable TV subscription. The others only get to watch cable TV in public places like lobbies of police stations, barangay halls and hospitals, or in the homes of their neighbours and relatives.

Successful Community Videos

If we set aside the limitations of video and cable TV, it is still considered powerful and effective when used for development work. Take the case of the Kayapo video in Brazil.

In 1985, filmmaker Monica Frola helped the Kayapo tribe in Brazil familiarise themselves with video technology. Initially, they used it as a tool for documenting and preserving their traditional culture, their rituals, dances and, songs for future generations.

Afterwards, the video was utilised to communicate to many villages and its chiefs. The video tapes functioned as mail that shuttled from one village to another. Soon, they started exchanging political speeches and documented their protests against the Brazilian state.

The Kayapo's image as "hi-tech" Indians quickly moved to the front pages of important journals, including the cover of *Time* magazine when they denounced the construction of a dam that would flood their land. The Kayapo became much more conscious of their own culture as an important component of their identity as a social group and a valuable political resource (Dagron, 2001).

Here's another successful case – TV Maxabomba of Brazil: TV Maxabomba is a project of the Centre de Imagen de Cerracao (CECIP) of Brazil. It started in 1980 aided by a video projector and an old van. TV Maxabomba presents documentaries to people in the streets, in public squares, schools, and open markets. Each screening easily gathers 200-300 people.

TV Maxabomba was used to record the experiences of the local people, appraise what had been done by grassroots or community organisations, and brought information necessary to the understanding of people's rights. As many as 100 video documentaries have been produced since 1986. The topics include democracy, citizen's rights, education, gender, environment, black culture, health, and sexuality (Dagron, 2001).

Community Cable TV and Environmental Conservation

Since video is an attractive medium and cable TV is a good channel to convey community messages and issues, several cause-oriented groups in the Philippines tapped video and cable TV in their endeavours. Among those groups are local government officials, firemen, health workers, religious groups, and environmentalists.

Several municipalities and cities in the Philippines saw the potential of cable TV for community broadcasts. The most common community-related cable TV broadcasts are community advisories and public service announcements. Upcoming civic activities of community organisations are written about and run across the screen during intermission time on local cable TV channels.

A few communities, one of which is Los Baños, put up "LB Talk", a community news-magazine programme which was a weekly programme, airing news and issues in an in-depth manner. Environmental conservation was one of the frequent topics in the segments of "LB Talk".

In one of the "LB Talk" 2001 episodes, an environmental video documentary was subjected to empirical study. The video documentary was entitled "Buhay sa Tabi ng Basurahan (Life in the Dumpsite)." It brought the viewers a comprehensive look at their own municipal dumpsite. The video showed images of the dumpsite – piles of garbage, and smoke, scavengers rummaging through the filthy mounds of waste, and a peep into their shanties. The video also featured several interviews with the scavengers, the residents in the vicinity of the dumpsite, and a government health worker. The documentary was seven minutes long and was broadcasted for four consecutive weeks in *"LB Talk"*.

The impact of "Buhay sa Tabing Basurahan" on the Los Baños community was determined by interviewing several viewers who were able to see the video. All of the respondents admitted that the video made them aware of the waste management problem of their town. The dumpsite is located on an isolated slope of a mountain hidden from people, thus, the video was an eye-opener for them. Furthermore, the video prompted them to act or participate in solving this community problem. They expressed various ways on how they intend to help solve the garbage problem of Los Baños. They also vowed to practise waste separation and recycling.

Although the study did not monitor if the respondents really implemented their plans, this research proved that cable TV is an effective channel in informing and educating the community on issues surrounding them. "Buhay sa Tabi ng Basurahan" served as an eye-opener and a catalyst for change.

Women and Video Production

In the past three years (1989-2002), female students outnumber male students in the video-production course at the UPLB College of Development Communication. The average ratio is 4:1. The female video students also get higher grades than their male counterparts, on the average.

In general, when they start as beginners, I observed that the women hold the camera better than the men. They shoot better footage primarily because of their delicate handling of the camera. Women produce smoother pans, tilts, and zooms than men. Men have this so-called "heavy hand" and so they press the record button hard and make abrupt camera movements.

Likewise, when it comes to conducting interviews, women are better interviewers than men. In the Philippines, particularly in man-on-the-street interviews (MOS), subjects are more comfortable with female interviewers. This is perhaps because the female interviewers look more "harmless" than their male counterparts. Women also have this special ability of building rapport with interviewees in a relatively short period of time.

207

Here is a case wherein women played important roles in successful community video productions:

The DevCom Development Society (DDS) of India conducted a video production training programme for the rural women of Medak District in Andhra Pradesh. The participants included seven women, four of whom were illiterate. They were taught the basics of video production for 30 days.

These women had various reasons for participating in the training: 1) to make the issues in their community known to the outside world; 2) to document the news events in their community; and 3) to document weddings and other special occasions. The training was done with one DV camera, and two VHS video cameras, and a makeshift editing set-up. The training culminated with a hands-on video project about pre-schools for the children and their significance to their lives.

Two months later, when these women were already on their own, heavy rains poured in their area and their crops were severely damaged. The women decided to tell their story on video. The group discussed their ideas and planned the story. The group also wanted to highlight that the video was produced by rural women. They assigned one of them to stand as reporter. They placed her in the midst of the flooded field as she delivered her piece on cam. She talked about the destruction and the dark future of the women and the farmers in their area.

DDS found the video impressive. They negotiated with the local cable TV to provide for air time. Two channels, namely Dordughan and the ETV channel, agreed to provide them space. The former provides them space on their women's programmes, while the latter provides a 5-minute slot per month for stories on organic farming.

BASIC VIDEO PRODUCTION EQUIPMENT

As video makers, let us familiarise ourselves with our tools. The following is a list of the basic video production equipment, and the hows and whys of using them:

Video Camera

Basically, there are two types of video cameras – the studio camera and the camcorder. For our purposes, we will use a camcorder or one that

combines a camera and a recorder in one portable unit. The studio camera
is big, bulky, and has a separate recorder unit. Make sure your camcorder
is clean and in good working condition and avoid getting your camcorder
wet or exposed to intense heat.

FIGURE 7.1 THE CAMCORDER AND ITS PARTS

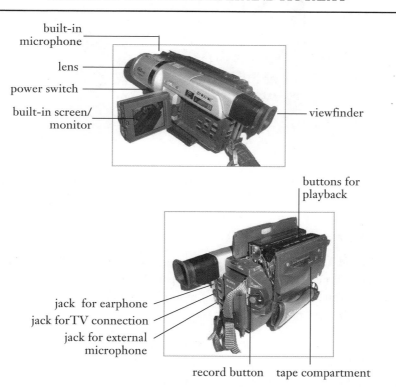

built-in
microphone

lens

power switch

built-in screen/
monitor

viewfinder

buttons for
playback

jack for earphone
jack for TV connection
jack for external
microphone

record button   tape compartment

Batteries

Before shooting, check if your camcorder's battery is fully charged. It is
also wise to bring along spare batteries that are fully-charged. You'll need
them in situations where you'll be shooting for several hours/days in
places where there is no electricity.

209

FIGURE 7.2 VIDEO PRODUCTION ACCESSORIES

Charger

Also bring along your battery charger all the time. You never know when you'll need it. If you don't have spare batteries, a charger is very valuable. You can also use it during indoor shots in order to conserve battery power.

Tripod

To minimise camera shakes, you need a tripod. It may be very bulky to bring along, but that's the sacrifice you have to make if you really want professional-looking footage. A tripod also helps you execute smooth camera movements.

External Microphone

Don't rely too much on the built-in microphone of your camcorder. Built-in mikes are usually omni-directional. This means they pick up sounds from all directions, even behind them. It is not good to use such mikes when conducting interviews in noisy places. In such situations you'll need a uni-directional external mike. This is a microphone that you attach to the "mike-input" hole of your camcorder. It picks up sound from just one direction – the direction it is pointing at. It eliminates background noise. It also extends the audio pick-up ability of your camcorder by several meters.

Earphones

In order to monitor the sounds that your camcorder is getting, you'll need earphones. Earphones for walkmans will do. Plug it in the "phones" hole of your camcorder.

Lights and Reflectors

If your budget allows, bring along some lights. They will be used to eliminate shadows on the faces of your subjects. If you don't have such lights, you can use reflectors. Find a shiny object, like a car's sunshield or a white piece of paper. Use it to reflect available light into the dark areas of your subject.

Gadgets for Cut IDs

It is important to have identification numbers for every cut in your tape. Don't rely too much on the tape counter. Some videomakers use a chalk board where they write the cut ID before shooting a particular sequence. Others use a small notebook with a number on every page. You are to aim your camera on the number and shoot it for 5 seconds before shooting what you really intend to shoot. You are to do this for every cut. These numbers will guide your post-production editor in locating the cuts to be included in your final video. So don't forget to bring along a chalkboard or a numbered notebook when you go on shooting.

Editing Machine

You'll need an editing machine to assemble your raw footage according to your desired sequence. Through an editing machine, you can also add music, sound effects, and narration to your video. You can further enhance your video by putting text, graphics, and visual transitions.

Basically, there are two kinds of editing machines:

1. **Analog editing machine** – It is also called the linear editing machine. It consists of a player and a recorder. The player plays the cuts from your raw footage tape and the recorder records them on a blank tape. You transfer the cuts into the blank tape in the desired chronological order. This system is called linear editing because you cannot interchange the order of the cuts once they are recorded on the blank tape. It's like pasting the cuts permanently on a time line.

FIGURE 7.3 LINEAR EDITING MACHINE

2. **Digital editing machine** – It is also called a non-linear editing machine. This is a desktop computer with a multi-media production function. The computer grabs your raw footage and stores it in its hard drive. From there, you arrange the cuts according to your desired sequence using the mouse. Its difference from the analog system is that you can interchange the order of the cuts anytime. When the assembly is done,

the computer will then record it on a blank tape. Generation loss is also minimal in this kind of editing.

FIGURE 7.4 NON-LINEAR EDITING MACHINE

THE VIDEO PRODUCTION PROCESS

The process of producing a video undergoes three phases – the **pre-production phase**, the **production phase**, and **the post-production phase**. Each phase is equally important and requires diligent planning, management, and supervision.

The Pre-Production Phase

This is the phase wherein you do all the necessary preparations before the actual shooting. There are several tasks involved here like scriptwriting, budgeting, making a distribution plan, preparing the shooting venue and the like. But before anything else, begin your work by studying your intended audience. Know their needs so that you can produce a video that is relevant to them.

Audience Analysis, Need Assessment and Objective Setting

Good producers often start by asking themselves if their video project would be relevant and would benefit their target audience. We should know our audience in terms of age group, occupation, interests, socio-economic status, educational level, language capabilities, lifestyle, religion, and ethnicity. When we know who we want to reach, we will be able to construct a video that will truly get into their hearts and minds.

FIGURE 5. THE VIDEO PRODUCTION PROCESS

PRE-PRODUCTION PHASE

Tasks:
- Audience analysis; Need assessment; and Objective setting
- Scriptwriting
- Distribution planning
- Budgeting
- Making shooting arrangements

PRODUCTION

Tasks:
   Shooting

POST-PRODUCTION PHASE

Tasks:
- Shot listing
- Transcribing interviews
- Determining cut-points
- Video editing
- Distribution
- Evaluation

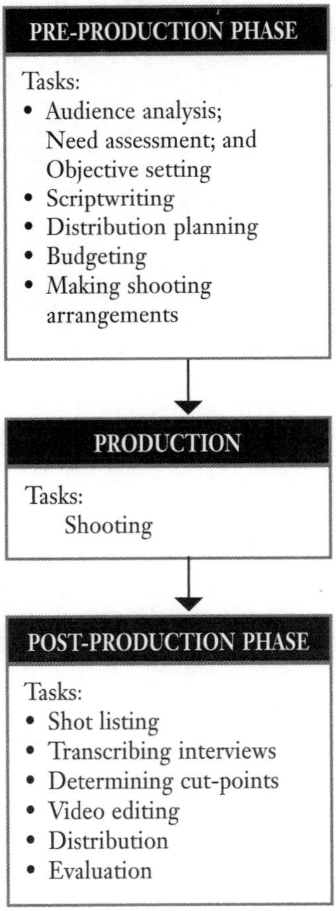

To help you in analysing an audience you can use this worksheet. Try answering these questions. Be as specific as possible:

SAMPLE AUDIENCE WORKSHEET

1. What is the age group of your audience?
   0-15 _____
   15-25 _____
   25-40 _____
   40 and above _____

2. Are you aiming at predominantly men or women?
   Men _____
   Women _____
   Both _____

3. What are their main occupations?
   Mostly professional _____
   Mostly non-professional _____

4. Is this community...
   Rural _____
   Urban _____

5. What kind of topics are they interested in?
   List at least 3
   _____, _____, _____

6. What is their social and economic status?
   They are barely able to meet basic needs of
   survival _____
   Easily meet basic survival needs _____
   Afford some luxuries _____
   Afford many luxuries _____

7. Their highest educational levels is...
    finished elementary school ___
    finished secondary school ___
    finished university ___
    a graduate degree holder ___

8. What languages do they know?

9. Describe their lifestyle, e.g., Are most of them
    married? With children? Who works in the family?
    Who usually makes the decisions?

10. What is their religion(s)?

11. Does this religion affect the way your audience views
    the world?
    Yes ___ No ___

12. Do most people have access to TVs? Yes ___No ___
    VCRs? Yes ___ No ___

13. What is the audience's current attitude toward your
    topic? How will this programme change this attitude?

14. What do you want your audience to think after
    watching the programme? To do?

After analysing your audience, you will be able to see their needs
and aspirations. Examples of needs are: livelihood, knowledge on family
planning, knowledge on environmental conservation, desire to increase
agricultural yield, or need to get rid of vices such as drinking and
gambling.

When you've identified the need you want to address, write down
in black-and-white the objectives of your video project. This list of
objectives will be your guide as you write your script. It will also be used
as an evaluation tool in the post-production phase. By looking at your
objectives, we will see whether you have been successful or not in your
job. Here are examples of good objectives:

A. Sample objectives for an environmental video
At the end of the video the audience must be able to:
1) List the causes of air pollution;
2) Describe the effects of air pollution; and
3) Explain some solutions to air pollution.

B. Sample objectives for a family planning video
1) Describe the benefits of having a small family;
2) Enumerate some family planning methods;
3) Explain the do's and don'ts of the rhythm method; and
4) Practice the rhythm method.

Remember that your objectives must be time bound, observable, measurable, achievable, and specific. Objectives are what you want your audience to do after watching your video. So always begin with the phrase: "At the end of the video presentation the audience must be able to…" Then write the specific actions that you want to see in them.

Team Building
Manpower requirement is another consideration in the pre-production phase. In small-format video production, the minimum manpower requirement is a team composed of two people – a reporter who appears on camera and a cameraman. But if you have more than two people who will work on your video project, you can assign them the following roles:

- **Scriptwriter** – somebody who will write the script.
- **Director** – somebody who prompts the people on camera on their speaking lines, acting (if necessary), and blocking.
- **Cameraman** – operates the camera.
- **Assistant cameraman** – helps in setting up the camera or the tripod, carries the tripod, cables, microphones and earphone.
- **Lightman** – in-charge of setting up the lights (if any).
- **Audioman** – monitors the sound during shooting.
- **Researcher** – gathers additional information that may be useful to the scriptwriter.
- **Production Assistant** – makes arrangements for the shooting sessions.

217

- **Video Editor** – edits/assembles the video.
- **Actors/Talents** – people who appear on camera.

If you don't have enough people to work with, you can assign several of the above tasks to one person in your team. Hold team-building meetings so that your video team will be familiar with their roles.

Scriptwriting

Another task under the pre-production phase is scriptwriting. The script will serve as a guide for your actors/actresses, narrator, and technical people like the cameraman and video editor. A script must be easy to understand and complete with instructions and specifications.

A basic video script is composed of two columns – the visual column and the audio column. The visual column describes what the audience will *see*, cut-by-cut. Parallel to it is the audio column. It contains what the audience will *hear*, cut-by-cut.

Below is an example of a two-column video script.

TABLE 7.1 TWO-COLUMN VIDEO SCRIPT

VISUAL	AUDIO
Medium shot: Mother working in the kitchen. She is wearing an apron.	MUSIC
Close up: Mother's hand slicing a carrot.	MUSIC
Close up: Mother's hand opening a can of mushrooms.	MUSIC
Medium shot: Mother throws carrot peelings and the tin can together in a trash bin.	MUSIC
Medium shot: 10 year-old daughter enters the kitchen. The girl is wearing school uniform.	GIRL: Mother, we learned in school that we should separate non-biodegradable wastes from the biodegradable wastes.

TABLE 7.1 (con't)

VISUAL	AUDIO
Close up: Girl talking, high angle.	GIRL: Biodegradable wastes like vegetable peelings can serve as fertiliser so let's put it in a separate garbage bin.
Close up: Two garbage bins with non-biodegradable and biodegradable labels.	GIRL: In this way, we will be able to reduce our garbage and in turn, help protect our environment.
Medium shot: Mother tapping her daughter's shoulder.	MOTHER: Don't worry, from now on, we will segregate our garbage.

END

Here are some scriptwriting tips:

1. Scriptwriting is like talking to someone. Don't sound academic.
2. Make your script simple – use short words and short sentences.
3. Use the active voice, not the passive.
4. Use the vernacular if you think it's the best way to get the message across.
5. Don't try to include too many parts, especially numbers.
6. The audio and the visuals must go together. It's like telling a story to a child using a picture book.
7. List your points in logical order.
8. Your script must not be too long. Time yourself as you read your script. A plug must not be more than 60 seconds; a news report must not be more than five minutes; a narrated feature story must not go beyond ten minutes including interviews; and a magazine programme must not be more than one hour, including commercials. If you're making a long documentary, break it into a series of ten-minute segments maximum. Put an intermission time in between segments.

ACTIVITY 7.1

Objectives

At the end of this activity, paticipants should be able to:

1. Identify an environmental problem in their community;
2. Describe an intended audience for an environmental video;
3. Set objectives for an environmental video; and
4. Write a two-column script for an environmental video.

Procedure

1. Think of one message that you want to tell the women of your community. It should be simple and specific.

   Examples:

   1) Segregate your garbage;
   2) Don't burn your garbage; and
   3) Help conserve our forests.

2. On a piece of paper, briefly describe your intended audience. What are their socio-demographic characteristics? What are their needs?
3. Write 2-3 objectives of your video project.
4. Write a two-column script for a TV plug conveying your message. It should be 30-60 seconds in length.
5. Have your trainer evaluate and approve your script.

Distribution Planning

How will you make your video reach your target audience? Will you buy airtime in a local TV station? Will you in VHS format or CD format in bookstores? Or would you video in video rental shops? Maybe school principals and teachers, then set-up a mini-theater in a village and invite the people to watch your video?

There are many ways to distribute your finished product. You may choose any of the ones we've enumerated, or choose a combination of ways. You may also come up with a better distribution plan than the ones listed above. The important thing to settle your distribution plan before you shoot your video. You should be decided on your distribution blueprint here in the pre-production phase, not when you get into the post-production phase.

Budgeting

Whether your video project is simple or grand, you will always spend money. Your budget will consist of many things – manpower, equipment, supplies and materials, distribution costs, and miscellaneous. Here is a sample budget plan for a 30-second TV commercial:

TABLE 7.2 SAMPLE BUDGET PLAN

		Unit Cost		Total Cost	
1.	**Manpower**				
	a. Crew – cameramen, video, editor, etc.	Php* 1,000	(2)	Php*	2,000
	b. Producer/director	5,000			5,000
	c. Actors/actresses/hosts/narrators	1,000	(5)		5,000
	d. Scriptwriter, artists, designers	1,000	(3)		3,000
2.	**Equipment**				
	a. Rental/purchase of cameras	100/hr.	(10)		1,000
	b. Editing facilities	100/hr.	(5)		500
3.	**Supplies and Materials**				
	a. Tapes	500	(3)		1,500
	b. Sets/props	1,000			1,000
	c. Graphics, artwork	1,000			1,000
4.	**Miscellaneous**				
	a. Transport	1,500			1,500
	b. Food	3,500/day	(1)		3,500
	c. Wardrobe/make-up	1,000			1,000
	d. Copyright of music, footage, story	3,000			3,000
	e. Photocopying	200			200
	f. Communication (telephone calls)	300			300
5.	**Reproduction and Distribution**				
	a. Duplication of tapes	100/tape	(5)		500
	b. Tape/CD jackets	100/tape	(5)		500
	c. Publicity materials	1,000			1,000
	d. Airtime	5,000			5,000
	*Philippine pesos	**GRAND TOTAL**			**36,500**

221

When planning your budget, consider time. Calculate how many days the whole process will take. If you have people who will be paid per hour or per day, determine how long you will need their services. Finally, always add 10% of the Grand Total on top of your estimated budget for contingencies.

Making Shooting Arrangements

Let's complete our pre-production checklist. Here the are other considerations and tasks we need to do before actual shooting:

1. **Check the location** – Be conscious of the audio and lighting conditions. Check the power supply. Make courtesy calls to authorities if necessary.
2. **Arrange accommodation for cast and crew** – If the shooting will take several days in a distant location, go there ahead of time and reserve a place to sleep for the cast and crew.
3. **Organise your team** – Make a final line-up of your cast and crew. Hold an orientation meeting. Be sure each one knows his/her role well.
4. **Obtain additional video and audio inserts** – These will be useful during the post-production. But to save time, it's better if you obtain them now. Look for file video, music, and sound effects that can make your video project more attractive and interesting.

If you're done with all of these, we are now ready to go to the next phase of the video production process – the production phase.

THE PRODUCTION PHASE

This is the phase where the shooting takes place. When taking video footage, there are many things to remember like lighting, audio, camera stability, camera movements and composition. Let's discuss them further one by one.

Lighting

You need the right amount of light in your shots. If your shot has too much light, it's called an overexposed shot. It's too bright then if viewer can't see the necessary details of the picture. On the other hand if it lacks light or is too dark, it is referred to as underexposed.

If you don't have artificial lights, the best time to shoot in the tropics, for example, is from 7 a.m. to 9 a.m., and from 4 p.m. to 6 p.m. Outside of these "golden hours", your shots will likely have dark shadows or be underexposed. Also avoid shooting your subject with the light source behind the subject. This will create a silhouette effect.

Audio

In modern videos, the audio is 50% of your work. That's how important it is to have good quality audio in your shots. If you're shooting an interview always use an external microphone. You can use either a lapel microphone or a hand-held microphone. This eliminates ambient sound which can be distracting. If there's a barking dog or if you're located beside a noisy street, the interview will not be as audible as you would want it to be.

If you're shooting a drama with many characters, you can use an overhead boom microphone. But if you don't have such a gadget, tell your actors/actresses to speak loudly when delivering their lines. Always wear headphones/earphones so you can monitor the audio that your camera is recording.

FIGURE 7.6 DIFFERENT KINDS OF MICROPHONES

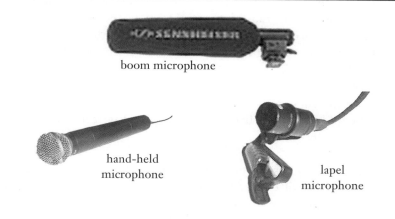

boom microphone

hand-held microphone

lapel microphone

Camera Stability

To make your shots look good, avoid camera shakes. Camera shakes give a dizzying effect. So, always use a tripod. It may take some time setting up the camera on a tripod, but the long wait is worthwhile as you are guaranteed professional looking shots. In case you don't have a tripod, learn to improvise. You can use a table, a chair, or any stable platform to hold your camera. If you still can't find an improvised tripod, learn the art of taking steady shots without any props. Hold the camera with both hands and avoid breathing heavily. It takes a lot of practice to perfect a steady shot. Be patient and keep on practicing. Also avoid overusing the telephoto lens. This creates a shaky image. Use a wide-angle lens as much as possible.

Camera Movements

Aside from the fixed shot, there are six basic camera movements. They are as follows:

1. **Pan** – the camera stays in one place but it swivels from left to right or right to left.
2. **Tilt** – the camera stays in one place but it swivels up and down. If it swivels up, it is called a "tilt up." If it swivels down, it is a "tilt down."
3. **Zoom** – The camera stays in position but its lens makes the subject seem closer (zoom in) or farther (zoom out) from the viewer.
4. **Track** – The camera and cameraman move from point A to point B. The line from Point A to Point B is parallel to the subject. It is like a pan, but the camera is moved from one point to another.
5. **Crane** – The camera and cameraman move from a lower plane to a higher plane, or vice versa as it shoots a subject. It creates a shot similar to the tilt.
6. **Dolly** – The camera and cameraman move closer to or farther from the subject. If the movement is toward the subject, it is called a "dolly in", If the movement is away from the subject, it is a "dolly out."

But remember this – do not abuse or over-use the camera movements. Too much of these will create a confusing video. Use the fixed shot 60% of the time. This will make your production viewer-friendly.

FIGURE 7. BASIC CAMERA MOVEMENTS

pan left/right

crane up/down

track left/right

dolly in/out

tilt up/down

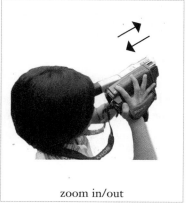

zoom in/out

Composition

Composition is the way you put your subject in the frame. There are basic tips on composition that you should remember:

1. **Rule of Thirds** – don't put your subject dead-centre in the frame. Put it slightly off-centre, either to the left or to the right. This gives us dynamism, and the shot will not look bland, flat, and boring.

2. **Line of horizon** – Don't let the horizon cut your frame in two equal halves. Position the line of horizon either on B or 2 part of the frame.

| Not okay | Okay | Okay |

3. **Headroom** – Give your subject ample headroom. A shot with too much headroom is not nice to look at.

Too much headroom Just right Too little headroom

226

4. **Line of sight/Nose room** – Give ample nose room. The space into which the eyes are looking should be bigger than the space behind the head.

Ample noseroom   Too little noseroom

5. **Close-up** – Crop your subject appropriately. Different sizes of your subject or the frame help tell different messages.

Long shot   Medium shot   Close-up shot

Extreme close-up shot

6. **Camera angles** – Use camera angles appropriately. Different angles give different messages too. A high angle shot (bird's eye view) dwarfs your subject while a low angle shot (worm's eye view) makes your subject appear bigger.

Low angle

High angle

7. **Distracting lines and objects** – Avoid putting your subject behind distracting lines and objects. These are things that seem to grow from your subject. Examples are electric cable and branches of trees in the background.

Additional Shooting Tips

Here are some more pointers that will be helpful to you in the production phase:

1. **Always have an ID number for every cut** – You'll use these cut IDs in the post-production phase. These numbers will make shot listing and locating cuts easier.
2. **Avoid a white background** – A white background is glaring to the eye. It will also "cut off" the head of your subject if your subject is wearing a white shirt.
3. **Advisable clothes** – There are some clothes that are not good for video. These are clothes with fine stripes or fine prints. They will make the clothes look as if were "dancing." Meanwhile, bright red clothes will make the edges of the shirt "bleed" or smudge. The best colour for video are pastel colours. As much as possible, if you and your host can afford such preparation, orient them on these things.
4. **Don't forget your white balance** – If your camera has a white balance button, press this as you aim the camera on a white object. Do this every time there's a change in the lighting condition. White balance orients your camera on the new lighting condition. If your camera has no white balance button, it means it has a built-in automatic white balance control. You don't need to worry about white balancing then. Most modern camcorders have this function.
5. **Manual focus vs. autofocus** – Minimise the use of autofocus. Most professionals use manual focus. In the autofocus setting, the camera will "look for the subject" on its own. This creates blurred moments in your recording.
6. **Add "pads" to every cut** – Every cut, whether it is a fixed shot or a shot with camera movement, must have at least two seconds of "establishing moment" before and after the sequence that you want to capture on tape. These are called "pads". It's a sort of allowance for the video editor doing post-production. The pads will ultimately be chopped off in assembling the final video.

Example:
When making a pan, do the following steps:
a) Press the record button to start recording;
b) Hold the camcorder still for two seconds;
c) Start panning;
d) When finished, don't turn off the record button. Hold your camera still for another two seconds.
e) Press the record button to end recording. The same principle also applies for fixed shots. Shoot your subject longer than you want it to appear on your final video.

7. **Use different tapes for different types of footage** – Put all the interviews in one tape. Likewise, put all the cut-aways (shots that are not interviews) in another tape. Don't mix them up in one tape. This is to make your raw footage organised and easy for the editor to work with. A given cut will be easy to locate if you follow this system.

ACTIVITY 7.2

Objectives
At the end of the activity, you should be able to:
1. Shoot video footage according to a script; and
2. Practice the shooting tips discussed earlier.

Procedure
1. Using your approved script (Activity 7.1), shoot the specified cuts of your 60-second TV plug. Follow the instructions in the script to the letter.
   Example:
   If the script asks for a medium shot, don't do a close-up, do a medium shot.
2. Follow the tips enumerated in this section (Production Phase). Remember your notes on audio, lighting, composition, camera movements, and camera stability.
3. Each cut should have a cut ID.
4. Organise your footage. Separate the interviews (if any) from the cut-aways. Label your tape properly.

The Post-Production Phase

When all the raw footage had been shot, we are now ready to proceed to the post-production phase. The activities under this phase are shot listing, video-editing, distribution, and evaluation of the video project.

Shot Listing

The shot list is a list of all the shots you've taken, including the bad takes. This list will help you when identifying the cuts to be included in your final video. It also helps the video editor locate the shots in the long roll of videotape.

After securing all the tapes containing the raw footage, view them carefully. List down all the cuts on a piece of paper. An entry will contain the respective cut ID number and a brief description of the cut/sequence/shot. Below is an example of a shot list:

TABLE 7.3 SAMPLE SHOT LIST

TAPE A Cut No.	Description
1	Panning of rice field
2	Tilt up: tree to sky
3	Fixed shot: façade of a church
4	Fixed shot: people walking on a busy sidewalk, medium shot
5	Fixed shot: reporter talking on a cam, medium shot
6	Zoom in: long shot of tractor to extreme close up of wheel
7	Tracking: Front of tractor to rear of tractor

When you're done with this list, mark the cuts that you will use for your final video. Don't worry about the discards. Keep them. They may be useful in your future video projects.

As for the good cuts, write their respective cut ID numbers on your two-column script. These numbers will tell your video editor where in the tape he can find a given cut. For example, say he needs cut 12 and

231

when he plays the tape, cut 30 is what appears. This then means he needs to rewind to get to cut 12. It makes his work faster and easier.

Thus, your two-column script will now be a three-column script because we added another column – the cut ID number column. In order to see what the script will now look like, let us go back to the script example we had earlier.

TABLE 7.4 THREE-COLUMN VIDEO SCRIPT

Title: **Let's Segregate Our Garbarge!**
Length: 3 seconds

CUT ID NUMBER*	VISUAL	AUDIO
7	Medium shot: Mother working in the kitchen. She is wearing an apron.	MUSIC
12	Close up: Mother's hand slicing a carrot.	MUSIC
5	Close up: Mother's hand opening a can of mushrooms.	MUSIC
3	Medium shot: Mother throws carrot peelings and tin can together in a trash bin.	MUSIC
8	Medium shot: 10-year-old daughter enters the kitchen. The girl is wearing a school uniform.	GIRL: Mother, we learned in school that we should separate nonbiodegradable from the biodegradable wastes.
10	Close up: Girl talking, high angle.	GIRL: Biodegradable wastes like vegetable peelings can serve as fertilisers, so we put it in a separate garbage bin.
11	Close up: Two garbage bins with nonbiodegradable and biodegradable labels.	GIRL: In this way, we will be able to reduce our garbage and in turn, help protect our environment.
12	Medium shot: Mother tapping her daughter's shoulder.	MOTHER: Don't worry, from now on, we will segregate our

-END-

*hypothetical numbers only

Determining Interview Cut Points

If your video has interview inserts, you should determine the interview cut points so your video editor will know what part of the interview will be included in the final video. Include only the most important parts of the interview. If you allow your interviewee to speak too much, he/she will be a talking head. It is thus important to review the tape interview, and if possible, make a word-for-word transcription of his/her speech.

Once you've identified the sentences that would be included in the final video, integrate them in your script. You can use a different ink color for the interview to differentiate it from the narration or highlight it with a coloured pen. Write the exact words/sentences that your subject said. Put them in the audio column. In the visual column, write "INTERVIEW INSERT. Medium shot of (your interviewee)."

Here is a sample script with interview inserts:

TABLE 7.5 SAMPLE SCRIPT WITH INTERVIEW INSERT

Title: **Save the Philippine Eagle**
Length: 30 seconds

CUT ID NUMBER*	VISUAL	AUDIO
4	Full shot: Philippine eagle sitting down Dissolve to....	NARR: The Philippine eagle is an endangered species.
1	Panning of forest: wipe to....	NARR: There are just a few dozens of them remaining in the forests of Mt. Apo.
3	Interview Insert: Medium shot of DENR Secretary Heherson Alvarez Cut to....	ALVAREZ: "The Philippine eagle is becoming extinct because of the destruction of its habitat."
5	Interview Insert: Medium shot of Mt. Apo tribesman. Dissolve to...	TRIBESMAN: "When I was a small kid, I used to see several Philippine eagles in the forest."

233

| 6 | Long shot: Trees being cut by loggers, dissove to... | TRIBESMAN: "But since the loggers came, I rarely see an eagle these days." |
| 2 | Super-imposed text: Let's save our forest. Let's save the Philippine eagle. Fade to black | NARR: Let's save our forest. Let's save the Philippine eagle. |

-END-

Visual Transitions

Continue completing your three-column video script by putting in instructions for visual transitions. Visual transitions describe what will happen in between shots. The most common visual transition is the **cut**. This is an abrupt change of picture, from picture A to picture B.

Another common visual transition is the **wipe**. Here, picture A is literally wiped or pushed out of the frame by picture B. Thus, there is a point in time when half of picture A is occupying the frame, while the other half of the frame is being occupied by picture B. A distinct line separates the two pictures. We usually use this kind of transition when there is a change in topic or sub-topic.

The **dissolve** is also a common visual transition. Here, picture B is superimposed with picture A. Then picture A dissolves or fades away, leaving picture B alone in the frame. This creates a dramatic effect. We use this when we want to stir the emotions of the audience. The dissolve is also used to show lapses in time. We use this when picture A and B are before-and-after shots.

Other visual transitions include the **fade from black, fade to black**, the **focus**, and the **defocus**. But with the development of non-linear editing programmes, there are countless visual transitions to choose from. However, it is still best to keep your video simple. Use only the appropriate visual transitions because too many fancy transitions may make your video look confusing.

Write the instruction for usual transitions in every block of your visual column or your three-column script. The "Philippine Eagle" script in the previous page serves as an example.

Video Editing

You are now ready for video editing once your three-column script is in order. Turn over the tapes and the three-column script to your video editor, but don't let him/her work alone. Sit beside your editor as he/she works because he may need to make crucial editing decisions (not presented by the script) along the way, and it's better if you're there to guide your editor.

Video editing involves grabbing the cuts/shots from the raw footage and transferring it to a blank tape. Music, sound effects, narration, visual transitions, visual effects, text, and graphics are added in the process. Video editing is a very tedious job. It usually takes one hour of editing work for every minute of the final video. For example, if your final video is five minutes long, it will most likely require five hours of video editing.

Alternative Video Editing

If you lack state-of-the-art video editing machines, or if you can't find a video editing shop in your vicinity, you can still edit the video on your own. Here are some ways by which you can edit on your own:

Crude Editing

One way is by transferring your raw footage on a blank tape cut-by-cut and according to your desired sequence. You can do this by connecting your camcorder to a VHS player with a record function. This gadget is the one you use when watching home movies. Check if it has a record button.

You have to first plug the cables of your camcorder into the "VIDEO IN" and "AUDIO IN" holes of your VHS player-recorder. Then cue your V8 or VHSC tape to the cut you want to get. Play that cut/shot in your camcorder while simultaneously pressing the record button of your VHS player recorder. Press the "pause" button of the VHS player-recorder at the cut-point of your raw footage. Then cue your V8/VHSC to the next cut. Release the "pause" button of the VHS player-recorder to record the next cut. Do these steps until you complete the whole video.

However, crude editing has its own limitations. First, you cannot add narration, music and sound effects into the final video. You just let the video speak for itself. Second, you cannot super-impose text on your visuals. For titles and sub-titles, you need to print your text on paper and shoot that paper with your camcorder. The text becomes part of the raw footage and can be transferred to the blank tape. Lastly, you cannot have fancy transitions like wipes or dissolves. You only have cuts to separate one shot from the other.

Shoot-Edit

Another alternative video editing process is the shoot-edit. Others call this "in-camera editing" because you edit your video as you shoot.

You begin shooting at the very first cut prescribed by your script. Follow it by the next cut, and so on. If you make a mistake, rewind your tape and erase that part by recording over that segment of the tape. Do this until you complete the whole video. Some camcorders provide wipes and fades. You can make use of these while you shoot. Most cameras also allow their users to type titles and super-impose them on the footage. You can also avail of this feature in your shoot-edit.

But like crude editing, additional narration, movie sounds and visual effects cannot be inserted into your footage. Shoot-edit requires a lot of thinking and preparation. But once you get used to it, it becomes easy. You just need to practice and practice. Your craft and skills improve the more videos you make.

Distribution and Evaluation

If you're done with your canned video, go ahead and distribute it according to the distribution plan you have set during the pre-production phase. You can submit it to the local cable TV network so that they can broadcast it in your community channel. Your video can now be seen by your community. It now serves as a mirror by which the community can see themselves. In doing so, problems can be identified and actions plans can be formulated to make living conditions better.

You can determine the impact of the video through evaluation. Remember the evaluation plan you did in the pre-production phase? It's now time to implement it. You can conduct interviews among viewers and find out their impressions about your video project. Look also at the objectives you drafted during pre-production. Were all of them met? Finally, look at your budget. Did you overspend? Do you have savings? Compared to the results of your interviews/impact of the video, was the video worth spending on? These are the factors that determine the over-all success of your video project.

ACTIVITY 3

Objectives

At the end of this activity, the participants should be able to:

1. Write a script for a 60-second TV plug; and
2. Edit and produce a 60-second TV plug.

Procedure

1. Finalise your 3-column script. Include cut ID numbers, instructions for transitions, and interview cut-points (if any).
2. Edit your video (60-second TV plug). If you have state-of-the-art equipment, try doing it yourself. If you have difficulty, you can ask a professional video editor to assist you.
3. If you don't have an editing machine, edit your video using the crude editing method.
4. Present your video to the class.

VIDEO PROGRAMME FORMATS

There are many kinds of video programme formats that you can use to deliver your message. Each one has it own strong points and limitations. Study each one and choose the best programme format for your ntended audience. You may also combine two or more of this types of videos in your time slot. Most of these video programme formats go through the process we have described earlier, as well as make use of the techniques we have likewise discussed.

1. **Narrative Video** – This is the most common type of video format. There's a voice-over who reports or narrates a story being shown on screen. The reporter may or may not appear on cam. Music and sound effects usually come in with the narration to enhance or help build the mood of the story. Interviews may also be inserted. Topics may also vary because anything under the sun can be presented using the narrative form. Examples are news reports, feature stories of all sorts, and documentaries.
2. **Drama** – This is like a stage play on video. Several people appear on screen with a rehearsed dialogue. Actors and actresses portray the different roles and characters. The message is in the moral of

the story. Music and sound effects are also useful in this program format. The story may be fictional or true-to-life. The treatment may vary – from serious to light-hearted – to a combination of both. It can also be taped inside a studio or even outdoors.

The drama format is very attractive for certain groups of people like housewives and rural folks. The beauty of the story/ script and acting skills of the cast are crucial factors to the success of a drama.

3.   **Talk show** – This programme format has a host who functions as interviewer. He/she presents a panel of guests who talk on a certain topic. The show revolves on the said topic. Questions are thrown to the guests by the host, and the guests answer those questions. The answers are usually unrehearsed. The guests may be interviewed one by one, or as a group. Sometimes, canned video segments are injected, as well as on-the-phone interviews. Some talk shows even include a live audience during taping. The success of a talk show depends greatly on the disposition and interviewing skills of the host(s).

4.   **Music Video** – The entirety of a song is played and visuals accompany it. The visuals tell a story, together with the lyrics of the song. Shots of the singer are usually inserted in the video from time to time. Some music videos provide lyrics. Other times one-line of text appears at the bottom of the screen so the audience can understand the song and sing-along if they want to.

The music video format is very popular among the young. It may not be preachy like the narrative script. Because it is not preachy like the narrative script, it can be a very powerful tool in disseminating developmental messages. However, you'll need professional equipment in editing a music video for it is difficult to assemble quality music videos using the crude method or shoot-edit technique.

5.   **Animation** – Puppets, stuffed toys, robots, paper cut-outs, drawings, and the like substitute for real people. These objects appear on screen and carry out the dialogue. This type of programme is very effective for children. Moreover, it requires a great amount of creativity, patience, and hard work.

In today's high tech world, most animation programmes are either purely computer-generated or computer-aided. But you can still make a simple animation video this way:

a) Mount your camcorder on a tripod and aim it in an inanimate object (e.g., a stuffed toy)

b) Shoot the inanimate object for a split second. If your camcorder has a remote control, use it to record.

c) Slightly move your inanimate object and shoot it for another split second. You can move it forward, backward or sideways, but only up to an inch away.

d) Repeat steps b and c several times until you record a minimum of 30 seconds of split-second shots.

e) Playback your video and your inanimate object now seems to move. All you need to do now is to put in some audio.

6. **Ethnovideo** – The ethnovideo is a non-traditional video programme format. The ethnovideo is the cheapest and easiest type of video to produce equipment-wise and manpower-wise. It is a type of documentary consisting of interviews and cut-aways on a certain topic. There is no narrator, sound effects, music, or fancy visual transitions. The video speaks for itself.

The ethnovideo is research-related. Ethnovideography is essentially "research using video." The idea here is to capture "slices of reality" and present them as they are in their pure form – without narration and background music which are considered by the ethnovideographer as "manipulative." Also, no script is involved in ethnovideography. The ethnovideographer just goes to the site to record people, places, and events. Afterwards, she reviews what she recorded in tape and selects the cuts and interview cut points to be included in the final video. Then the selected cuts are assembled using the crude editing method. Text sub-titles are injected to introduce the sub-topics of the presentation.

One of the earliest applications of ethnovideography was done by Matela (1992). In his undergraduate thesis, he went to the Mountain Province to document and study parts of the oral tradition of the Ibaloi tribe. Cagampang (1992) made a similar study by using ethnovideography to study myths and folklore of the Ibaloi tribe in Benguet.

A number of foreign graduate students in UPLB also took ethnovideography to their countries to conduct their respective Master's thesis. They are Hardono (1993) and Maya (1993) from Indonesia, and Bandara (1994) from Sri Lanka.

239

Since then, ethnovideography has slowly evolved as an effective research instrument within the Los Baños research community. It was primarily used for documentation by the then UPLB Institute of Development Communication (Librero et al., 2000). It has also been a fixture in the DEVC 143 course (Fundamentals of Video Production) offered by the College of Development Communication in UPLB.

One of the latest applications of ethnovideography was done by this author for his master's thesis (Castillo, 2001) at UPLB testing the viability and acceptability of the ethnovideo as a cable TV programme segment.

Together with a camera crew, Castillo documented the lives of people living inside and around the municipal dumpsite of Los Baños. He then broadcasted the ethnovideo through cable TV. The 7-minute ethnovideo contained interviews and cut-aways showing how miserable and dangerous the lives of the dumpsite people were. "Buhay sa Tabi ng Basurahan" reaped a common reaction among the different age groups and social groups of Los Baños. They all became concerned about the waste management problem of their town, and they vowed to participate in various ways to help solve that problem.

Though very simple, the ethnovideo can be an equally-effective programme format compared to the more traditional ones.

LINKING WITH THE LOCAL CABLE TV PROVIDER

As mentioned earlier, Los Baños put up a community news-magazine programme entitled *"LB Talk"* through the partnership of the University of the Philipines Los Baños (UPLB) College of Development Communication (CDC) and the local cable TV network. Since its conceptualisation in 1998, it has kept the Los Baños community abreast with local events and issues.

In the next few years, several towns and cities are expected to follow *LB Talk's ex*ample. With more and more households subscribing to cable television, the opportunity to facilitate development through community broadcasting continuously expands.

This trend is also starting outside the Philippines, as in the case of the Deccan Development Society mentioned earlier in this module.

You too can start your own community-oriented video programme that you can broadcast through your local cable TV channel. You can start by having a meeting with the owner of your local cable TV provider. Share your ideas on a creative, development-oriented cable TV news-magazine programme, or whatever format you'd like to air. Stress the "development" or "environment" angle. Point at the NEED of having such videos/programmes on your local channel.

Try to negotiate for free airtime since your videos are non-profit oriented. Cable TV providers will usually agree to this, especially if you will give them the tapes in their final form. It's better if you do not task them to help in the production. All that you ask of them is to air your video tape.

When talking with your local cable TV provider, also tell them what they'll get in return. Point out that they'll probably get more subscribers because of your community programme. People are always hungry for information, especially that which concerns them. They like to hear and watch community news and issues. A programme that brings such information will spark curiosity among the community. More people will then be interested in having cable TV at home.

Another benefit of having a local cable TV programme is that "community-ness" will be instilled among the people. They will have a sense of unity, belongingness, and pride in their community.

Finally, stress to your cable TV provider that they have nothing to lose, but everything to gain in such an endeavour. This is a win-win situation for them (cable TV provider), you (video producer), and the community.

Let us now look at the case of a successful community cable TV program in the Philippines, Alah-Eh TV. In Lipa City, a cable TV news-magazine programme was launched in 1999. *Ala-Eh TV* is Lipa Cable Television Corporation's own version of *LB Talk*. The programme's title is taken from the famous Batangeño expression "*ala eh*". This phrase is commonly used by Batangeños at the start of their sentences and discourses (Lagrimas et al. 2000).

The programme's main thrust was to inform Lipa city residents about current events in their city and neighbouring towns in the province of Batangas. It also aimed to entertain and educate the people by trying to adopt the documentary approach in presenting local issues. Lastly, *Ala-eh TV* aimed to promote Lipa City and the whole of Batangas by showcasing the various interesting places in the province. *Ala-eh TV* is now watched by more than one-half of the households in Lipa City (Lagrimas et. al., 2000).

INVOLVING OTHER COMMUNITY ORGANISATIONS IN YOUR PROGRAMME

Initially, producing and maintaining a community program is difficult because 100% of the production is in your hands. But as your programme gains a following among the viewers, the work will become easier because other community organisations and individuals will volunteer to help you by volunteering information and topics for your next episodes. They may also express their interest in having their own segments/time allotment within your programme. Such is the case of *LB Talk*.

During *LB Talk*'s first two years, all the pre-production and production work was done by the UPLB College of Development Communication. But because of the "community" nature and noble objectives of the programme, other organisations and individuals volunteered to take part. A private video editor volunteered to do all the post-production work, for free. Students and alumni of UPLB also worked for free. A handful of organisations asked if they could produce canned segments for *LB Talk*. Among them were Haribon Foundation, an environmental group; Kaakbay, an association of disabled people; ARTIST Inc., an organisation of alternative theatre people; and CABHRIBA, a school in Los Baños.

In addition to these, other individuals and institutions would always call the news director of *LB Talk* and ask for news coverage of various developmental events in their vicinity. Today, *LB Talk* further enhanced community participation by featuring the different barangays, or villages, in Los Baños and sometimes inviting someone from the community to co-host the show.

When you come to this point in the life of your community programme, start training these people (the volunteers) on video production. You can invite them to a training course where you'll share with them your knowledge and skills in video production. Give them hands-on experience in writing their own stories, shooting, and if possible, editing their footage. Pass on to them not only technical know-how, but also your vision. This will ensure that your work becomes sustainable. Your community programme will be a program that is for the community, and by the community.

242

FACILITATOR'S GUIDE

TOPIC	OBJECTIVE/S	TEXT	ACTIVITY	DURATION
The Production Phase	• To enumerate and explain the various post-production tasks	• Lighting • Audio • Camera Stability • Camera Movements • Composition • Additional Shooting Tips	Lecture/ Discussion/ Demonstration	1 hour
	• To shoot footage prescribed by a script	• Activity 7.2	Shooting workshop	4 hours
The Post-Production Phase	• To enumerate and explain the various post-production tasks	• Determining Interview Cut-points • Visual Transitions • Video Editing • Distribution & Evaluation	Lecture/ Discussion	1 hour
	• To edit a video as prescribed by a script	• Activity 7.3	Video editing workshop	**Day 2** 3 hours
Types of Video Programmes	• To enumerate and explain the various types of video programmes	• Types of video programmes	Lecture/ Discussion	30 minutes
Linking with Other Organisations	• To discuss the guidelines on how to link with other organisations in line with improving their community video programmes	• Linking with other organisations	Lecture/ Discussion	30 minutes
Presentation of Video Projects and Closing Ceremony	• To present the video projects to the plenary	• Presentation and closing ceremony of video production module	Video showing/ Sharing of experiences/ insights	1 hour

243

FACILITATOR'S GUIDE

TOPIC	OBJECTIVE/S	TEXT	ACTIVITY	DURATION
Nature of Video	• To describe the nature of video • To cite cases of successful community videos	• Nature of Video • Case Studies of Successful Community Videos	Lecture/ Discussion	**Day 1** 1 hour
Basic Video Production Equipment	• To enumerate the different types of video production equipment • To identify the parts of the camcorder	Basic Video Production Equipment	Lecture/ Discussion/ Demonstration	1 hour
The Pre-Production Phase	• To enumerate and explain the different pre-production tasks	• Audience Analysis • Needs Assessment • Objective Setting • Scriptwriting • Distribution • Planning • Budgeting	Lecture/ Discussion	1 hour
	• To write a script for a 30-second cable TV spot	• Activity 7.1	Scriptwriting workshop	2 hours

SUMMARY

In the module, we have studied the nature, potential, and limitations of small format video and cable TV in development work. We also looked into several case studies of successful community and environmental video and cable TV programmes. Some of these women as producers. We also had an overview of the whole video production process. We tackled several tips for each of the three phases of video production – the pre-production phase, the production phase, and the post-production phase. We then discussed the different types of videos you can use to communicate your message. And finally, we talked about the pointers on how to establish linkages with your local cable TV provider and involve other community organisations in your programme.

GLOSSARY

Camcorder
A one-piece video recording system in which the camera and videocassette recorder are combined into one unit.

Character generator
An electronic device that generates letters, numbers, or symbols for use in video titles. Also a device that converts electronic time code into visible numbers displayed on a TV monitor. It allows you to key in titles, lettering, and basic designs in a variety of styles and sizes.

CU (close-up)
A close shot of a person or object.

Cue
To instruct the computerised editing system to shuttle a video tape reel to a predetermined location.

Cut
A straight edit from one audio or video source to another, resulting in instantaneous change. The most common transition.

Cut-away
A shot inserted to either explain a part of the action or to provide a transition to the next scene.

Dissolve
A video transition in which the existing image is partially or totally replaced by superimposing another image.

Dolly
The camera moves closer to or farther away from the main subject in the shot.

Dub
To make a copy of a video recording.

Electronic news gathering (ENG)
Using portable video equipment to record news events from field locations.

Establishing shot
It establishes setting and location; generally a wide shot.

Extreme close-up (ECU)
The tightest shot possible on a person or object.

Extreme wide shot (EWS)/extreme long shot
The widest shot possible of the location on TV, the EWS is used to establish setting and location.

Eyeline
Describes the direction in which a person is looking across the screen. Also called "line of sight."

Fade
A gradual transition from black to an image or sound (fade up) or from an image or sound to black (fade down or fade out). Usually, a dissolve from full video to black video or from full audio to no audio.

Fill light
Non-directional light used to fill in but not eliminate completely the shadows created by the subject from the key light.

Generation
Copy of original video programme material. The original material is the first generation. A copy of the original is a second generation tape, and so on. Generally the edited master tape is a second generation tape.

Generation Loss
Video clarity/resolution lost after dubbing it.

Head Room
Space between the top of the head and the upper edge of the screen.

Medium close-up
A shot which consists of a head and shoulders that ends at the chest. One of the most frequently used shots.

Medium shot (MS)
A half shot of the object or person in the scene.

Man-on-the-Street Interview (MOS)
An ambush interview with common people.

Phase Alternating Line (PAL)
A color TV standard used in Europe and Asia. PAL consists of 625 lines scanned at a rate of 25 frames per second. Compare NTSC color video standard.

Pan
Horizontal movement of the camera head only.

Preroll
Process of rewinding video tapes to a predetermined cue point, so the tapes are stabilised and up to speed when they reach the edit point.

Preview
To rehearse and edit without actually performing (recording) it. Looking at an edit before actually making it to be sure it is what you want.

Storyboard
Graphic representation of the planned shot sequence of shooting, with a brief written description of each shot's action, size, and type.

Tilt
Movement of the camera head similar to the movement of a person's head when he/she looks up or down.

Time code
Electronic indexing method used for editing and timing video programs. Time code denotes hours, minutes, seconds, and frames elapsed on a video tape.

Track
The entire camera moves left or right parallel to the main subject in the shot.

Video tape
Oxide-coated plastic based magnetic tape used for recording video and audio signals.

Voice over (VO)
Talking over the video without ever seeing the person speaking.

VTR
Video tape recorder.

White balance
Enables the cameraman to adjust the relative intensity for the red, green, and blue channels to allow the camera to produce an accurate white signal in the particular light in which you are shooting.

Wipe
Special effect transition in which a margin or border moves across the screen; wiping out the image of one screen and replacing it with another.

Zoom in or out
Brings the scene closer or farther away from the viewer.

REFERENCES

Asia-Pacific Media Ministries. 1999. **Workbook for the 1999 Workshop on Video Production.**

Castillo, O.C.T. 2001. **Viability and Acceptability of an Ethnovideographic Method in Producing a Segment for Cable TV.** Unpublished master's thesis, University of the Philippines, Los Baños, Laguna.

Dagron, 2001. **Making Waves: Stories of Participatory Communication for Social Change.** Rockefeller Foundation, New York.

http://www.dds.cover

CHAPTER **8**

Preparation and Production of Media Resources: Community Theatre

VANESSA P. EBRON

OBJECTIVES
After the training, the participants should be able to:

1. Explain the significance of community theatre as a means of promoting environmental awareness and conservation in their respective communities;
2. Discuss the basic elements and techniques in mounting community theatre productions; and
3. Utilise community theatre for environmental awareness and conservation.

249

INTRODUCTION

In this technology-driven generation, wherein using state-of-the-art media forms is a must in keeping the people in sync with the rest of the world, it is somewhat inevitable to notice the backwardness of isolated communities in Asia. Apparently, there are still groups of people trailing behind these technology-dependent individuals. This can perhaps be attributed to the fact that modern technology can only reach so far. Hence, it is high time for us to consider alternatives to the more technologically advanced media and go back to where we started – folk or community media. Of these, theatre is one of the most enduring.

Theatre has existed perhaps from the time human beings started to inhabit the earth. Though our ancestors might view it in a different way, their mimetic dances – dances that depicted their daily activities manifested in the artful bodily movements accompanied by chanting and/or musical instruments – and rituals can be considered as the earliest form of theatre. Considered a form of indigenous theatre, these mimetic dances have been used to imitate rituals and customs the tribe conducted in honour of their gods or in celebration of a birth, their mourning for the dead, or any routine they had in their communities. Thus, theatre has been used in to convey realities of existing societies.

Asia is a continent rich in culture. Its art forms reflect the cultural heritage of each nation. Theatre in different regions of the continent provides people an overview of the lifestyles existing in the society. Their identity as a community is established by what they present to the public, by their language, and through the intricate design of their sets and costumes. Men, as well as women, partake in this event of promoting their culture to various audiences. Isn't it good to know that there are still communities that choose to preserve what the Creator had given them in the very beginning, instead of the man-made gadgets we have at present? Unfortunately, only a few of those groups are left. Especially at a time when Asia is faced with one of the most pressing problems at the moment: environmental degradation.

On that account, this chapter will aim to address this matter by giving the community of women their most righteous mission of promoting environmental awareness and conservation through theatre.

LESSON 1. COMMUNITY THEATRE: DEFINITION AND NATURE

Community theatre, also known as folk media and a community cultural practice, has been a vital tool for social change. But before we delve further into the significance of community theatre, we must first have a clear understanding of its nature. According to Valbuena (1986), community theatre involves the "verbal, action, aural, and visual forms which are known or familiar to the folk, are accepted by them, and are addressed to or performed by and/or for them for the purpose of entertaining, informing, enlightening, instructing, and educating".

In a community theatre, the residents of a particular community produce their own play – from the script down to the actors who will be performing in the production–integrating with it the cultural heritage, beliefs, and traditions of the community. The people produce something that is unique to their community. They present themes that are socially relevant to them and topics that the people can easily relate to.

Remember this: involvement and participation of the community people are the most important factors for a successful community theatre production to occur. A successful production may lead to an effective communication transfer which can be truly instrumental in bringing about social change (Valbuena, 1986). Take the case of *Suntok sa Buwan*, a play produced by the Arts Research and Training Institute in Southern Tagalog, Inc. (ARTIST, Inc.). The play was a success in itself mainly because it was able to transcend the barrier between the stage and the spectators by bringing the audience "into" the whole production.

As you can see, unlike the other forms of mass media, i.e., print, radio, and video, community theatre can readily reach most of the Third World population with credible and relevant information that the people need for real social change to take place in their lives. It can easily penetrate areas that are not easily accessible to the modern mass media. With its flexible nature, community theatre can adjust its treatment without much difficulty depending on the needs of its audience.

In addition to this, community theatre makes use of the very basic form of folk-level communication – the verbal and non-verbal cues, the humour, melodies, and themes that reflect situations in the community.

Aside from its portable and inexpensive nature using resources available in the community, community theatre is capable of eliciting instant feedback from its audience. They can immediately evaluate the production face-to-face. In certain situations, audience participation in a production is always a possibility. Community theatre is considered to be "alive" or intimate in its immediate communion with its audience. "The only thing disheartening about any community theatre production, or any theatrical event for that matter, even as it is taking place, it is lost forever" (Barranger, 1995).

LESSON 2. FORMS OF COMMUNITY THEATRE

As mentioned earlier, Asia is one continent notable for its rich and diverse culture. Asia's cultural heritage is like a sumptuous palate – unique, gratifying, and at the same time, nurturing.

The following is an overview of the most common forms or styles employed in a theatrical production.

Children's Theatre. As the name implies, children's theatre refers to plays with children as actors. Or it can also be described as a play performed by adults for children. "Its aims go beyond self-expression, towards the encouragement of creativity and self-esteem, and beyond entertainment, towards value and cultural formation" (Fernandez, 1994). The children's theatre is an effective means of promoting appreciation of the country's history, culture, and artistry.

Drama. Popularised during the 19th century, a drama consists of performances in verse and/or prose and usually in one act (Fernandez, 1994). Basically of the soap opera type, drama focuses on themes regarding contemporary life wherein the conflict between young and old, between new, emerging values and age-old, traditional patterns are heightened. Drama not only entertains but also provides a venue for people to gain new insights in life, for learning lessons about man's relationships, and their implications for personal as well as communal welfare (Valbuena, 1986).

The drama can be an allegorical drama, a dramatic monologue, or a dance drama.

An **allegorical drama** is sometimes described as seditious, especially when used to inculcate a spirit of hatred and enmity towards a specific organisation, institution or a government for the purpose of overthrowing them and setting up another instead (Fernandez, 1994).

A **dramatic monologue** on the other hand is a type of modern play which features one actor speaking and acting out his or her innermost thoughts and emotions as the main character of the play (Fernandez, 1994).

The **dance drama** makes use of bodily gestures or pantomime, and narratives, usually done in a poetical manner or simple dialogues in conveying the message to the audience. Predominant in India, it is in fact the country's oldest form of theatre.

Mimetic Dances. Prolific among the ethnic communities of the Philippines, mimetic dances are dances that imitate the movements of animals and plants or of human beings at their various occupations (Fernandez, 1994). It differs from a dance drama simply because the themes manifested in mimetic dances are of the daily activities and rites a certain ethnic community conducts, such as fetching water from a nearby riverbank and funeral rituals among others. Moreover, if narratives are evident in a dance drama, chanting usually accompanies mimetic dances.

Musical Theatre. In this form, music is an integral part of the play. Some of the most established forms are the following: *zarzuela* and the opera.

The *zarzuela*, introduced in the Philippines by the Spaniards in 1900 and institutionalised in 1940, is a musical play similar to light opera presented in three acts. The main appeal of the *zarzuela* lies in the "satire and the biting social criticism underlying the sharp, witty, humourous, and often earthly language of the dialogue" (Valbuena, 1986). The most common themes of a Filipino *zarzuela* include: relationships between husband and wife and between in-laws, and the love between young master and servant girl among others.

The opera, on the other hand, is a classic theatre of the Chinese wherein the dialogue is punctuated with arias and recitatives.

Play Poem. This consists of a poem which is dramatised by the use of a narrator who reads all the parts, and one or more actors who mime all the roles and provide all the sounds and special effects (Fernandez, 1994).

Political Theatre. This type includes plays which aim to change or improve existing systems of government, directly or indirectly (Fernandez, 1994). Classified under this is the allegorical drama mentioned earlier in this lesson. Actually, any form of theatre can be considered political as long as its main objective is that of social change.

Puppet Theatre. It is a form of drama in which the characters are puppets — flat figures that throw shadows on screen as in *Wayang Kulit* and *Wayang Golek* of Indonesia, or rounded miniature figures controlled from below of above the stage by the operator's hands, rods, strings, or wires (Fernandez, 1994).

Another alternative to hand or string puppets is through the use of the so-called "Black Theatre". Actors wear a basic black costume and paint their props and costumes with luminous paint. For a more dramatic effect, black light is used to make objects glow in the dark.

Stage Show. Also referred to as *vaudeville* which has its origin in France, a stage show is a stage presentation that consists of a variety of musical and comedy acts, skits and monologues, novelty and acrobatic numbers, solos and chorus lines (Fernandez, 1994). Stage shows became very prominent in the Philippines during the 1940s when the country was under Japanese colonisation. This is because the presentations bore hidden messages of encouragement for the war-weary people. The stage show still lives on in the country's town-fiesta celebrations, film musicals, radio variety shows, and even in political theatre in rural and urban areas.

Street Theatre. This form of theatre draws its material from the experiences of the streets and is presented outside of theatre structures such as the church, building lobbies, marketplaces, plazas, roads, assembly points for rallies, etc (Fernandez, 1994). Mobility is an important aspect of this form. Hence, the use of elaborate props, set, and costumes are usually minimised in this type of theatre. Furthermore, the spontaneity of the performers plays a powerful force for an effective message transfer. The performers should be sensitive to the needs of the audience and can readily adjust to what the situation dictates. Creativity in dealing with matters that the audience might perceive as repulsive is another prerequisite in mounting such production. A perfect example of this is the Aarohan Street Theatre of Nepal.

LESSON 3. FUNCTIONS OF
COMMUNITY THEATRE

Now, with a bird's eye view of the different forms of theatre, it is important to realise the effectiveness of using a more traditional approach in promoting social change in a community, eventually in a country.

Community theatre has been an effective way of communicating social issue, particularly in rural areas. Our ancestors witnessed the essence of community theatre as a forceful tool in mobilising communities toward action. It has always been the perfect venue for individuals to seek entertainment as well as enlightenment on relevant social issues confronting the society.

From the time the very first theatre presentation was staged – not professional theatre productions but the indigenous ones of the ancestors – community theatre was used to mirror familiar details of everyday culture. In that way, people are able to validate the rituals and institutions of culture, thus, strengthening the heritage of their community. People are brought back to and reminded of their roots, enabling them to resolve community matters based on their acknowledged norms. In the process, the community is able to maintain conformity to accepted patterns of behaviour.

Finally, community theatre recognises the need to educate in non-literate societies such as the rural communities of the Third World nations. The topics, the language, and the process exemplified in a community theatre production are those that the people can undoubtedly empathise with.

ACTIVITY 8.1

Objectives
After the exercise, the participants should be able to:
1. Define the meaning of community theatre;
2. Enumerate the forms of community theatre in the ASEAN regions; and
3. Explain the uses, advantages, and disadvantages of using each form.

Procedure
Note: It is important for you, the facilitator, not to spoon-feed all the information to the participants. Elicit ideas from the participants and let them speak from their experiences. Use this chapter as a supplement and guide for wrapping up discussions.

1. Open the discussion about theatre. Begin with what they already understand about community theatre and how they see its potential as an agent of social change.
2. Group the participants according to the country or community they belong to.
3. Provide each group with sheets of paper and pens. Then ask them to jot down at least three forms of community theatre they are familiar with. Allow them to discuss among themselves the significance, relevance, and efficiency of each form in communicating developmental messages. Inform the participants that they will have to demonstrate each form briefly.
4. Allot 30 minutes for group discussion and preparation. Each group will present their output to the rest of the participants in the training session.
5. Give the rest of the group at least five minutes to voice their feedback after each presentation.
6. When all the groups have reported, wrap-up the discussion by giving a summary of all the information acquired from the group.

LESSON 4. BASIC ELEMENTS AND TECHNIQUES IN MOUNTING A COMMUNTY THEATRE PRODUCTION

In preparing for a community theatre production, you must at least have a clear understanding of the basic elements and techniques in mounting a play in order for you to satisfy your audience. Below is a list of the things you must consider in producing a theatrical presentation:

1. Plot
2. Script
3. Language
4. Character
5. Theme
6. Spectacle
   a. Costumes
   b. Sets

    c.   Music

    d.   Lighting

7.   Audience, Time, and Space

8.   Acting

9.   Directing

Now let's take a look at each one in depth.

1. Plot

Before you can mount a theatre production, it is important to at least have a plot in mind. This will serve as the "seed" of your production. A plot is a scheme of action that includes the selection, arrangement, and progression of events from beginning to the end of the play. This consists of the beginning, which introduces the charactres in the story; the conflict or the problem that arises in the story; the climax which is the height of all the course of actions in the story, the significant decisions, revelations, and twists in the story; and an ending that will tie up the whole story to a unified finish.

The plot can be one of three kinds: simple, complex, and compound (Albright et. al., 1968).

Simple plot. The simple plot represents a direct progression of events from some acceptable starting point to some predictable conclusion, with no major deviation from expectation. Take a look at the example below:

> The story begins with a family–a father, mother, and their 4-year old daughter. They live in a valley teeming with wildlife and lush forest. The father works as a logger for a foreign logging company in their area. The mother is a plain housewife and devoted to taking care of the household and rearing their daughter. The conflict arises when the logging company orders the loggers to cut down trees in a protected area of the valley. The mother, realising the consequences uncontrolled logging would impose on them, tries to talk to her husband about this. However, the husband refuses to listen to the wife since logging is the only way he knows to support his family. So, the father continues on with his job... until one incident when a fierce storm reaches their area. It was one night when the father was up in the mountains doing his job together with other fellow loggers. The rain was

pouring hard and seemed to show no sign of stopping. The soil started to erode. Landslide. Flood…The father, realising what was about to happen, tried to search for his family. But it was too late. Homes nestled at the foot of the mountain were being washed away by the raging waters. Nothing could be done to save the community… As guilt started to envelope him, he sees two familiar bodies floating towards him. There, lying in front of him, were the lifeless bodies of his wife and daughter. It was then that he realised what his wife told him a long time ago…that they should protect the area they live in…nurture their environment and it will do the same for them. His loved ones suffered because of him…And it was then when the words of his wife came echoing to his mind as regret slowly filled his soul…nurture the environment and it will do the same for you…

Complex plot. The complex plot represents an outcome that is different from the expected, the progression being complicated by one or more unexpected shifts in direction.

An example of this type of plot can be seen in one of the subplots of *Igway sa Ulnan* (Song from the Mountain).

The Iraya Mangyans are confronted by a very sensitive issue regarding their plight to protect the land given to them by their ancestors. Their crusade against the illegal mining of the lowlanders is going well until Inakay, the youngest daughter falls in love with a handsome young man from the lowlands. Their relationship was kept in secret since it was against their community values to fall in love with someone different from them. The tribe continues to fight until Inakay discovers that the man she fell in love with happened to be the son of the chief miner (unexpected shift in the story). She was caught in a dilemma—who would she choose: her tribe and join them in upholding the virtues of their community, or Bobi, the man she'll love for the rest of her life. In the end, Inakay decides to follow her heart and chose Bobi. As a result, she was cast out from the tribe. The Iraya Mangyans were forced to leave their abodes but with a promise of regaining their land.

Compound plot. The compound plot is a combination of two or more progressions of events compounded in such a way as to produce a satisfying whole. An example of this type is a play conducted by a non-government organization of the Philippines, the Arts Research and

Training Institute in Southern Tagalog, Incorporated or ARTIST, Inc. Entitled *Igway sa Ulnan* (Song from the Mountain), the play is composed of more than one subplot—the plight of the Iraya Mangyans, a native tribe of Mindoro, Philippines, against the corrupt miners from the lowlands, the essence of preserving the tribe's cultural heritage, and the love stories of the three main characters: Tala, Aldaw, and Inakay.

> The plot...the Iraya Mangyans of Mindoro fight for their right to protect the land their ancestors had passed on to them against the corrupt miners from the lowlands. And because of the ill effects of illegal mining—tribesmen are starting to get sick, animals were being dispersed in search for a better and safe sanctuary—families are being forced to leave their homes. Added to that, the loyalty of fellow Iraya Mangyans is being questioned. Some of the tribesmen were being bribed by the lowland miners to join their group in exchange for a better urban life. The story is even complicated when two sisters fall in love with the lowlanders. Tala, the elder one and already married to a fellow Iraya, falls in love with a journalist conducting a research about the mining. And the younger one, Inakay, falls in love with the chief miner's son—Bobi.

The story moves to a unifying finish when Tala decided to be with her tribe, while Inakay, unfortunately was banished from the tribe for choosing Bobi. The Iraya Mangyans, left with no other choice, leave their land...but they will come back to regain what used to be theirs.

2. Script

With a working plot in mind, the next thing you have to accomplish is the script. This is where you make your ideas tangible to others. It is a written plan or scheme according to which a play is performed. It includes stage direction, cast list, and possibly production and other notes. Written by a playwright, the script may or may not constitute the final playscript since it may be modified in production or given final revisions when prepared for publication. Hence, the author's text, working script, and the published play may or may not be identical (Fernandez, 1994).

Below is a sample script to guide you in writing your own.

WHEN NATURE STRIKES BACK
BART SABULARSE

Characters:

Pris - A single female. Lives in a subdivision located near a factory. Very handy with hand held pistols.
Trinidad - A Farmer. Mother of two boys. A woman versed with Arnis, a farm of martial arts.
Sining - A priestess in a nearby mountain. Master of powers from Mother Nature.
Giya - Spirit of the Earth. Will bring the three women together.
Michael - A businessman who drove the owner out of his own company for his personal wants.
Kamil - Original owner of the corporation.
3 Farmers
2 Guards

Setting
The stage is separated by different levels.

Stage left is an office table, which is the main office of Kamil (later to become Michael's).

Stage right, located on a higher level, is a mountain where Sining worships Giya.

Below the mountain is Trinidad's hut and resting place.

While centre and most of the stage is a rice field.

Time
Mid 90's

Act 1 (Intro)

Lights open on Kamil's office. She sits on her chair with Michael on the opposite side.

Kamil: How are things going Mike?

Michael: Business is good but slow.

Kamil: Excellent.

Michael: But ma'am, with all due respect, I can double our profit or even triple it.

Kamil: And how is that?

Michael: By reducing the pollution control measure we have been...

Kamil: Mike! If I told you million times, that is not an option. How many times do we have to discuss this?

Michael: But Ma'am I'm only proposing that it is not efficient and nothing will be heard from our neighbour when we...

Kamil: I heard enough! (Raises her voice and stands up.) Leave now before I loose my temper.

(Michael turns around and this part freezes. Lights turn on to Giya with Sining chanting before her. Giya is shown as a statue.)

Sining: Oh Giya! Thank you for all the riches you have given us. We are truly grateful! Our Spirit of the Earth. (Continues her chant and this part fades to black.)
(Then in the middle is shown a group of farmers planting rice.)

Farmers: Mag-tanim ay di biro maghapong naka- upo... (*Planting rice is never fun...*)

Farmer 1: Hey Trinidad!!! Leaving so early?

Trinidad: My work is done here. Now got to attend to my daughters.

Farmer 2: Why don't you hang out with us?

Farmer 3: Yah, Huwan's got a gallon of lambanog buried in the ground, is ready to drink at this time of the year.

Farmer 2: He even put a few raisins and a bunch of grapes in it to make it taste really great.

Farmer 1,2 & 3: We just butchered the old man's dog from down the street. Ha! Ha! Ha!

Trinidad: Don't you guys have anything else to do but drink after a hard days work? Huh!

Farmer 1: No!?!

Farmer 3: Should we?

Trinidad: How about your wives and children? I'm getting out of here before my mind melts and I turn into a mindless drone. (Trindad exists stage right.)

Farmer 1: Must be a girl thing.

(Farmers laugh their way out the opposite direction.)

(Stage light open on Pris.)

Pris: (Sigh!) Hard day at school. Got one term paper left to do. But before that, I must go to my night job. Now off I go to the assembly line. I never see the finish products or get to use them. But when I get my degree, its bye-bye to the factory and the rest of this hell hole.

(Lights turn back on Kamil's office.)

Michael: Guards, take her!

Guards: Sir yes sir!
(They rush to Kamil's side before she could reach for her gun. The guards hold her tight.)

Kamil: What the hell is going on?

Michael: I'm making things more efficient — for the benefit of the company. Or should I say me.

Kamil: You won't get away with this. If the authorities don't get you, Mother Nature will.

Michael: But I just did. Now lets call this, your early retirement. Ha! Ha! Ha! (Then Mike puts a bullet in her head.)

Guard 1: You killed her!

Michael: Wanna be next? (Points the gun to the guard's head) Then shut up and follow my orders.

Guard 2: What to do with the body sir?

Michael: Get rid of it and show no traces of our operation. Now get down to business. Get rid of those money wasting pollution control entrapments. The waste water treatment system and garbage segregation blah-blah-blah. It's too time and money consuming. It also reduces our income. You know what I mean. Now, get to work!!! Move your butts out of here!!!

Guards: As you command! (The two rush out with Kamil's body. Leaving Michael while he laughs as he lights a cigarette.)

- End of Act 1 -

ACTIVITY 8.2

Objectives

At the end of the exercise, the participants should be able to explain the first two basic elements and techniques in mounting a community theater production, i.e., the plot and the script.

Procedure

1. Explain the importance of community theatre to the group.
2. Discuss the significance of having the proper knowhow of the elements and techniques as well as continuous training in mounting community theatre productions for an effective theatrical presentation.
3. Group the participants. Let the participants count-off from 1-5, depending on the density of the group. The groupings should be different from the first one they had. This new group will now be their permanent team for their final output (brief theatre presentation) to be performed at the end of the training for this module.
4. Instruct them to go to their respective group numbers and prepare a plot for their group. The theme should revolve around the current situation of the environment in their community – the problems encountered, and how women can partake in preserving the environment. From there, they will create a script to use in their short production number the following day. This doesn't need to be submitted immediately to you. If there isn't enough time for the script to be finished, the participants are free to finalise their stories until the end of the day.

3. Language

There are two ways of conveying your message to your audience, through bodily movements or gestures and the dialogues. Language includes the spoken word, symbols and signs, and movements and gestures that actors use in a specific play. Language is customised for a particular character in a play so as to enhance its substance as well as add up to its consistency (Albright et. al., 1968). It is an important part of a theatre production for without it, no one would be able to comprehend the play.

The voice, the body, and the senses contribute to the efficiency of language. The voice should be projected from the diaphragm for better enunciation. The words should be audible since it is one of the actor's channels in relaying the story to the audience. The movements created by the body should be definite and must always be consistent with the charactre the actor is portraying. The basic rule of thumb for this is exaggeration and "no movement without a purpose" (Albright et. al., 1968). The senses–imagination and reactions to other characters in the play–should be logical and justifiable to the character of the actor.

ACTIVITY 8.3

Objectives
At the end of the exercise, the participants should be able to:
1. Describe language as the third basic element and technique in mounting a community theater production;
2. Demonstrate the three levels of shape;
3. Explore various shapes, gestures, and movements that can be performed using our bodies;
4. Use their imagination; and
5. Explain the value of team effort.

PROCEDURE

A. Basic Shapes
1. Discuss and demonstrate the three types of shapes: high, medium, and low. An example of a high shape is a person standing in an erect position; medium shape is shown when a person is slightly bending; and the low position is achieved when a person is lying on the floor. See Figure 1 below.

FIGURE 1. BASIC SHAPES

(Illustration as described in #1)
HIGH

(Illustration as described in #1)
MEDIUM

(Illustration as described in #1)
LOW

2. Explore the variations of these shapes through out the exercise.
3. Then instruct the group to think of an action or shape that they have never done before. At the count of three, the participants execute the action and then freeze. Ask them again to think of another shape, this time using a different level from their first one. At the count of three, the participants freeze to their second action. Repeat the same process for the third action.
4. Now, each having a high-medium-low shape of her own, command them to do their high shape, then their medium, then their low, depending your preferences. Instruct the participants to have bigger and defined movements of their bodies.

B. Story Shapes
1. As follow-up exercise, instruct the participants to shut their eyes and relax. Then, let them execute what you will instruct them to perform.
2. Begin the Seed Story…

To the participants: "Imagine yourselves as a seed (low shape). You are buried deep within the rich soils of a certain land. You cannot see anything. It is very dark. Then suddenly, you see a light and it is warm and soothing. Sunshine came to help the little seed grow into a seedling. (Slowly, the participants should be transforming into a seedling; arms still tucked in but not too much than before.) Seeing that sunshine's efforts are not enough, rain came to quench the thirst of the little seedling with some water to drink. Days passed and the seedling has now turned into a shrub. Years passed, the little seedling is now a tree (high position). A soft breeze lightly moves her branches and leaves. Unfortunately, the soft breeze turned into a strong wind, as if a typhoon is about to arrive. The wind is blowing hard. Thanks to the tree's strong roots, she survived the storm. Suddenly, there was that irritating noise…That irritating noise…Where is it coming from? Worried, the tree suddenly felt something slice her sturdy trunk. As the tree looked down, she saw two men starting to cut her down. The tree tried to cry for help but the men were deaf from the noise the chainsaw is making or worse deaf from reason. Slowly, the tree starts to fall on her side...and die (transition from high to low position)."

3. Encourage them to continue exploring the action further during the process. Commend the participants for a job well done.

C. Object Shapes

1. After the story, group the participants into five, maybe different from their theatre production group.
2. Explain the importance of team effort in creating a unified movement.
3. Instruct the participants to show her a house. The participants should use their bodies to represent one house. One participant can be the post, the other the door, and so on and so forth. Give them at least five objects to imitate.

4. Character

Another aspect is the character. The character refers to the physiological and psychological make up of the persons in the play. The character should possess the following characteristics: aesthetic acceptability, identification, consistency, motivation, and revelation.

Aesthetic acceptability refers to the extent to which the character is recognisably human, interesting to watch and presentable within the limitations of performance. What distinguishes the character from the human beings that we see and hear in daily life is the vitality he or she manifests on stage (Albright et. al., 1968).

A character has **identification** if he/she can be distinguished as some certain kind of person and as an individual being apart from his/her real identity off-stage. This can be best described by what other characters in the play say about him/her, by what he/she says about himself/herself, by what he or she does, and by his/her appearance (Albright et. al., 1968).

Consistency is crucial in justifying a character in a play. It is the way in which the various manifestations of personality, actions and speech, principally fit together, and that which is observed throughout the presentation (Albright et. al., 1968).

Motivation refers to the way in which the author has accounted for the character's behaviour. In real life, we usually see only one side of the story. "But drama is not life. It is a simulation of life in which we see not only the actions of humans but the causes of their behavior" (Albright et. al., 1968). Carefully established series of events for a character creates a valuable motivational factor for the actor.

Finally, **revelation.** "On stage, as in life, character is never static" (Albright et. al., 1968). Gradual revelation of character — or at least be sustained to the end of the play — helps build up interest on the part of the audience.

The character is of two types: flat and round (Barranger, 1995).

Flat characters are those of a single trait and are highly predictable. A treacherous villain, a faithful wife belong to this type.

Round characters, on the other hand, are more complex. Their motives, insights, and behaviour, though sometimes unexpected, are credible and provocative.

5. Theme

Also denoted as meaning or thought, the theme is the play's underlying idea — its general and particular truths about experience (Barranger, 1995).

The moral viewpoint of a play concerns the individual human being whose actions are shown and explained to the audience. The actions are usually interpreted in terms of his or her own ideas of what is brave or cowardly, generous or selfish, and right or wrong (Albright et. al., 1968).

The ethical viewpoint of a play concerns the relation of people to each other and to the community in which they exist. Issues concerning loyalty, duty to the family, duty to country, humanitarianism are some of the examples of this type (Albright et. al., 1968).

The theme can be inferred through the plot, the character, verbal expressions, and symbolisms integrated in the play (Albright et. al., 1968).

6. Spectacle

The spectacle involves all the visual and aural elements in the production (Barranger, 1995).

Costumes
These are distinctive dresses used by an actor in order to authenticate a role in performance (Fernandez, 1994).

Sets

The sets include the scenery and properties or the physical context created for theatre performance (Fernandez, 1994).

Music

Included here are the background music, incidental music, songs that are part of the dialogue, songs that replace dialogues, music that eliminates the need for dialogue, or a combination of the above (Fernandez, 1994).

Lighting

This involves the use of lights and other related equipment for the purpose of illuminating the stage, creating atmosphere and mood, producing special effects, and highlighting character and action. Some of the most common types of lighting used in a theatrical presentation are footlights, sidelights, overhead illumination, and spotlights (Fernandez, 1994). However, in the absence of electricity, which is usually the case of rural and depressed areas, lanterns, kerosene lamps, sparklers, torches are the best alternatives.

ACTIVITY 8.4

Objectives
At the end of the exercise, the participants should be able to:
1. Enhance imaginative skills of the participants;
2. Incorporate movement and action, with props, set, and costume in character development; and
3. Practise reaction skills of participants.

Procedure
Silent Movie
1. Place a wooden block large enough for two to three individuals to sit on it. Place it in the middle of the room. On one corner of the room, provide a "goody box". Inside the box are hats, canes, shawls, and other props, which the participants may need.
2. Instruct the participants to choose one prop or costume that they like. Give them one minute to do this.

3. After the participants have chosen their prop or costume, give them another minute to think of a character other than that of their real self that would suit the prop they have at hand.

4. Tell them to fall in line. Your support staff should be responsible for creating mood music from bamboo, bottles, etc.

5. Instruct the first person on the line to start walking in character towards the wooden block. The participant may sit on it, lie on it, or even move towards another area in the "stage". The next person then walks toward the scene and from there create impromptu responses. The process continues until everyone in the group is on the stage. Actually, there is no established story from the very beginning. The story starts the moment the first person walks in. And the next characters create a series of events. The participants should be sensitive to the actions of the other characters since they are only using movements and gestures in conveying their message — as if they are in a silent movie. Do this until everyone had her chance of showing off her character.

7. Audience, Time, and Space

A play is not complete without these three. The audience are the viewers and spectators. Time is the occasion or time/s set aside for performance, length of performance, and the time or period the play presented was supposed to have taken place (symbolic time). The space is the location of the physical set-up of the whole production (indoor or outdoor, enclosed or open). These help define the context of the theatre and to some extent, shape it (Fernandez, 1994).

8. Acting

The beauty of a playwright cannot be seen in the absence of brilliant acting. Acting is the art of representing a charactre in a play (Fernandez, 1994). It demands flexibility of both voice and body, responsiveness in both intellect and emotion. It assumes insight as well as technique, imagination as well as judgment. It deals with inner content as well as outward form (Albright et. al., 1968).

An actor serves as a sort of middleman between script and observer in a process of projecting theatrical values from a playwright to an assembled group of spectators and listeners (Albright et. al., 1968).

A good performance of an actor is rooted deeply in the play from which it springs. Patterns of action, of dialogue, and of character are not only congruous one with the other, but uniquely suited to a particular playscript. They are carefully integrated details characteristic of the style and form of the manuscript at hand (Albright et. al., 1968).

In addition to that, a good performance is continuously clear. There is consistency in motivation or in the emotional tone and always and everywhere in character (Albright et. al., 1968).

A good performance is continuously interesting. An actor should learn to innovate, explore, and search for fresh and varied appeals in the treatment of a character for the audience's satisfaction (Albright et. al., 1968).

Lastly, an effective performance is that of team performance. Actions, rhythms, responses, and group developments should always be a team effort and contribute to a unified and consistent production (Albright et. al., 1968).

ACTIVITY 8.5

Limbering Exercise
Objectives
At the end of the exercise, the participants should be able to relax and prepare for the activities to be conducted throughout the day.

Procedure
1. Let the group form a circle. You, as facilitator, will stand in the middle. The participants should be standing, feet slightly parted.
2. Start the exercise with eight counts of inhale and exhale.
3. **Isolation of the head.** Feet apart. Bend head right-centre-left-centre-right. Do two sets done in eight counts. Twist head right-centre left-centre-right. Do two sets done in eight counts. Bend head forward-centre-back-centre-forward. Do two sets done in eight counts. Rotate head clockwise, eight counts, then reverse (counterclockwise), eight counts.
4. **Isolation of the shoulders.** Feet apart. Move both shoulders up-centre-down-centre-up. Do two sets done in eight counts. Move both shoulders forward-centre-back-centre-forward. Do two sets done in eight counts. Rotate shoulders, inwards, eight counts, and outwards, eight counts. Then raise arms sideward, hands flexed. Rotate arms,

271

FIGURE 8.2 ISOLATION OF THE HEAD

Head Bend   Head Twist   Head Rotation
(Right-Centre-Left)   (Foward-Centre-Back)

creating small circles with palm of hand, inwards, eight counts, and outwards, eight counts. Then rotate fully whole arms inwards, eight counts, and outwards, eight counts. Shake arms after.

FIGURE 8.3 ISOLATION OF THE SHOULDERS

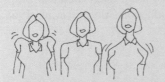  

Up-Centre-Down   Foward-Centre-Back   Shoulder Rotation

5. **Isolation of the upper torso.** Feet apart. Bend knees. Move upper torso right-centre-left-centre-right. Do two sets done in eight counts. Move upper torso forward-centre-back-centre-forward. Do two sets done in eight counts. Rotate upper torso clock-wise, eight counts. Then reverse (counterclockwise), eight counts. Slowly stand and shake legs.

FIGURE 8.4 ISOLATION OF THE UPPER TORSO

First
Position:
Feet Apart

Right-Centre-Left   Foward-Centre-Back

272

Second
Position:
Knees
Sightly Bent

Rotation

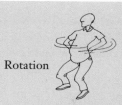

6. **Isolation of the lower torso.** Feet apart. Bend knees. Move lower torso right-centre-left-centre-right. Do two sets done in eight counts. Move lower torso forward-centre-back-centre-forward. Do two sets done in eight counts. Rotate lower torso clockwise, eight counts. Then reverse (counterclockwise), eight counts. Slowly stand and shake legs.

FIGURE 8.5 ISOLATION OF THE LOWER TORSO

Right-Centre-Left   Foward-Centre-Back

7. **Isolation of the knees.** Feet apart. Bend knees. Rotate knees inwards, eight counts, then outwards, eight counts.

FIGURE 8.6 ISOLATION OF THE KNEES

Inward Rotation   Outward Rotation

8. **Isolation of the feet.** Raise right foot forward. Point and then flex foot, eight counts. Then rotate, clock-wise, eight counts, and reverse (counter clockwise) eight counts. Do the same for the other foot.

FIGURE 8.7 ISOLATION OF THE FEET

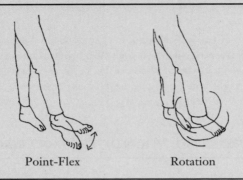

Point-Flex   Rotation

9. Stand and shake whole body. Then inhale and exhale.

Breathing and Voice Exercise
Objectives
At the end of the exercise, the participants should be able to apply the proper way of breathing and voice modulation techniques.

Procedure
1. Instruct the participants to stand up straight. Feet apart. Inhale. (Stomach should enlarge which means that the air fills the diaphragm). Avoid raising shoulders when inhaling. Then exhale. (Stomach should tighten, which indicates that the air is let out). Inhale again, this time holding breath for five counts. Then exhale and push all the air out: HAH! Repeat process.
2. To perform the staccato for volume, inhale then exhale, producing a series of sounds: HAH! HAH! HAH! until you tell them to relax.
3. Instruct the participants to focus on your hand signals. The higher your hand is, the louder is the volume. The lower your hand, the softer the volume. Staccato for pitch follows the same direction. Only, the higher the hand, the higher the pitch, and vice versa.
4. Inhale then exhale. Relax.

Scene-Building Exercises
Objectives
At the end of the exercise, the participants should be able to:
1. Apply the skills in scene building, i.e., definite movements and gestures; and
2. Incorporate the proper use of voice, movement, and reaction to events in performing on stage.

Procedure
A. Paint Me A Portrait
(Note: This exercise is an advanced form of the exercises in movements and scene building).
1. Divide the participants into five groups.
2. Instruct them to re-enact an illegal-logging scene, for example. Give them one minute to discuss among them which one would play a certain character. When you shout "Click!", the group should freeze in action based on the scene given to them. Take note of the levels, the blocking and the overall impact of the "portrait".
3. Repeat the exercise this time using a different scene.

B. Talkies!
1. Maintain the groups.
2. Pass a box around. Each group draws one piece of paper from the box. The piece of paper contains the scene they have to perform.
3. Pass another box. This box includes lines from famous movies, names of characters, expressions blurted when surprised, body parts, anything under the sun. The contents of the box should be enough for the whole group. Now, the information in the piece of paper will serve as the lines or dialogue of each participant in the scene that they are about to perform. The talkies they are about to conduct will totally have no sense in relation to their specific scenes. The trick here is to use the various intonations of voice to convey fear, excitement, despair, etc., in their performance.
4. Give the groups 15 minutes to prepare. Take note that the other groups have no idea what scene will be presented. The task of the groups not performing is to guess what scene is being re-enacted for them.
5. After each presentation, give a critique of the performance based on the guidelines presented in this module.

9. Directing

Directing is the over-all supervision and coordination of the elements of a theatrical production, including acting and design of sets, props, costumes, lights, and sounds. It is the director who calls rehearsals, gives instructions about acting and staging, and has the judgment to revise scripts (Fernandez, 1994). A commendable director is sensitive to the needs of his team. Truly it can be said that there are no bad actors, only bad directors.

All these elements and techniques in mounting a community theatre production coupled with discipline and passion will make for a successful theatrical production.

To reiterate some important points, I have provided a table below as a guideline in teaching this part of the module to the participants.

As a final output for the chapter on community theatre production, kindly consider the activity below:

**TABLE 8.1 BASIC ELEMENTS IN MOUNTING A
COMMUNITY THEATRE PRODUCTION AND TIPS
ON HOW TO DO IT EFFECTIVELY.**

ELEMENTS	TIPS
1. Plot	This should have a clear storyline from start to finish. Add twists in the story to prevent a monotonous tone.
2. Script	This should have all the necessary information such as cast list, stage direction, and other production notes. The script can always be revised during the course of the production so do not be afraid to experiment with given situations.
3. Language	The language used in a play contributes to the degree of authenticity of the play. Be consistent with the type of language used in the play.
4. Character	Be consistent in portraying a character. This can be achieved through practice and internalisation of the role.
5. Theme	This can be inferred through the plot, character, verbal expressions, and symbolism integrated in the play.

TABLE 8.1 (con't)

ELEMENTS	TIPS
6. Spectacle a. Costumes b. Sets	This helps to authenticate a role in performance. The scenery and properties or the physical context created for theatre performance. You can use elaborate sets for major productions. However, minimal use of sets will help in provoking the imaginative skills of the audience. For example, a wooden block can be pictured as a boat with the use of bodily movements.
c. Music d. Lighting	Music can enhance the mood depicted in the play. Always improvise. In the absence of electricity, use lanterns, kerosene lamps, sparklers, and torches.
7. Audience, Time, and Space	These help define the context of the theatre and to some extent, shape it.
8. Acting	Be consistent with it since the actor is the middleman between the script and observer. Poor acting eliminates the success of an effective message transfer.
9. Directing	A commendable director is sensitive to the needs of his team. There are no bad actors, only bad directors.

ACTIVITY 8.6

Group Theatre Production
Objectives
At the end of the exercise, the participants should be able to:
1. Integrate all the basic elements and techniques in mounting a community theatre production; and
2. Understand the current status of the environment in Asia.

Procedure
Instruct the groups to produce a short production number based on the scripts they have created during the first session of the workshop. They have to incorporate all the things they have learned in the training through the presentation that they are about to conduct.

SUMMARY

Community theatre as compared to the other forms of mass media, is a very viable instrument for implicating social change. Through its use of folk-level communication, i.e., verbal and non-verbal cues, language, humour, situations, and themes familiar and relevant to the community, community theatre readily touches the intellect and emotions of its audience.

A noble goal of enlightening the community, however, is not enough for an effective and efficient communication transfer to occur. Knowledge of the basic elements and techniques in mounting community theatre productions is a must. They must be fully understood and applied by the team, practised religiously in order to give satisfaction to the audience. Education and entertainment should never be set apart from each other.

As for the conduct of the activities, the facilitator/s should be vigilant in encouraging the learners to participate and involve themselves intellectually and emotionally in the activities. The participants should be keen in observing what transpires for each moment will be a learning experience for them.

Furthermore, the facilitator/s should refrain from spoon-feeding all the information that the learners need to know. Instead, it should be an exchange of ideas between the facilitator/s and the learners, and the learners among themselves.

FACILITATOR'S GUIDE

Note: for the duration of this training, the participants, as well as the facilitator/s are required to be in workshop clothes. To be more comfortable in conducting the activities, the participants are requested to be barefoot.

TOPIC	OBJECTIVE	TEXT	ACTIVITY	DURATION
Getting to Know You	1. To get to know the learners in the training; and 2. To allow them to be comfortable with one another.		Character in a name	**First Day** AM 15 minutes
Leveling Off	1. To determine the expectations of the		Leveling Off	20 minutes

FACILITATOR'S GUIDE (con't)

TOPIC	OBJECTIVE	TEXT	ACTIVITY	DURATION
Leveling Off	participants regarding the facilitator/s, co-participants, and subject matter of the workshop; and 2. To give an overview of what the workshop would cover.		Leveling off	20 minutes
Community Theatre Nature and Definition Forms and Functions	1. To define the meaning of community theatre; 2. To enumerate the forms of community theatre in ASEAN regions; and 3. To explain the uses, advantages, and disadvantages of using each form.	Lessons 1-3	Group report on forms of community theatre, functions, relevance, and efficiency in communicating development messages	1 hour
Basic Elements: Plot and Script	To explain the first two basic elements and techniques in mounting a community theatre production.	Lesson 4	Scriptwriting	1 hour
Limbering Exercise	To relax and prepare for the following activities.	Lesson 4	Limbering exercise	**PM** 15 minutes
Icebreaker	To prepare for the following activities on movement.		Icebreaker: The Boat is Sinking!	15 minutes
Basic Element: Language	1. To describe the third basic element and technique in mounting a community theatre production; 2. To demonstrate the three levels of shape; 3. To explore various shapes, gestures, and movements that can be performed using our bodies;	Lesson 4	Basic shapes, Story shapes, Object shapes	1 hour

TOPIC	OBJECTIVE	TEXT	ACTIVITY	DURATION
Basic Element: Language	4. To tap the imagination skills of each participant; and understand the value of team effort.	Lesson 4	Basic shapes, Story shapes, Object shapes	1 hour
Basic Elements... Character, Theme, and Spectacle	1. To enhance imaginative skills of the participants; 2. To incorporate movement and action, with props, set, and costume in character development; and 3. To tap reaction skills of participants.	Lesson 4	Silent movie	1 hour
Insights	1. To evaluate the course of activities for the day; and 2. To pinpoint areas that they need to improve.		Insights	15 minutes
Limbering Exercise/Acting	To relax and prepare for the following activities.		Limbering exercise	**Second Day** AM 15 minutes
Breathing and Voice Exercise/ Acting	To apply the proper way of breathing and voice modulation techniques.	Lesson 4	Breathing and voice exercise	10 minutes
Mounting a Community Theatre Production	1. To demonstrate the basic techniques in a theatre production; and 2. To discuss how these techniques can be effective in communicating a developmental idea.	Lesson 4	Brief presentation from facilitator's group	15 minutes

TOPIC	TOPIC	TEXT	ACTIVITY	DURATION
Basic Element: Acting	1. To apply the skills in scene building, i.e., definite movements and gestures; and	Lesson 4	Paint Me A Portrait	
	2. To incorporate the proper use of voice, movement, and reaction to events in performing on stage.		Talkies!	
Basic Element: Synthesis	1. To integrate all the basic elements and techniques in mounting a community theatre production; and	Lesson 4	Preparation for production Group Theatre Production	2-3 hours
	2. To understand the current status of the environment in Asia.			10-15 minutes each group
Insights	1. To evaluate the course of activities for the day; and	Lesson 4	Insights	15 minutes
	2. To pinpoint areas that they need to improve for succeeding training sessions.			

CASES OF COMMUNITY THEATRE*

Philippines: Suntok sa Buwan

Written by Carlos Palanca awardee Edward Perez, *Suntok sa Buwan* is characterised as a montage of short comedy plays. Stories in the said production are woven through the involvement of the audience from start until the end of the performance. Its first part dramatises the realities of the displaced tribes due to continuous mining and illegal logging. The second part depicts the injustices a poor farmer endures due to the insufficient compensation he receives for all the hardships he experiences in tilling the land of tyrants. Added to that, new chemical pesticides are introduced to them that resulted in increased production but with the possibility of damaging the environment. The journey goes on to the third story about two fishermen comparing their sickly catch with usually healthy fishes they used to have. The fourth part moves on to the urban areas wherein the people only see huge factories emitting ugly smoke and mountains made of trash. Moreover, mangrove sanctuaries are being transformed into industrial areas and more factories are being established. Finally, the actors ask the audience what environment related problems they are currently experiencing in their communities. The actors act out the situation thus providing more entertainment and enlightenment for the group.

Suntok sa Buwan was produced by the Arts Research and Training Institute in Southern Tagalog, Incorporated or ARTIST, Inc.. Established in 1987 as a non-stock, non-profit, non-government organisation, ARTIST, Inc. aims to proliferate arts and culture in the Southern Tagalog region through training, research, and production of original pieces that depict relevant social issues.

First staged in April 1992 the *Korido Theatre Ensemble*, the theatre arm of ARTIST, Inc. during a protest rally for the Earth Day celebration in Manila, *Suntok sa Buwan* posed the following questions: 1) What is the significance of environmental conservation if oppression is still rampant within the society? 2) What is the essence of freedom if the society's environment is lost forever?

This just implies that Filipinos will not be able to recover from the illnesses of the society – even if the natural resources are conserved and environmental awareness among the citizens is high – if the government will not eliminate its corruptive and oppressive nature. Likewise, even if we eliminate this negative image of the government, and our environment continues to suffer from human abuse, then that harmonious relation between man and his environment will never exist.

Nepal: Aarohan Street Theatre

The Nepalese people are very elusive regarding the issue of leprosy – a disease rampant in their country. In order to cure this negative response towards leprosy, the Aarohan Street Theatre made use of a street theatre production in changing the behaviour of the people towards the said disease.

Hence, the group used the character of a magician since the people enjoy magic performances conducted in their areas. So, the street magician at first uses his magic tricks to entertain the village people. Audience started gathering around, even women who are not allowed to come out in public. Slowly, another character is introduced in the show and the dramatic conflict begins. The whole story builds up and the issue of leprosy is introduced in the play when the magician's assistant discovers a symptom of leprosy on himself. He told the magician about this and immediately the latter accompanies the assistant to a health post — that no magic can cure it, only medicine (Dagron, 2001). The play ends in an open forum about the symptoms of leprosy, that there is nothing to be afraid of as long as you understand the disease, and that it is helpful to have regular check-ups with the health post (Dagron, 2001).

It was a rewarding move for the Aaron Street Theatre since they were able to enlighten the minds of the village people regarding leprosy. Since their performance in 1999, many people turned to the hospital for check-ups and treatment. The majority of the patients asserted that they were prompted by the play (Dagron, 2001).

The Aarohan Street Theatre was established in 1982 and is still active in promoting social change in the country.

The following activities will prove helpful in levelling off with your participants as well as the participants among themselves. Since this is a workshop on community theatre production, you have to incorporate in every activity the significance of bodily gestures, the voice, on how we express our ideas towards other people. Furthermore, the activities listed below will enable your participants to loosen up and feel more relaxed during the conduct of the training.

CHARACTER IN A NAME

Objectives

At the end of the exercise, the participants should be able to:

1. Get to know the learners in the training; and
2. Allow them to be comfortable with one another.

Instructions for the Facilitator

1. You, your support staff, and the participants – form a huge circle.
2. One by one introduce yourselves. State a nickname and a corresponding action to remember you by. For example, " I am Indira!" Then jump and clap your hand. The next person to your right says your name, as in "She is Indira!" and then mimics your action. Then says her name and performs an action of her own. The process is repeated until each one has introduced herself.

LEVELLING OFF

Objectives

At the end of the exercise, the facilitator/s should be able to:

1. Determine the expectations of the participants regarding the facilitator/s, co-participants, and subject matter of the workshop; and
2. Give an overview of what the workshop would cover.

Instructions for the Facilitator

1. Give the participants small pieces of paper. On the yellow pieces of paper, instruct the participants to write down their expectations on the subject matter. On the pink pieces of paper, they are to write down their expectations on their co-participants. And on the blue pieces of paper, their expectations on the facilitator/s.
2. When they are done with the task, first collect the yellow pieces, then the pink pieces, and the blue pieces of paper and post them on a board under their corresponding headings.
3. Examine the output and discuss the expectations of the participants. Also, tell them what the training would cover and things they are expected to do.

ICEBREAKER: THE BOAT IS SINKING!

Objectives
At the end of the exercise, the participants should be able to prepare for the following activities on movement.

Instructions for the Facilitator
Shout "The boat is sinking! Form into groups of three, knees together." Those who won't be able to make it to the "lifeboat" will have to swim. Repeat the process using different actions to be performed.

INSIGHTS

Objectives
At the end of this activity, the facilitator/s should be able to:
1. evaluate the course of activities for the day; and
2. pinpoint areas that they need to improve.

Instructions for the Facilitator
1. Group the participants into five. There should beat least two facilitators or support staff for each group, one to moderate and one to annotate.
2. Consider the following questions:
    a) How do you feel about the day?
    b) Were your expectations met?
    c) What do you like/dislike in the way the workshop was conducted?

REFERENCES

Albright, H.D., Halstead, W.P., and Mitchell, L. 1968. **Principles of theater Art,** 2nd ed. Houghton Mifflin Company, Boston.

Barranger, M.S. 1995. **Theater: A Way of Seeing,** 4th ed. Wadsworth Publishing Company, California.

Cameron, M. 2001. **Who Were You.** http://www.alltheaterarts.com/article1019.html

Coseteng, A.M.L., and Nemenzo, G.A. 1986. **Folkmedia in the Philippines,** in V.T. Valbuena's Philippine folkmedia in development communication. The Asian Mass Communication Research and Information Centre, Singapore.

Dagron, A.G. 2001. **Making Waves: Stories of Participatory Communication for Social Change.** The Rockefeller Foundation, New York.

Fernandez, D.G. 1994. "Aspects of Production", in N.G. Tiongson's **CCP Encyclopedia of Philippine Art.** Cultural Center of the Philippines, Manila.

Fernandez, D.G. 1994. **"Forms"** in N.G. Tiongson's **CCP Encyclopedia of Philippine Art.** Cultural Center of the Philippines, Manila.

Valbuena, V.T. 1986. **Philippine Theater Arts as Development Communication,** in V.T. Valbuena's Philippine Folkmedia in Development Communication. The Asian Mass Communication Research and Information Centre, Singapore.

Valbuena, V.T. 1986. **Using Folkmedia in Development Communication,** in V.T. Valbuena's Philippine folkmedia in development communication. The Asian Mass Communication Research and Information Centre, Singapore.

FINAL WORD TO THE FACILITATOR

Before you close this training manual, consider how the whole training course is to be conducted. Below is your **guide for the whole training course.**

TOPICS/MODULES	DURATION	TIPS FOR THE FACILITATOR
Opening Ceremonies	Day 1: 1 hr	• You will have to prepare your own opening programme. This depends on your knowledge of your participants and the preferences of your sponsoring organisation. • You may choose to do a brief introduction of your organisation, if the participants are not yet familiar with it. You may also ask the participants to conduct a "getting-to-know-you" exercise if they do not know each other yet. Chapter 8's Appendix contains one such exercise. You can try that one or come up with your own.
The ASEAN Environmental Scenario	Day 1: 4 hrs	The uses of visual aids like maps, pictures, etc. will help the participants better understand the present environmental problems of the ASEAN region.
Environmental Communication	Day 1: 5 hrs	Tips for conducting this session are found in the facilitators' guide of Chapter 2
Women and Environment	Day 2: 8 hrs	This is rather long because the concepts about why women should be advocates for the environment are found in this chapter. An advance reading for the participants will facilitate the smooth flow of discussion. Thus, it would be best if you give the lessons of this chapter (in the form of a hand-out) to the participants before they retire at the end of Day 1. This should be enough time for them to do an advance reading before the lessons begin on Day 2.

TOPICS/MODULES	DURATION	TIPS FOR THE FACILITATOR
Communication Planning	Day 3: 8 hrs	Tips for conducting this session are found in the facilitators' guide of Chapter 4
Preparation and Production of Media Resources: Low-Cost Print Media	Day 4: 8 hrs Day 5: 8 hrs	Tips for conducting this session are found in the facilitators' guide of Chapter 5
Preparation and Production of Media Resources: Community Radio Broadcasting	Day 6: 8 hrs Day 7: 8 hrs	Tips for conducting this session are found in the facilitators' guide of Chapter 6
Preparation and Production of Media Resources: Small Format Video and Community Cable TV Programmes	Day 8: 8 hrs Day 9: 8 hrs	Tips for conducting this session are found in the facilitator's guide of Chapter 7
Preparation and Production of Media Resources: Community Theatre	Day 10: 8 hrs Day 11: 7 hrs	Tips for conducting this session are found in the facilitators' guide of Chapter 8
Closing Ceremonies	Day 11: 1 hr	• You will have to prepare your own closing programme. Once more, this depends on your knowledge of your participants and the preferences of your sponsoring organisation. • It would, however, be best if you include an activity where the participants can share their insights and experiences during the training course. • Since this training course is about equipping women to be better advocates for the environment, it is a good idea to include an activity during the closing where the participants can make a public commitment about what they will do for the environment now that the training is through.

What we have provided in this training manual is the basic framework of the training. We have included the lessons, discussions, cases and activities you can use to make the training effective BUT much is still left to you. We have provided the bare essentials, you would have to fill in the gaps. You can modify the training course in the way you see fit. After all, you know your participants better. So you can tailor the training to their needs.

You may stretch or shorten the time allotted for each module as you see fit. Only, consider that the chapter on production really require more time than the modules about concepts. Since no visual aids have been provided for you, you may use available training materials or produce your own like Overhead Transparencies, or power point presentations or flipcharts, whichever is appropriate to your participants and their community.

You may also have the training materials/hand-outs/cases photocopied and distributed to the participants beforehand so that they have a chance to do advance reading and be able to participate better during the actual sessions.

Lastly, we also suggest that you provide more opportunities for the participants to learn such as taking them on field trips, or arranging for them to present their output to the other community members who are not part of the training. These will all enhance their learning.

Now you're ready to conduct the training. We hope that it will not only be successful, but that your efforts, ours and those of your participants will all contribute in creating environmental awareness and strengthening environmental conservation efforts not only in our region but also in the rest of the world.

THE PRODUCTION TEAM

Project Coordinator

Mildred O. Moscoso
*Department of Educational Communication College of Development Communication,
University of the Philippines Los Banos*
Ms. Moscoso is a member of the GPRD at UPLB and was co-host of a women's
radio programme titled Sandigan at DZLB-AM. She was also a participant of
the Training Workshop on Capacity Building of Women Communicators to
Promote Environmental Awareness and Conservation in Bangkok, Thailand,
which was the derivation of this project. Aside from being coordinator, she also
wrote two chapters and served as instructional designer in this project.

Project Co-Coordinator

Ma. Rovilla C. Sudaprasert
*Department of Educational Communication College of Development Communication,
University of the Philippines Los Banos*
Currently an assistant professor, Prof. Sudaprasert specialises in development,
design and production of instructional, information, education, and
communication (IEC) materials. She is also an expert in courseware development
for distance education, scriptwriting for audiovisual media, basic photography,
video production, and desktop publishing.Likewise, she served as chapter writer
and worked on the instructional design of this book.

Chapter Writers

Oliver Carlo T. Castillo
*Department of Educational Communication College of Development Communication,
University of the Philippines Los Banos*
Aside from producing segments for the local cable television, Mr. Castillo also
studied the Viability and Acceptability of the Ethnovideographic Method in
Producing Program Segment for Cable TV. He has also attended several local
and international video production workshops.

Dinah Pura T. Depositario
*Department of Agribusiness Management College of Economics and Management,
University of the Philippines Los Banos*
Women and environment are just two areas Dr. Depositario specialises in. She
has written various published and unpublished papers on women empowerment,

gender dimensions, and coastal resource management, among others. She also served as resource person on various topics regarding both women and environment.

Vanessa P. Ebron
ARTIST Inc. Los Banos, Laguna
As a member of the Korido Theater Ensemble of the Arts Research and Training Institute in Southern Tagalog, Inc. (ARTIST, Inc.), she has assisted in facilitating trainings and workshops such as Creative Pedagogy for Teachers and Children's Literary and Arts Performances.

Alexander G. Flor
University of the Philippines, Open University
Dr. Flor is an expert in environmental information, education and communication (IEC); development communication, social marketing and strategic communication; participatory approaches, process documentation and social mobilisation; distance learning and instructional materials development; information resources, knowledge networking and multi-media systems development; and training and technology transfer.

Ma. Teresita B. Osalla
Department of Development Broadcasting and Telecommunication College of Development Communication, University of the Philippines Los Banos
Aside from planning, writing, producing, and hosting her regular programme at DZLB, Ms. Osalla also entails in packaging project proposals on radio production and development. She was involved in the implementation of an action project on women's participation in development broadcasting and is currently pursuing her masters degree in Development Communication, with cognate in Environmental Science.

Content Reader

Delia P. Mariano
Department of Social Development Studies College of Human Ecology, University of the Philippines Los Banos
Aside from being the study leader of the Gender Program for Rural Development (GPRD) at UPLB, Prof Mariano was involved either as resource person or facilitator in different gender and development projects. She coordinated various research, extension, and action projects on environmental consciousness, enhancement, protection, and conservation.

Leah P. Arboleda
Institute of Agroforestry College of Forestry and Natural Resources, University of the Philippines Los Banos
Ms. Arboleda has been working in the Institute of Agroforestry for almost ten years. As a researcher, she was involved in numerous projects dealing with forest conservation and environmental education. Aside from research, she also does training and extension work, and is in-charge of the production of most of the print materials in their institute.

Editor

Maggie Rose B. Almoro
Department of Science Communication College of Development Communication, University of the Philippines Los Banos
Ms. Almoro graduated cum laude and is presently employed as instructor at the College of Development Communication (CDC), University of the Philippines Los Baños (UPLB). Aside from being actively involved in local and international trainings, she has served as editor for various publications and proceedings of conferences and symposia.

Artist-Illustrator

Venancio P. Escobin
Department of Educational Communication College of Development Communication, University of the Philippines Los Banos
Mr. Escobin spent almost 20 years of his career at the CDC as an expert in sketch drawings. He has created numerous drawings and illustrations for different publications, communication materials, and visual presentations.

Bernabe M. Remoquillo
Department of Educational Communication College of Development Communication, University of the Philippines Los Banos
Mr. Remoquillo started out as artist-illustrator. Today, he is one of the experts at CDC in desktop publishing, computer graphics, web page design, and basic digital videography. He assists the faculty and staff with visual production and provides services for other units in the University in their needs in diverse forms of illustrations and graphics.

Lay-out Artist

Apichart P. Sudaprasert
Bayog, Los Banos, Laguna
Mr. Sudaprasert is an expert in desktop publishing and computer graphic design. He has a wide experience in Pre-press and Offset printing which he has learned from a training that he attended in Germany. He has served as layout artist on various publications, both local and international. He obtained his degree in Economics in Thailand.

Support Staff

Charito C. Cabrera
Department of Development Broadcasting and Telecommunication College of Development Communication, University of the Philippines Los Banos
Ms. Cabrera has served as data entry machine operator for more than 20 years at CDC. Because of her loyalty and reliability, she has been involved in various projects of the College either as secretary or data encoder.

Romeo C. Estimado
Department of Educational Communication College of Development Communication, University of the Philippines Los Banos
Constantly dependable, Mr. Estimado was awarded as CDC's Outstanding Administrative Employee for Technical Category in 1999. Though he is officially employed as an audio-visual technician, he can be relied upon to do any job assigned to him.

Laila M. Garcia
Department of Development Broadcasting and Telecommunication College of Development Communication, University of the Philippines Los Banos
Ms. Garcia is presently working as university extension associate at CDC, UPLB. Having a strong background and experience in research and extension work, she has worked as research assistant on various projects of the College. She has also served as technical editor and writer at the International Rice Research Institute (IRRI).

Index

air pollution, 15-17
ASEAN environmental scenario module, 1-22
  ASEAN background, 2
  ASEAN view of environment, 2
  atmosphere (**Lesson 3**), 15-17
    air pollution, 15-17
    El Niño Southern Oscillation (ENSO), 16
    transboundary haze, 15-17,
    key environmental issues and causes, by country, 18-19
  objectives of module, 1
  problem tree analysis of key environmental issues (**Activity 1**), 20-1
  terrestrial ecosystems (**Lesson 2**), 9-15
    biological diversity, 11-12, 14
    deforestation rate, 11, 14
    forest cover and deforestation, 11
    hazardous wastes, 13, 15
    land degradation, 9-10, 14
    soil contamination, 11, 14
    soil erosion, 10
    soil fertility, 10
    solid waste management, 12-13, 14
  water and aquatic ecosystems (**Lesson 1**), 3-9
    coastal and marine resources, 4, 9
    coral reefs, 6-8
    fishery resources, 8, 9
    mangroves, 4-6
    quality of freshwater bodies, 3-4, 8-9

Brazil
  Kayapo video, 208-9
  TV Maxabomba, 209
Brunei Darussalam
  haze pollution, 16
  key environmental issues and causes, 18

Cambodia
  key environmental issues and causes, 18
  mangroves, 4-5
  role of women, 34-5
  soil contamination, 11
Campo, Josefina: case study, 64-7
China
  aquaculture, 8
  toxic substances, 41

coastal and marine resources, 4, 9
Coastal Environment Project (CEP), 56-61
  CEP-GAD programme, 58-61
comics, 118, 120, 143
  concept, 143-4
  illustrations, 146-7
  script writing, 144-6
communication planning module, 76
  advantages/disadvantages of different media (Appendix), 108-11
  the convergence model of communication (**Lesson 2**), 80-3
    Berlo's SMCR Model, 82-3, 85
    communication models, 80-3
    Kincaid's convergence model of communication, 81-3
  facilitator's guide, 107
  objectives of module, 76
  the steps to communication planning (**Lesson 3**), 83-4
    communication planning, 83-4
    communication planning process, 84-93
      audience analysis, 85-7
      communication resources, 91-3
      getting to know your audience (**Activity 1**), 87-8
      organisations, 89-90
      policies and programmes, 88-89
      wrapping up the analysis, 93
    strategic design, 93-102
      developing a communication plan (**Activity 2**), 105
      development, pretesting, revision, and production, 99-100
      GANTT chart, 96
      identifying implementing organisations, 98-99
      impact evaluation, 102-3
      important considerations, 97-8
      management, implementation and monitoring, 100-2
      planning for documentation and evaluation, 99
      planning for continuity, 103-4
      positioning, 95-6
      setting objectives, 93-5
      SMART objectives, 94-5
      strategising to achieve objectives, 96-8
      summary of module, 106
      work plan, 101-2
  the value of a good communication strategy (**Lesson 1**), 77-79

**community radio broadcasting module,
167-201**
defining, 168-9
facilitator's guide, 197-198
objectives of module, 167
programme planning, 170-6
determine and allocate resources,
172-3
identify the priority messages,
175-6
identify programme objectives,
171-2
know the intended audience, 170-
1
select an appropriate format, 174-
5
programme production, 176-95
auditioning talent, music and
sound effects, 176-7
gather broadcast materials, 177
interviewing for radio, 181-3
guidelines, 184
planning and conducting expert
interviews (**Activity 2**), 184
planning and production of
developmental radio plugs, 189-193
what are plugs?, 189
the motivated sequence, 191-2
planning the plug's message,
189-190
production, 193
scripting, 190
structuring the plug, 190-1
types of presentation, 190
writing the message, 193
planning and production of radio
magazine progammes, 193-5
contents of magazine
programmes, 194
steps, 195
types of magazine
programmes, 194
planning and writing news for
radio (**Activity 3**), 188
planning and writing radio plugs
(**Activity 4**), 193
script writing, 176, 178-181
principles, 179-181
types of scripts, 178-9
radio news, 185-88
interview, 186-7
news gathering techniques, 185
news sources, 185
news writing, 187-9
observation, 186
on-the-spot coverage, 186
research, 186
tips on news reporting, 188
what is news?, 185

taping, mixing and dubbing, 178
writing a short radio talk (**Activity
1**), 181
summary of module, 196
women's radio (survey: Philippines),
199-201
coral reefs, 6-7

deforestation, 11, 14, 39

environmental awareness project, 49-50
**environmental communication module,
23-31**
core messages (**Lesson 2**), 25-6
informal "laws" of ecology, 25-6
definition/nature (**Lesson 1**), 24-6
environmental communication,
definition, 24, 25, 29-30
general systems theory (GST), 24
essentials (**Lesson 3**), 26-8
ability to network effectively, 26
appreciation and practice of
environmental ethics, 27
conflict resolution, mediation, and
arbitration, 27-8
efficiency in using media for social
agenda-setting, 27
knowledge of ecological laws, 26
sensitivity to the cultural
dimension, 26
facilitator's guide, 30-1
forms (**Lesson 4**), 28-9
communication campaigns, 28
cultural interventions, 28
indigenous communication, 28-9
popular culture, 29
objectives of module, 23
summary of module, 29-30
environmental issues and causes, by
country,18-19
evaluation, 102, 236

fishery resources, 8, 9, 39
case study: Pangangan Island, 55-60
flyers, 116, 146-7
Food and Agriculture Organization (FAO), 11
forests, 11, 14, 36, 50-1, 63-5,
Forest Protection Association, 50-1
forest protection project, 50-1

Gender and Development (GAD)
programme, 57
gender sensitivity training, 59-60
guides for *facilitators*
ASEAN environmental scenario
module, 22
communication planning module, 107
community radio broadcasting
module, 197-198

environmental communication
module, 30-1
final word: *guide* for the whole
training course, 287-9
preparation and production of media
resources community theatre module,
176-8

hazardous wastes, 13, 15
haze pollution, 15, 16-17, 17
health problems, 40-1

India
deforestation, 39
DevCom Development Society
(DDS), 208
Indonesia
air pollution, 16
biodiversity, 14
coral reefs, 6-7
forest cover, 11
hazardous wastes, 13, 15
haze pollution, 16
key environmental issues and causes,
18
mangroves, 5
land degradation, 10
water purification project, 86-7
International Potato Center (CIP), 90

land degradation, 9-10, 14, 47
land ownership, 46, 47
Lao PDR
key environmental issues and causes,
18
soil contamination, 11
leaflets, 117, 147-59
appearance, 147
design, 149
information, 148
review, 149-150
text, 148
title, 148-9

Malaysia
advocacy work initiated by women
(Bakun project), 51-2
air pollution, 15
biodiversity, 14
coral reefs, 7
hazardous wastes, 13, 15
haze pollution, 16
key environmental issues and causes,
18
land degradation, 10
mangroves, 5
pesticides and health, 40
solid waste management, 13

mangroves, 4-6
Myanmar
key environmental issues and causes,
18
land degradation, 10

Nepal
case study (community theatre):
Aarohan Street Theatre, 283
newsletters/newspapers, 117, 118, 150-7
decide on page layout, 154-5
decide where the article belongs, 153
identify the elements, 150-1
identify the staff and functions, 152
know what news is, 150
printing, 155
write the article, 152-3
non-government organisations (NGOs), 51,
57

Pangangan Island, case study, 50-60
Participatory Rural Appraisal on Gender
and Environment Concerns
(PRAGEN), 57
Philippines
agricultural project (Pinagdanglayan),
89-91
air pollution, 16
biodiversity, 14
cable TV, 203
case study (community theatre):
Suntok sa Buwan, 282-3
case study (community cable TV):
Alah-Eh TV, 241-5
case study (radio station): Ang
Bandilyo, 161-6
production process, 164-6
coral reefs, 7
Council for Agriculture, Forestry and
Natural Resources Research and
Development, 90
ethnovideography (Los Baños), 240
Farming Systems and Soil Research
Institute (FSSRI), 90
fishery resources, 8, 39
hazardous wastes, 13, 15
key environmental issues and causes,
18
land degradation, 10
"LB Talk" (Los Baños), 206-207, 240,
242-3
mangroves, 5
Municipal Ordinance 2001, 78, 79
newspaper communication, 119
soil erosion, 90
solid waste management (Los Baños),
77-80
women's radio (survey), 199-201

Platform for Action, 34
posters, 117, 155-7
    design slogan or message, 156
    determine colour combination, 157
    determine image or content, 156
    interesting slogan, 155
    make sure there is balance in design, 156
preparation and production of media resources community theatre module, 249-86
basic elements and techniques in mounting a community theatre production, 256-77
    acting, 270-271
    audience, time and space, 270
    character, 267-8
    complex plot, 258-9
    directing, 276
    language, 264-5
    levels of shape, 266-8
    plot, 257-8
    script, 259-3
    spectacle, 268-9
    summary of basic elements, 276-7
    theme, 268
case studies:
    Aarohan Street Theatre (Nepal), 283
    Suntok sa Buwan (Philippines), 282-3
character in a name, 284
community theatre: definition and nature (**Lesson 1**), 251-2
enhancing imagination, incorporating movement and action, practising reaction skills
    (**Activity 4**), 269-70
explaining the plot and the script elements of community theatre (**Activity 2**), 263
describing language, demonstrating and exploring levels of shape and explaining the value of team effort (**Activity 3**), 264
facilitator's guide, 278-83
forms of community theatre (**Lesson 2**), 252-4
explain the uses, advantages and disadvantages of forms of community theatre (**Activity 1**), 255-6
functions of community theatre (**Lesson 3**), 255
group theatre production (Activity 5), 277
icebreaker (**Activity**), 285
limbering exercise (**Activity 5**), 271-5
objectives of module, 249
summary of module, 278

print media materials production module, 113-66
case study: Ang Bandilyo (Philippines), 161-6
design and production of print media/materials (**Lesson 4**), 119-58
    4P-E-R Process of Designing and Producing Print Materials, 119-58
        design visual material (**Activity 2**), 127
        plan, 120-4
        prepare, 124-39
        prepare production plan (**Activity 1**), 125
        present, 157
        produce, 140-57
        revise, 157
        valuate, 157
facilitator's guide, 160
identification and design of print material (**Activity 3**), 158
nature of print media materials (**Lesson 1**), 115-16
objectives of module, 113
redesign visual material (**Activity 3**), 140
summary of module, 158
types of print media/materials (**Lesson 2**), 116-7
uses of print media/materials (**Lesson 3**), 117-9
print production
    colour, 135-7
        combinations, 136
        guidelines in using colours, 135
        layout, 135-7
    designing the material, 126-34
    illustrations/graphics, 130-4
        cartoons, 154
        forms of illustrations, 131-2
        levels of visualisation, 130-1
        photographs, 132-4, 154
        KISS (Keep It Short and Simple), 139-40
        visual design principles, 138-9
production team: *Strengthening Women's Voices*, 290-1

radio, 167-200
    case study: Ang Bandilyo (Philippines), 161-6
references, 22, 31, 74-6, 111-2, 168, 200, 286
Russia
    water pollution, 41

Singapore
    air pollution, 15
    coral reefs, 7

hazardous wastes, 13, 15
haze pollution, 16
key environmental issues and causes,
18
solid waste management, 13
**small format video and cable TV
production module, 202-48**
community cable TV and
environmental conservation, 206-7
facilitator's guide, 245-6
glossary of terms, 242-3
historical development of cable TV,
204-5
involving other community
organizations, 240-1
limitations of cable TV, 205
linking with the local cable TV
provider, 238-40
the nature of video, 203-4
objectives of module, 202
shoot video footage (**Activity 2**), 229
successful community videos, 205-6
summary of module, 241
video editing machine, 2
video production accessories, 210-1
video production equipment, 209-13
video production process, 214-7
    post production phase
        alternative video editing, 233-4
        determining interview cut
points, 232
        distribution and evaluation,
234-5
        sample script with interview
insert, 232
        shoot-edit, 234
        shot listing, 230
        3-column video script, 231
        video editing, 233
        visual transitions, 233
    pre-production phase, 214-21
        budgeting, 220-1
        distribution planning, 219-20
        making shooting arrangements,
221
        scriptwriting, 217-8
        team building, 216-7
    production phase, 221-9
        audio, 323
        camera movements, 223-7
        camera stability, 223
        lighting, 221-2
        shooting tips, 228-9
video program formats, 235-8
women and video production, 207-8
write a script for and edit a 60-second
TV plug (**Activity 2**), 235
write a script for an environmental
video (**Activity 1**), 219

soil conservation project, 51
soil erosion, 10, 40, 91
solid waste management, 12-13, 14
    Los Baños project, 78-81
        questions for discussion, 80
Straits of Bali
    fishery resources, 8
Straits of Malacca
    fishery resources, 8
Sudan
    pesticides, 41

Thailand
    air pollution, 15, 16
    coral reefs, 7-8
    "Environmental Awareness among
Homes" project, 50-1
    fishery resources, 8
    forest cover, 11
    Government Agricultural Department
Project, 50-1
    hazardous wastes, 12, 15
    key environmental issues and causes,
18
    mangroves, 5
    solid waste management, 12-13
theatre, community, 249-86
    allegorical drama, 253
    children's theatre, 252
    dance drama, 253
    drama, 252-3
    dramatic monologue, 253
    mimetic dances, 253
    musical theatre, 253
    play poem, 253
    political theatre, 254
    puppet theatre, 254
    stage show, 254
    street theatre, 254
tourism, 17

United Nations Development Program
(UNDP), 91
United Nations Environment Program, 16,
41
USAID, 51

video, 202-48
    animation, 236-7
    drama, 236
    ethnovideo, 237-8
    music video, 236
    narrative, 235-6
    talk show, 236
Vietnam
    air pollution, 16
    forest cover, 11
    key environmental issues and causes,
18

mangroves, 6
land degradation, 10
soil contamination, 11

water pollution, 3-4, 8-9, 87-8
women and the environment module, 33-75
effect of environmental issues on women, 36
guide to discussion 1, 35
facilitator's guide, 71
objectives of module, 32
role of women in environmental protection, 51-4
advocacy work initiated by women and a NGO (Malaysia), 51-3
case study no.1: coastal resource management, 55-60
case study no. 2: the case of Josefina Campo, 63-65
examples of how women can participate, 53
forest protection project, (Cambodia), 50-1
forest protection (Binogsayan), 64-5
guide questions case study no. 1, 61-2
guide questions case study no. 2, 66-7
guide to discussion 43-5
forms of women participation in environmental protection, 53
Government Agricultural Department Project (Thailand), 49-50
soil conservation project (Philippines), 50
strategies for involving women, 53

summary of module, 68-70
synthesis activity (group discussion and role-playing), 67-8
what are the constraints on women's sustainable use of natural resources? 46-8
agricultural services bias towards men, 46-7
development activities, 47
guide to discussion 48
land degradation, 47
national law or local customs, 46
poverty, 47
value of ideas, 47-8
what is ecofeminism? 37-8
ecofeminism, definition, 36
guide to discussion 37
why should women be concerned with the protection of the environment? 38-43
childbearers and health caretakers, 40
examples of the impact of environmental degradation on women activities, 39
guide to discussion 43-5
knowledge of problems and needs, 41-2
most affected by environmental degradation, 39
users and nurturers, 38-9
women's involvement needed for sustainability, 42-3
Workshop on Capacity Building of Women Communicators to Promote Environmental Awareness and Conservation, background, vii
World Health Organization (WHO), 15, 16